Acknowledgements

This book is the result of doctoral research on the interrelationship between the African and Western, specifically Irish, literature. It is equally an attempt to meld disparate but intense personal experiences into a coherent whole, to replicate the unique harmony that defines the differences of our lives, and celebrate that unity in diversity which was the goal of the Creator as He spoke the universe into being. I wish to acknowledge the special contributions the following people who in their own special ways enhanced my understanding of this process:

First, to Professor Emmanuel N. Obiechina, my academic mentor and the supervisor of the doctoral dissertation that is the primogenitor of this book. The range and depth of his scholarship, which he willingly shared with all of his students, inspired this book.

To Professor Onuora Ossie Enekwe, who put his knowledge and vast library on the theater, traditional and modern, at my disposal, and for his kind revisions of the work.

To Professor Michael J. O'Neill of Waterford, Ireland, formerly of the University of Ottawa, who provided invaluable, structured insights on Irish culture, and acted as my external examiner.

To Professors D.S. Izevbaye, Ernest Emenyonu, Ogbu Uke

Kalu, the late Edith Ihekwazu and Kalu Uka for their critical contributions at the various stages of the process.

I am equally grateful to friends made during my sojourn at the University of Nigeria, Nsukka – Gladys Agusiegbe, Dr. Virgy Anohu, Brown Okeiyi, Caroline Uchendu, Roumyana Paunova.

To colleagues and friends at the University of Calabar, who encouraged me through periods of frustrations with a seemingly intractable project – Dr. Nana Wilson-Tagoe, Drs. Akomaye and Emelia Oko, the Ezes, the Umenyis, E.D. Akpan, Dr. Ede Iji, Julia and Gerry Oku, and Eno Nta. Special thanks go also to Eno James, Okon Okon, John Ikebuiro, and Josephine Isamade – for their diligent secretarial support.

I wish to especially thank members of my family – my husband, Alex Akporji, for his support and love at every stage; to my beautiful children: Chinedu, Obinna, Yvonne (Nnenne) and Nnamdi, who endured the vicissitudes of a mother caught in the work/home dialectic, and without whose cooperation this work would not have been possible. To my great parents, Max and Loretta Ochu; siblings, Sonny, Ify, Nikki, Obi and Chuma, for their constant love and support throughout the years.

To Chivuzo Bertram Ude, founder of NOK Publishers, for introducing me to the world of publishing, and for enabling an opportunity for me to study at Harvard; to Tanya Hume-Sotomi, Tunji Olaewe, Njide Ejikeme, Felix and other encounters at Minaj Publications, who believed in me, and showed me so in no mean terms.

I wish to particularly thank and dedicate this work to Margaret Funmi Adebija (4/1962–6/2001), a friend indeed. May your gentle, beautiful soul continue to rest in the perfect peace of the Lord, Amen.

Ultimate thanks go to Almighty God: This book is another aspect of his immutable will for my life; to Him I submit, always.

Foreword

F*igures in a Dance: The Theater of Yeats and Soyinka* draws our attention to similarities and differences between Yeats and Soyinka, prominent dramatists from quite different environments. Dr. Akporji takes us through the geopolitical terrains of Ireland and Nigeria in order to reveal what inspired and motivated the two authors.

Yeats and Soyinka achieve their success as dramatists by immersing themselves in their traditional milieu, but not equally. Whereas Yeats creates poetic dramas integrating and improvising Irish and borrowed religious and esoteric elements, Soyinka, for the most part, reinterprets and adapts Yoruba myths, rituals and conventions. Yeats' poetic and symbolic drama is intensely suggestive, and lyrical, while Soyinka's drama is full-blooded and sensuous, and filled with the intense rhythms of communal living. Although he was preoccupied with the crisis ridden Irish experience, Yeats wrote symbolic plays that are passionate, archetypal and metaphysical. On the other hand, Soyinka chronicled, in the words of Albert S. Gerard, "Africa's dizzy descent toward the murky depths of despotism or anarchy," in eclectic styles, determined by themes and social environment.

The author gives considerable emphasis to politico-historical and social factors, without disregarding the creative initiatives and originality of the authors. She is quite convincing in her analysis of the major works of the authors. By highlighting essential qualities of their works, she has increased our interest in the two authors and improved our understanding of the nature and functions of art. *Figures in a Dance* is a lucid and engaging work.

Akporji demonstrates profound understanding of Irish and Nigerian histories, and is very much at home in dealing with both Celtic and Yoruba myths and traditions. This is not surprising, because as a young Nigerian girl, she had her secondary school education and did her first degree in literature in Ireland. She seems to have enjoyed writing this book, despite the enormous sacrifice it must have entailed. This is a good example of subject and author choosing each other.

Onuora Ossie Enekwe MFA, *Ph.D. (Columbia)*
Professor of Dramatic Arts
University of Nigeria
Nsukka, Enugu State
Nigeria.

Contents

Chapter one
Introduction:
The Artist and Zeitgeist

To the greater poets everything they see has its relation to the national life, and through that to the universal and divine life; nothing is an isolated artistic moment; there is a unity everywhere; everything fulfils a purpose not its own; the hailstone is a journeyman of God; the grass blade carries the universe on its point.

William Butler Yeats

A distinctive universal quality in all great poets does exercise ghostly influences on other writers — however different in background — at moments when a similarity of particularized experience is shared.

Wole Soyinka.

The nature of an artist's relationship with his or her society has been central to critical debate for centuries, and will probably remain so as long as the creative impulse and its expression remains an inexorable fact of life. The issue attains even more multiplex dimensions in this age of Information, with its re-definitions of *zeitgeists* that are at once global and communal. This chapter does not set out to revisit the age old, intractable controversy; the brief examination which follows is however, pertinent to the ensuing comparative study of the major plays by Yeats and Soyinka, two definitive artists of the twentieth century.

Erich Auerbach's seminal work, *Mimesis*, inaugurated what has been termed the *mimetic* side of the controversy.[1] In which garb does the artists most fully actualize his value? As a faithful reflector of the *zeitgeist*? Or as a demigod, an omnipotent creator accountable only to his or her innermost feelings. A survey of Western literary thought from classical times to the twentieth century reveals the pre-eminence of the mimetic view up until the Romantic period, when the subjective view took hold as a conscious reaction against the classicism and the rationality of the Age of Reason. The lines of division from then onwards became blurred, as various points of intersection appeared to dot the grand canyon between the two views. This was, arguably, a natural corollary to the increasing existential uncertainties generated by new scientific discoveries, sensibilities and assimilation of new world views that marked the Age of Enlightenment. These extended into the distinctive permutations of the controversy with regards to writers in the developing world.

The representation of reality, of life as lived, in Western literature, as Auerbach attempts in the works of such artists as Tacitus, Petronious, St. Augustine, St. Francis, Dante, Boccaccio, Rabelais, Montaigne, Saint Simeon, Goethe, Schiller, Balzac, Stendhal, Flaubert, Proust and Virginia Woolf, emphasizes their imitative or mimetic roles. Auerbach traces the origins of this perception of their function to the classicism of Aristotle, the reverence for which attained its apogee during the Renaissance period and the seventeenth century. Aristotle's *Poetics* projects a view of poetry as an imitation of human beings not only as they are in real life, but as either better (*beltionas*) or worse than they are; and not only of things as they were or are, but things as they ought to be.[2]

Renaissance images of the artist were basically more systematized re-echoes of classical attitudes. Sir Philip Sidney's *Apologia for Poesie* (1595), for example, conceives of poetry first as the educator and mental nourisher of primitive human beings, gradually leading them into a more civilized state, and a more sensitive receptivity to knowledge of every sort. Secondly, poetry is seen as an imitation of reality of human experience, in a vivid and persuasive form, and thirdly, as a formative molder and enlarger of the human mind and nature.[3]

Seventeenth to eighteenth century neo-classicism, in strict adherence to precision, correctness and detail in the manner of Horace's *Ars Poetica,* modified the classical bias of the earlier Renaissance period. Literature was conceived as an imitation of human life, a mirror held up to nature, a conception aptly encapsulated in Pope's injunction in *Essay on Criticism* (1711): "First, follow Nature, and your judgment by her just standards set."[4] "Wit" was proffered as the chief prerequisite for the experience of nature. Wit was the imaginative faculty, not the "decaying sense" of Hobbes' *Leviathan,* but the poetic capacities for objective discernment and judgment. True wit, to Pope, was "Nature to advantage dressed,/ What oft' was thought, but ne'er so well expressed."[5]

In 1794, however, Longinus inaugurated the "art for art's sake" theory by arguing that when "nature ushers us into the vast universe as into some great assembly to be as it were, spectators of the mighty whole and the keenest aspirants for honor, forthwith she implants in our souls the unconquerable love of whatever is elevated or more divine than we."[6] Thus, it was more natural for human beings to trust their feelings than to believe in a rationally ordered universe. Encouraged by the authority of Longinus, the Romantic poets emphasized artistic sensitivity and reaction. In his *Preface to the Lyrical Ballads* (1800), Wordsworth makes his famous definition of poetry as "the spontaneous overflow of powerful feelings". The essential ingredient in poetry therefore, is feelings, emotions; the process of composition, being "spontaneous", is in direct opposition to the conscious artistry stressed by the neo-classical poets. Romantic emphasis on spontaneity, immediacy and originality continued into the latter part of the nineteenth century and laid the framework for a new aesthetic conception of literature propelled in the main by Immanuel Kant's *Critique of Judgment* (1790).

Kant evolved the mediational concept of aesthetic values, the beautiful and the sublime, both of which are subjective, as the median point between the world of necessary physical events conditioned by time and space and ordered according to the categories of scientific understanding, and the free moral world of our choice. The beautiful is that which "brings with it a purposiveness in its form by which the object (of contemplation) seems to be, as it were, pre-adapted to our Judgment, and thus constitutes itself an object of satisfaction." The sublime, on the other hand, the more subjective of the two concepts, is "that which excites in us, without any reasoning about it, but in the mere apprehension of it, the feeling of the sublime, which may appear as regards its form to violate purpose in respect of Judgment, to be unsuited to our presentative faculty, and, as it were do violence to the imagination".[7] The aesthetic experience consists of a disinterested contemplation of an aesthetic object without reference to its reality, or to the external ends of its utility or morality.

The product of an artist's consciousness of reality, the resulting expression in art form, is of supreme value because it is self sufficient and self serving, and has no other aims beyond its own existence. The artist becomes a priest who renounces the mundane and self seeking concerns of ordinary existence in the service of the religion of beauty, in pursuit of the epiphanic moment when, as Stephen Daedlaus, the supreme aestheticist in Joyce's *Portrait of the Artist as a Young Man* observes, "that supreme quality of beauty, the clear radiance of the aesthetic image, is apprehended luminously by the mind which has been arrested by its wholeness and fascinated by its harmony – a spiritual state called the enchantment of the heart."[8]

Running at times parallel, and at other times cross cutting its aesthetic counterpart, the mimetic school of thought was furthered in the late eighteenth to early nineteenth century by the search for material, scientifically tested connections between facts such as climate, geography and literature. Giambattista Vico, in *Scienzia Nuova* (1744) avers that the social world was largely the work of humans, not of divine providence, and that, therefore, its literature, must be analyzed in material terms. He analyzed the two great Homerian epics, *The Iliad* and *The Odyssey*, in terms of the geographical, historical and climatic factors within which their author was working, concluding that the former epic belonged to the north-east of Greece, since it describes the Trojan Wars and the period "when Greece was young and consequently burning with sublime passions such as pride, anger and vengeance." *The Odyssey*, on the other hand, belongs to the south-east, since it "celebrates Ulysses who reigned there, during a period when the passions were somewhat cooled by reflection."[9]

Vico's argument was echoed by Hippolyte Taine, often credited with the formulation of a sociological theory of literature. Adjudging literature to functionally reflect certain ascertainable facts and emotions, he called the emergent novel form a "portable mirror which can be conveyed everywhere and which is most convenient for reflecting all aspects of life and nature."[10]

Marxist conceptions of the artist centered on a composite conception of the craft as the "embodiment of man's essential strivings for a sense of community and authenticity, an attempt to grasp the meaning of a world which was being emptied of genuine values through the progressive incursions of the division of labor."[11] The literature which is a byproduct of this process should reflect these strivings, the class stratifications and struggles produced by the division of labor. In *Art and Social Life*, Plekhanov avers *inter alia*, that "Art begins when the writer recalls within himself feelings and ideas that he has had under the influence of the reality surrounding him and gives them a certain figurative expression."[12] Art is predominantly a reflection of social life, and the mainspring of social life is the fact of class struggle. The writer who ignores this fact, according to George Lukacs, "closes his eyes to the future, gives up any chance of assessing the present correctly, and loses the ability to create other than purely static works of art."[13]

Colonialism and its Discontents

The debate over the relationship between the artist and society assumes even more complex dimensions in the context of societies coming to grips (or attempting to) with their identities. The often torturous rite of passage that this process entails invariably stems from years of suppression of inherited traditions by a foreign power, under the guise of the colonialism.

The term colonialism has been subject to varying interpretations by the historian, the political scientist and sociologist alike, and its exegeses need not concern us here. What we need is a simple comprehension of the term as the situation where one nation imposes its own political and cultural systems upon another, and exploits its human, economic and cultural resources. With the advent of the Age of Discovery and the Renaissance man, colonialism became entrenched in most West European government systems and became the moral as well as the political *raison d'etre* for survival.

Ireland and Nigeria were subject to British colonial rule. The Irish experience of colonialism dates from the fifteenth century when it was subjected to a more systematic and protracted application by the English of the inhuman conditions characteristic of the earlier Viking and Norman incursions. The Tudor monarchy of the time pioneered the re-settlement program of thousands of restless and pioneering Protestant English, Scots and Welsh peoples, a campaign known in Irish history as the "Plantations." Much like the Boers in South Africa, these settlers dispossessed the indigenous Celtic population of their lands and attempted to obliterate their culture. Over the centuries, these same settlers evolved an Anglo-Irish identity, a composite personality comprising aspects of the English and the Irish cultures, resulting in the psychological crisis of divided allegiance between England and the Anglo-Saxon Protestant way of life, and the cause of the Catholic Irish, with whom they were continually being lumped by their erstwhile brothers in England.

To ensure the continued success of the plantations, successive English monarchies introduced a series of harsh laws to quell any agitation on the part of the Irish, the most infamous of these laws being the Penal Laws of the seventeenth to the late eighteenth centuries, which denied the indigenous Irish of such fundamental freedoms as the right to land or farm ownership, freedom of language and religious practice. It also produced the sustained exploitation of the Irish economy which culminated in the Great Famine of 1845 to 1848, caused by the blight of the potato crop, the staple food of the colonized Irish. The major consequence of the Famine was the decimation of approximately a third of the entire Irish population, either through starvation or emigration to the Americas, Australia and elsewhere.

In Nigeria, the exploitation of human and natural resources was undertaken under two heinous forms, the slave trade and the so-called "scramble for Africa". The slave trade was predicated on a Hamitic conception of the black African as God's own reject, a natural servant. It persisted mainly in the forcible capture and transportation of the physically fittest Africans under the most inhuman conditions imaginable, from the shores of West Africa to the new colonies in the Americas, initiating the Black Diaspora. There, they were sold to the highest bidders and carted off to work on the various plantations. The "scramble for Africa" was a natural corollary of the abolition of the slave trade subsequent to the Berlin Conference of 1888, but was still a mild euphemism for the trade in humans. Empire-hungry European nations, to compensate for the loss of most of their colonies in the Americas, turned once more to Africa under the pretext of enlightening a dark continent to Western civilization; then invaded and carved up the continent to suit their own ends.

In the vanguard of the scramble were Bible-wielding missionaries who came and overturned age long ontological beliefs and hierarchies in favor of Christianity. They were followed by the administrators who set up systems of government in diametric opposition to existent ones. The British colonial policy of indirect rule overturned traditional administrative hierarchies, so that leadership in the various communities was based on the acceptance and the pre-disposition of the indigene to the colonial regime, rather than on qualification or natural order. In northern Nigeria the wildfire distribution of Islamic fervor ignited in the fifteenth century by Arab nomads and merchants and fanned by the Sokoto caliph, Uthman Dan Fodio, proved a final nail in the coffin of traditional administration.

In both the Irish and Nigerian contexts however, the most debilitative aspect of colonialism was cultural imperialism, the conscious derogation of indigenous culture which manifested itself most succinctly in the propagation of pejorative images of the colonized and his culture. For example, Count Gobineau's *Essai sur l'inegalite des races humaines* draws upon the Darwinian placement of the Blackman at the bottom of the evolutionary scale to deny the existence of the creative faculty in the Negro; Lucien Levy-Bruhl's *Les fonctiones mentales dans les societies inferiueres* distinguishes between the "primitivity" of Africa and the "civilization" of the West, and between the "logical" mentality of civilized societies, and the "pre-logical" mentality of primitive ones.[14]

The Irish experience of cultural strangulation, with its pejorative definition of the Irishman was perhaps more intense and protracted than its Nigerian counterpart. Benjamin Disraeli, Victoria's Prime Minister, for example, characterized his restive Irish subjects as follows:

> The Irish hate our free and fertile isle. They hate our order, our civilization, our enterprising industry, our sustained courage, our decorous liberty, our pure religion.

> This wild, reckless, indolent, uncertain and superstitious
> race have no sympathy with the English character. Their
> fair ideal of human felicity is an alternation of clannish
> broils and coarse idolatry. Their history describes an
> open circle of blood and bigotry.[15]

The portrayal of the Irish as savage, with attendant poverty, indolence and brutality became, as Patrick O'Farrell asserts, "entrenched in English imagery from medieval times and provided moral justification for continued English efforts to destroy or dominate the Celts".[16] A twentieth-century equivalent of this concerted erosion of the preexistent, native psyche is perhaps, apartheid South Africa.

The psychological effects of this systematic erosion of indigenous psyche are legion, the most obvious of course being insecurity and extreme self-consciousness, a constant and inconclusive assessment of self and values. These only serve to exacerbate the vulnerability of the colonized to the machinations of the colonial oppressors. Frantz Fanon's *Black Skins, White Masks* details in uncompromising terms some of the physical and spiritual baggage that colonial cultural suppression imposes on the colonized:

> The Negro's behavior makes him akin to an excessive
> neurotic type. There is a constant effort to run away
> from his own individuality, to annihilate his presence.
> Having been made inferior, he proceeds from a humiliat-
> ing insecurity, through a strongly-voiced self-accusation
> to despair. The attitude of the Black man towards the
> white, or towards his own race, often duplicates almost
> completely a constellation of delirium, frequently bor-
> dering on the region of the pathological.[17]

Given such conditions of economic exploitation and cultural degradation, the artist functioned primarily to mobilize the various facets of society into one, whole, coherent consciousness united in intent by opposition to the colonial experience. This perception of his/her role was not predicated solely on the urgent colonial imperatives. Rather, it originated in the pre-colonial, traditional "communalism" which defined the life of the society, as opposed to the "individualistic" societies of the colonials. In a communalistic society the collective, the community's systems and values held absolute sway; they are often closely associated with the agrarian or rural aspect of man as opposed to the urban profile of the colonials, and with the mystical or spiritual attitude towards nature and the cosmos, as opposed to the dry rationalism of the individualistic colonials.

Communalism defined traditional Irish and African society, a lifestyle where for example, the craftsman or artisan did not produce art for the mere aesthetic pleasure derived from it, but for its relevance to the community's values and systems of belief. In much the same manner, the ballads sung by the wandering bards in traditional Irish society projected the society's hopes and beliefs. The *seanchai* or local storytellers knew local genealogies and the origins of the names of towns and other locations. They could tell family sagas and recite the old heroic legends of Finn and his forest warriors. In both the Irish and Nigerian contexts the artist functioned as the mover or organizer of communal consciousness. Hence, the concept of aestheticism, deriving from the conflicting ideologies and class interests of modern industrialized, capitalist, colonial societies was anathema to the state of what Warren d'Azevedo calls the "harmonious connectedness" which the traditional artist had with the world around him.[18]

With the advent of colonialism, this communal role for the artist became circumscribed by exposure to the literary tradition of the colonials, which apart from being alien is written, in contrast with the traditional culture which was based primarily on the spoken word. As mentioned earlier a concerted suppression of the indigenous languages often attended the superimposition of a written literary culture. For example, in both the Irish and Nigerian experiences, English became the official language; success in business or administration was predicated on proficiency in that language. The artist was subsequently thrust in the ambiguous position of using an alien medium for expression. The artist however, often manipulated this tenuous situation to his/her advantage. The colonial literary culture facilitated confronting the oppressors with the unsavory truths of their regimes. In African countries such as Nigeria, characterized by a variety of peoples and languages, it led to a broadening of communal consciousness and a linguistic homogeneity that was hitherto lacking. Jean-Paul Sartre aptly sums up the colonized writer's strategy as follows:

> To the guile of the colonizers' claims the black poets reply with a similar but inverse guile. Since the oppressor is present even in the language that they speak, they will use that to destroy him. The European poet of today tries by dehumanizing words to return them to nature. The black herald however, will strip from them their Frenchness, will shatter them, will destroy their traditional associations and will juxtapose them with violence.[19]

In Ireland the use of Gaelic, the native Irish language was restricted to the remote and sparsely populated "Gaeltacht" areas in the extreme west and northwest of the country. The rest of the country spoke an English language characterized by a profusion of Gaelic speech inflexions which people had incorporated over the centuries. In his plays, J.M. Synge manipulates this new English dialect to celebrate the peasant ideal in Ireland, saying: "In a country where the imagination of the people and the language they use is rich and living, it is possible for a writer to be rich and copious in his words, and at the same time to give the reality which is the root of all poetry, in a comprehensive and natural form.[20] Chinua

Achebe in a similar vein, recognizes the dilemma of having to use the language of the colonials, but asserts "that if colonialism did not give the African peoples a song, it at least gave them a tongue, for singing."[21]

Having circumvented the obstacle of language, the artist invariably spearheaded the formation of indigenous-based intellectual groups designed specifically to raise the consciousness of the colonized community to the destructive forces at work within. The emergent "cultural nationalism" was predicated on a process of cultural affirmation, on "the expressing and affirming of the past of the colonized peoples, validating their autochthonous values, often at the expense of the received new values".[22] The Irish experience of cultural nationalism to counter aggressive British cultural imperialism is echoed in most African American and African responses.

The Young Ireland Movement for example, with Thomas Davis and Charles Gavan Duffy as their chief-spokesman, concerned itself with the propagation of a "Romantic Ireland", as a corollary to its agitation for a political nationalism. Its members proclaimed a doctrine, "Racy of the Soil", which they described as "a nationality of the spirit as well as of the letter", and which they communicated through their newspaper, *The Nation*. They addressed themselves to the whole past civilization of Ireland her language, history, and her literature, and insisted that this civilization was something to which all Irishmen were heirs, the common ground on which their conflicting sectional interests might eventually unite:

> Did the history of Ireland forbid her to hope for a great career? Not so. Her enemies allege that it was the annals of a people who had not bequeathed one great name to posterity. But rightly understood. the history of Ireland abounded in noble lessons, and had the unity and purpose of an epic poem. It exhibited an unbroken determination to maintain their national

existence, which every generation of Irishmen took up anew, from the twelfth century to the nineteenth.[23]

The Young Irelanders' "romanticization" of Ireland spawned Celticism, a more formalized movement for the propagation of such.

The context within which this movement took maximum hold of the Irish imagination is often referred to as "the Celtic Twilight." Throughout the 1890s, writers, mostly Anglo-Irish in origin, attempted to define the elusive concept known as "the Celtic imagination". They perceived the John Stewart Parnell scandal and his subsequent failure to win Home Rule for Ireland as an indictment of their contribution towards Irish nationalism.[24] In the pervading atmosphere of betrayal and disappointment they turned towards the rediscovery and affirmation of Celtic tradition. Celticists such as T.W. Rolleston, Douglas Hyde, Katherine Tynan and George Russell (whom Yeats frequently referred to as A.E.) variously celebrated the Irishman's simplicity, spirituality, emotionalism and irrationality, the very qualities for which their race was disparaged, at the expense of English rationality and materialism. Celticism also persisted in the celebration of what Ann Saddlemyer calls the folk-spirit, "marked by the heightened passions and superstitions common to all literature rising from the people," and of Irish myths and legends.[25]

The publication in 1878 of Standish O'Grady's *History of Ireland: Heroic Period,* with its discovery and imaginative recounting of old Irish myths and legends, particularly fuelled bourgeoning Celticism. On first reading O'Grady's book, George Russell wrote that he had felt like a man "who suddenly feels ancient memories rushing at him, and knows he was born in a royal house and that he had mixed with the mighty of heaven and earth and had the very nobles for his companions".[26] Yeats himself saw O'Grady's book as "the starting point of what may yet prove a new influence in the literature of the world."[27] It did prove a new influence, for it was directly responsible for the tautological Irish literary renaissance, of which he was the prime figurehead. Together with compatriots Lady Gregory, John Millington Synge, and Douglas Hyde, he considered his primary duty to be the propagation of the Celtic ideal, in which lay the hope for the expression of an Irish national character, distinct from and infinitely superior to the English one. In the essay, "Nationality and Literature," Yeats asserts:

> I affirm that we are a young nation with unexhausted material lying within us in our still unexpressed national character, about us in our scenery, and in the clearly marked outlines of our life, and behind us in our multitude of legends—. All that is greatest in literature is based upon legend upon those tales which are made by no one man but by the nation itself through a slow process of modification and adaptation, to express its loves and hates, its likes and dislikes.[28]

The African writer was also concerned with the definition and propagation of a national ideal. In the late eighteenth century James Africanus Horton of Sierra Leone, John Casely-Hayford and Mensah Sabah of Ghana, and probably the most prominent of them all, Edward Wilmot Blyden, spearheaded the definition and celebration of the African essence. Blyden coined the term "African Personality", which was given great rhetorical and ideological force in the writings of the Negritude poets and intellectuals of French expression. French-speaking West African writers were generally more vociferous in the celebration of the African essence, concomitant with the condemnation of colonialism, than their English-speaking counterparts. This was perhaps an upsurge of the French colonial policy of assimilation, whereby the colonized was forcibly assimilated and turned into a Frenchmen and women. The militancy among writers arose out of their perceived disconnect between the policy's claims of one race, one French nation and one civilization and the reality of third class citizenship for Africans.[29] Furthermore, linguistic affinities with French Caribbean students whose journals were the only available outlets for anti-colonial expression facilitated their militancy.

La Revue du Monde Noire, founded in 1930 by two Haitians, Safons and Nordal, infused the black French colonized with the ideas of the Black Renaissance Movement in America. As Lillian Kesteloot asserts, "it was in the salon of Miss Nordal that the Black African writers went on to found the negritude movement".[30] Another journal, *Legitime Defense,* founded in 1932 by the Martiniquans, Jules Monnerot, Etienne Lero and Rene Menil, advocated the exploration of "one's authentic self, abundant in dynamic reserves from which spring the Black personality. This is the way of the discovery of the African heritage".[31] These two French journals prompted three assimilated French Blacks, Leopord Sedar Senghor, Aime Cesaire and Leon Damas to found *L'Etudiant Noir* in 1934. The journal quickly became the medium for the policy of cultural assimilation and formulated the concept of Negritude as basic framework for African cultural nationalism.

In its immediate sense negritude refers to the movement which took form as a distinctive and significant aspect of the comprehensive reaction of the colonized African to the colonial situation. In its general reference however, it refers to what Abiola Irele calls the entire Black world in its historical being, in opposition to the west.[32] Aime Cesaire first defined Negritude as "the simple recognition of the fact of being Black, and the acceptance this fact, of our destiny as black people, of our history and our culture".[33] However, a more erudite and concise exegesis of the term was provided by its chief theoretician and practitioner, Leopold Sedar Senghor. Senghor's exposition stems from an empirical concept of Negritude as a collective soul of the black race, constituting the unifying concept of the collective personality of the black peoples. He discusses, *inter alia,* the emotive disposition of the African, and argues that the African's response to the external world is an upsurge of the sensibility, an intense engulfing experience in which the whole organic being of the self is involved. Senghor attributes this extreme sensibility of the African to the action of the hot and humid climate of his tropical milieu upon his nervous system, which results in a "Negro temperament". This temperament reveals itself particularly in the African's highly developed sense of rhythm. The African reacts to a perceived object with his own particular orientation and rhythm, which expresses itself through "the most material, the most sensuous means; lines, surfaces, colors, volumes in architecture, sculpting and painting; accents in poetry and music, movements in dance." In this respect, the Negro-African mode of perception differs from the Western mode: "I think, therefore I am", wrote Descartes, the European par excellence: "I feel, I dance the other," the Negro African would say.[34]

Senghor then interprets the cosmologies and social institutions of traditional Africa in spiritual terms. The Negro-African ontology identifies being with life, the vital force. By virtue of this vitalist philosophy, as well as by an emotive and mystical disposition, the African is naturally a religious being, in whom the sense of the sacred is acutely alive, one who communes directly with nature and with the elements, and through these with the absolute fountain-head of vital force, "God" Himself.[35] African society is, in turn, a complex network of individualized incarnations of the vital force, and social participation is a complex of relationships between these. The family is primarily a religious, mystical union and extends into the clan. African art and literature are functional and collective; they are committed in the sense that they commit the artist to a future which will also be the present, an essential part of his/her ego; art for art's sake does not exist; all art is social.[36] Senghor's exposition of a distinctively African mode of consciousness birthed a "Negritudinist" literature in West Africa, reflected in the works of Senghor himself, Birago Diop, David Diop, Cheikh Hamidou Kane, among others.

Paying lip-service to the concept of a Negro-consciousness, some writers in English speaking West African countries, in Nigeria particularly did not adhere faithfully to the idealistic postulations of the African expounded by the Negritudinists in their writing. They advocated a more muted and much more pragmatic cultural nationalism. British colonial policy of indirect government did not demand the same total submission of indigene to the colonial culture as it did in Ireland or as did French colonial rule in Africa. Most Nigerian writers regarded their cultural heritage as needing no apology and no idealization. Their primary concern was to ensure that traditional life and culture be portrayed with fidelity. In contrasting the approaches to the colonial question by the English and French-speaking writers, Obiechina observes that:

> (T)here was always an effort (on the part of the English-speaking writers) towards objectivity and balanced judgment, a desire to see the question dispassionately, to weigh the evidence, to establish the position and to pin down the causes and effects. There was no attempt to visit all human disasters on some abstract monster called colonialism or on some sinister and monstrous humans called colonialists. The problem was seen in terms of a clash of systems, a clash in which the system supported by superior coercive sanctions wins over the other. The conflict, because it signified the imperatives of fundamental differences, generated unhappiness and tragedy.[37]

Chinua Achebe's *Things Fall Apart* (1958) and *Arrow of God* (1960) are highly representative of the English-speaking West African artist's approach to cultural nationalism. The missionaries and colonial administrators in these novels were misguided but Achebe's attitude is that they could not have been otherwise since they "were not natives and certainly did not understand the African way of life. Young Ox-bridge graduates obsessed with their self-approving mission of empire and civilization seize and imprison traditional rulers and inflict grave wounds on the traditional order."[38]

The Impact of the Theater

The most effective and certainly the most well-known expression of a distinctly national culture, as part of a general cultural nationalism in both the Irish and Nigerian contexts, is through the medium of the theater. In its most fundamental aspect, the theater constitutes a social framework, within which the actors are integral parts. According to Georges Gurvitch, the prominent sociologist of the theater:

> We go to the theater in order to re-experience certain social situations which have occasionally been oppressive, and to free ourselves from that oppressiveness; or perhaps we go because some driving enthusiasm which we used to have and which is beginning to fade requires revising by some spectacle which will rekindle it.[39]

In enabling a close and intimate interaction between the dramatist, the actors and the gathered audience the theater fundamentally alters the lives of all parties involved, making the people concerned, the spectators, weep, laugh or come to some decision with increased resolution.

The form and functions of pre-colonial theater in both Ireland and Nigeria were basically similar. As in all agrarian-based societies, there was no division into a playwright and his audience. Everybody was involved in the ritual enactment of the myths deriving from the community's attempts to externalize and to communicate its collective inner doubts and fears. The ritual performances were, therefore, functional, acting as a cleansing, binding communal and re-creative force. A protagonist actor known as the *fili* in the

Irish context, and the *babalawo* in the Nigerian (*Yoruba*), often performed the functions which were to be later assumed by the dramatist. In embodying the spirit of the myth, the actor became a mediator between the community and its psyche, presiding over the communal rites, divining the future and the fate of the community.

One such ritual drawn from Yoruba mythology is the festival of Obatala, the Yoruba god of creation to whom *Olodumare*, the all-powerful Deity, conferred the task of fashioning men with clay. Obatala however, got drunk during the execution of his duty and created albinos, blind men and cripples. This error is often proffered as the pretext for persistent reenactment of his rites of passage, in which it becomes a drama of his spiritual essence through capture, ordeal, ransoming, and triumphal return, communicating the interrelatedness and continuity of the world of the gods or the ancestors with that of mortals and of the unborn, fundamental to Yoruba world view. Obotunde Ijimere's *The Imprisonment of Obatala* amply exemplifies the ritual bias of the Obatala festival.

The rituals of *Samhain* in traditional Celtic society were enacted to communicate an essentially similar world view. *Samhain* was celebrated at the beginning of the Celtic New Year, every November 1, to appease the gods of the *Tuatha De Danaan*, and the people of the *Sidhe,* supernatural beings who wandered into the world of humans on the eve of the feast. The tribute to the gods was particularly significant coming as it did at the beginning of winter, to a people whose agricultural economy was still liable to failure.[40] Indeed, the agricultural cycle of sowing, strengthening, reaping and harvesting formed the basis for the division of the year into four quarters: *Sainhain* (November 1) *ImboIc* (February 1), *Beltaine* (May 1), *Lughnasa* (August 1).

With the advent of colonialism and an alien culture of the theater, playwrights in both contexts, initiated into the basic tenets of the colonial theatrical traditions, predictably manipulated these to nationalist imperatives. Language for example, was adapted to incorporate an indigenous flavor to better express the subject matter which invariably was drawn from traditional mythological heritage. The Irish example of this experience differed slightly from its Nigerian counterpart. Prior to the Irish Dramatic Renaissance, the theater functioned basically to entrench the prevalent Anglo Saxon Protestant values. Writers, such as William Congreve and Farquhar, Brinsley and Sheridan propagated the "waspish" values they had imbibed at Trinity College, Dublin and from elsewhere, to develop their "comedy of manners." Congreve's famous satire, *The Way of the World* (1700) for example, hardly acknowledges the existence of the native Catholic majority of the country he depicts in the play. In the late eighteenth century, the populist plays of Dion Boucicault such as *The Shaughraun* and *Myles-na-Copaleen*, inaugurated the image of the stage Irishman, whereby the typical Irish Catholic was projected as an imbecile, a filthy, spud-consuming, drunken lout with nothing better to do than sing *airs* (ballads) and play with his club stick or *shillelagh*.

Plans to counter this negative image of the Irishman began in the summer of 1897 when Yeats, Edward Martyn and Lady Gregory discussed plans for the creation of an Irish national theater which was to be a vehicle for the dramatic expression of Irish life and culture. In May 1899, the newly chartered Irish Literary Theater, with its home at the Abbey Theater, held its maiden performances of Yeats' *The* Countess *Cathleen* and Edward Martyn's *The Heather Field* to favorable reviews. The preamble to the theater's constitution reads:

> We propose to have performed in Dublin, in the spring
> of every year, certain Celtic and Irish plays, which what-
> ever be their degree of excellence will be written with
> a high ambition, and so to build up a Celtic and Irish
> school of dramatic literature. We will show that Ireland
> is not the home of buffoonery and of easy sentiments,

as it had been represented, but the home of an ancient idealism.[41]

Plays staged by the society drew from the rich storehouse of Irish traditional culture to effect both an affirmation of that culture and a condemnation of British colonialism.

John Millington Synge's debut on the Abbey Theater scene fuelled the nationalistic intentions of the society. At Yeats' instigation, Synge spent six months with the peasants of the Aran Islands, off the West Coast of Ireland. His impressions of the Islanders inform the six plays he wrote during his short lifetime: *Riders to the Sea* (1903), *The Tinker's Wedding* (1908), *The Well of the Saints* (1905), *The Playboy of the Western World* (1907), and *Deirdre of the Sorrows* (1909). Synge captured the spirit of rural Ireland, and propagated an image of the Irishman and Irishwoman which spurred many national audiences to take up arms for the Irish national cause.

In Nigeria, initial attempts at the evolution of a dramatic forum celebrating indigenous culture were undertaken by the breakaway African Christian churches in the early years of twentieth century. The secession from the mainstream Christian churches was the inevitable consequence of the disillusionment and alienation experienced by their educated African members, conscious of the disparities between doctrinal claims and practice. In tandem with the general aspirations of cultural nationalism, they began to inject elements of the indigenous culture into the traditional church service. The lead for such innovations were taken by the Yoruba Christian churches, members of whom adapted their histrionic sensibilities to the new religious and political imperatives. In 1902, under the joint sponsorship of the Bethel African Church and St. Judes's Church, Ebute-Metta, D.A. Oloyede's *King Elejigbo and Princess Agbeje of Kontangora,* was performed, and became the prototype for most of the plays produced by these breakaway African Christian churches. These plays are characterized by their mild satires, the dialogues mingled with songs, the hymn tunes immersed in Biblical themes, the opening and closing glees.[42]

However, their limited audience appeal mitigated against not only their theatrical foundations but also worked counter to their cultural nationalistic objectives. The target audience comprised mainly an elite circle of people Michael Echeruo calls educated or "Victorian" Lagosians, while the majority of the "natives" were "illiterate and uncultivated."[43] The exclusivity of these shows was guaranteed further by the exorbitant gate fees charged for these performances. With the lack of grassroots support, these theaters sponsored by the breakaway Christian churches collapsed, to be replaced by more strident demands for a national theater movement. The demands were often fuelled by newspapers belonging to the political nationalist groups. *The West African Pilot* of the Nnamdi Azikiwe-led National Council of Nigeria and the Cameroons (NCNC), for example, called for a theater movement that would "preserve our customs and encourage out art, and literature. Let us do this now for the glorification of tomorrow's youth".[44]

The clear, precise aim for a national theater was, "to arouse and re-activate a feeling of cultural nationalism among Nigerians, through the glorification of African culture above the alien culture of the colonial rulers".[45] Theater groups which responded to these calls included those led by Hubert Ogunde, Kola Ogunmola, P.A. Dawodu and G.T. Onimole; of these, Hubert Ogunde's theater is probably the most well-known. As Ebun Clark has illustrated in her seminal study of the development of Ogunde's theater, Ogunde was actively involved in the struggle for self-rule, an involvement which was reflected not only in the subject and themes of his works, but also in his several brushes with the colonial authorities. He inaugurated the tradition of the traveling theater in Nigeria and broadened the popular base of his theater group by embarking on well-publicized national tours. His conscious use of the Yoruba operatic form, with its revelatory opening glee, the interspersion of dialogue with song and chant and dance, the mingling of Biblical and indigenous themes to condemn colonialism ensured a very broad appeal for his plays. Three of his operas: *Isreal in Egypt* (1945), *Nebuchadenezza's Reign* (1945) and *Darkness and Light* (1946) are "covert political attacks on colonial rule"; while others such as *Journey to Heaven* (1945), *The Black Forest* (1945), *Mr. Devil's Money* (1946), *Half and Half* (1949) were deliberately written to instill cultural consciousness into Nigerians".[46]

In the Eastern part of the country, Onitsha market pamphleteers early recognized the effectiveness of the dramatic form in reaching the public. Obiechina has undertaken extensive studies of the various socio-economic and historical factors which led to the brand of popular literature known as Onitsha market literature.[47] Some of the pamphlets are plays that deal with a wide range of subjects and themes, from the imprisonment of Adolf Hitler, through dramatized biographies of African leaders, love themes, to straight forwardly didactic pieces. The most prolific playwrights in this tradition are perhaps Thomas Orlando Iguh and O.A. Ogali. The former's *Dr. Nkrumah in the Struggle for Freedom* was just as impactive in its dramatization of the nationalist struggle and the significant contribution of the African leader, as the other plays which deal with marriage, family tussles and religious and moral themes.

Independence and After

Independence presented artists in both countries with an even greater sense of responsibility to action. In Ireland, independence was immediately followed by a protracted and bloody civil war between the negotiators of the Anglo-Irish Treaty of December 1921, and those who felt cheated out of a promise of a United Ireland, comprising the total thirty-two counties, not just the current twenty-six counties which excluded Ulster (Northern Ireland). Moreover, the political programs of de-colonization and reconstruction following the cessation of hostilities in 1923 were merely cosmetic, and served to only prop up the images of the new leaders.

The hoped for improvements in the welfare of the majority were also not forthcoming. Living conditions for the greater majority of the Irish populace, mainly farmers and low-income city-dwellers, worsened while those of the Catholic middle-class to whom power had devolved, improved dramatically. The economic war with Britain between 1932 and 1938, during which the British government imposed tariffs on agricultural imports from Ireland and vice versa, did not help matters either. Disillusionment with the realities of independence on the part of the Irish populace was reflected in the disinterestedness and low turnouts that characterized general elections in the Free State, and the strong support enjoyed by such anti-government groups as the Irish Republican Army (IRA), and the Blue-Shirts. Disillusionment did not however, produce the political intrigues, military coups and life-time leaderships that have characterized post-colonial life in most African countries.

In Nigeria, the initial period of civilian rule from Independence in 1960 to 1966 was marked by frequent changes of government and by the proliferation of coalitions of ethnic groups easily identifiable by their loyalty to and economic preference for their ethnic regions rather than to the elusive abstraction, Nigeria.[48] The situation was exacerbated by the excesses of the new national elite who filled the upper echelons of the political hierarchy. These, comprising the entrenched traditional rulers of the north and the Western-educated nationalist leaders from the south exploited the meager resources of the fledgling economy for political and personal *aggrandisement*, at the expense of the welfare of the largely rural and illiterate electorate. Fanon's prognosis of the neo-colonial mentality in *The Wretched of the Earth* (1965) bears mentioning here; he describes the emergent elitist upper middle-class as "only a sort of little greedy caste, avid and voracious with the mind of a huckster, only too glad to accept the dividends that the former colonial power hands out to it. The get-rich-quick (elitist) class shows itself completely incapable of great inventiveness."[49]

From 1966, the year of the first military intervention, corrupt and inept civilian leadership was replaced by a militocracy which bears an even more terrible aspect. With brief interludes of civilian rule which they themselves sponsor, members of this new military elite have through, the force of the gun, continued to traumatize an increasingly beleaguered populace into perfect resignation to their rule. Given these post-colonial developments the artists had to assume and project a morality higher than that of the politician, the priest and the military class, to take a firm stand against the new injustices. Ayi Kwei Armah's *The Beautiful Ones Are Not Yet Born* (1969) captures the mood of despair which casts a shadow over the gains of independence and which threatens to plunge Ghana into a darkness greater than that of colonialism. In Ireland, it is reflected in the literary preoccupation with such themes as emigration and rural depopulation, urbanization, increasing social mobility, the questioning of frail old gods and of strange new ones, of old dogmas and new fashions, all features characteristic to post-colonial Ireland.

Traditional heritage now became the matrix from which the artist drew to address the neo-colonial imperatives. Sometimes, a return to the past virtues of communalism and the quest for the heroic ideal was urged as a means of circumventing the materialism and the greed that were threatening to overwhelm the new society. Yeats' concern with the heroic ideal in the Cuchulain cycle of plays for example, reflects his belief that the virtues of the Irish traditional past could be used to direct the course of the present. In other instances, the artist used the past as a springboard for their criticism of contemporary society. Soyinka for example, reinvigorates the traditional Yoruba world-view with a new consciousness, in response to contemporary socio-political imperatives.

The recourse to the medium of the theater became even more widespread, though differences in approaches emerged. Independence in Ireland exacerbated the schism between those playwrights who argued for a fidelity to the past as a guide to the contemporary malaise of materialism and greed and those who rejected that past as unrealistic and irrelevant to the urgent need to address the social ills. The original inaugurators of a national theater movement, Yeats, Lady Gregory and George Russell among others urged and practiced a continuing fidelity to the propagation of peasant and noble ideals rooted in the mythological heritage of Ireland, in the belief that this ideal would counter the materialism, greed and a-spirituality which had entrenched itself in the new Free State. Their arguments, however, ran counter to that proffered by the so-called Realist dramatists, Lennox Robinson, T.C. Murray, Padraic Colum and Seumas Kelly, who were influenced by the drama of Henrik Ibsen and the trend towards realism in literature; they rather pledged absolute fidelity to depiction of life as lived. J. Bernard MacCarthy's comments in the preface to his play, *The Long Road to Garranbraher,* is representative of the basic doctrines guiding the realistic dramatists:

> To many honest persons the so called 'Abbey' peasant in a serious play is anathema. They are sunny well-fed folk, who stoutly refuse to think that the Irish peasant is anything else save a good natured giant singing at his work all day long out of sheer joy in his existence, and dancing merrily at the crossroads in the evening. It is a pleasant picture: pity it is not a true one.[50]

The insistence of the realistic dramatists on the nonmythopoetic and non-intellectual "frills" ensured popular support and demand, as exemplified particularly by the plays of Sean O'Casey.

A similar schism in the definition of aims and approaches to the new post-colonial imperatives also characterizes post-independent theater in Nigeria. On one side of schism are the two so-called fathers of modern Nigerian drama, Wole Soyinka and J.P. Clark, who advocate and practice a basic grounding in aspects of the traditional heritage of the country, as a means to raising national awareness to new injustices. In the formulation of a dramaturgy in response to his consciousness of the Nigerian situation, Soyinka immerses himself totally in the traditional milieu of his own Yoruba people. This conscious immersion in specifically Yoruba myths has "little to do with popularizing the archaic", but rather stems from an innate belief that mythic history embodies certain principles upon which "the chaotic nature of social behavior in our time" may be "legitimately judged."[51] J.P. Clark merges his traditional Ijaw culture and that of ancient Greece to evolve a fundamentally African world-view in his plays.

On the other side of the schism are a different crop of dramatists, often referred to as second generation dramatists, including Femi Osofisan, Bode Sowande, Kole Omotosho, Wale Ogunyemi and James Iroha. Characterized by a conscious ideological framework and an unwavering conviction that social change can be effected only by the playwright's ability to raise mass awareness to a positive revolutionary alternative to social decadence, they roundly reject their predecessors' transmutation of social concerns into universal truths and metaphysical profundities, as well as their essentially tragic vision of human life. They attribute this obsessive vision to their predecessors' concern with animist metaphysics and with individual as opposed to the collective heroism. In its place Bode Sowande, for example, proffers a socialist belief in collectivism:

> Revolution has to be collective. If any man believes he can go it alone he is fooling himself. The forces that he is fighting are enormous. Let us start from history; none of the revolutionaries worked alone. The kind of characters you have in Soyinka's plays who are individualist are so perhaps because of Soyinka's ideals. But I don't think it is realistic. You cannot make it as an individual.[52]

This does not mean the complete abnegation of their traditional heritage. Rather, they practice what can best be described as a "cultural vandalism", where they subvert the mythical heritage to their political ideologies.[53] Osofisan elaborates as follows: "Obviously, I may use myth or ritual but only from a subversive perspective. I borrow ancient forms specifically to unmask them, to use theatrical magic to undermine the magic of superstition. All these gods and their inviolability, one is tired of them."[54]

As with the Irish realistic dramatists the premium placed by these second generation dramatists on collectivism and a revolutionary approach to social decadence in Nigeria has ensured a wider based popular support than that of their predecessors. However, as artists who identify with the fundamental social tendencies of their times in a way which allows them to achieve a world vision, a coherent universal expression of reality, Yeats and Soyinka find themselves at a higher remove than these; this is the genesis of their international appeal. As Soyinka sums up with his characteristic *fait accompli,* "all socio-political systems believe that many facets of experience in the process of catalyzing the status quo into a new level of society are understandable and explicable through a recourse to myth."[55]

Chapter two
Stimulus and Response: Yeats, Soyinka and the Idea of a Theater

Difficult times in the life and times of a nation demand urgent redress, on both the practical and sublime levels. A writer's soul at such moments is particularly stirred and stimulated to react and to express that reaction in an art form; the result of a deep seated commitment to positive change. This sense of commitment in face of national crises has generated tremendous controversy in the criticism of Yeats and Soyinka, where it has been variously described as non-existent, naive, distorted and ideologically imbalanced.

In Yeats' case there has always been this notion held by a number of Irish critics that he was little concerned with the socio-political issues of the Ireland of his time; that at best, he was an infuriating Anglo-Irish Protestant aristocrat, with a condescending attitude towards the native Irish that was anathema to the militancy necessitated by the times. For example, Seamus Deane, the Ulster poet and critic attacks him for giving dignity and coherence to the Irish Protestant Ascendancy tradition, and calls for the abandonment of the literary myths of the Revival which Yeats spearheaded in collaboration with Lady Gregory and others. Another critic, Brian Farrington attacks Yeats along the same lines as his "Realist" contemporaries, for "cultivating the cult of a pseudo-peasant."[1]

Soyinka's commitment in turn has been lambasted by many critics for its lack of an ideological fulcrum, especially one that should take into consideration the dialectics of class stratification and of struggle of the masses. Biodun Jeyifo for example, compares him unfavorably to his contemporary first generation artists and asserts that the lack of an informing ideology results in the failure of purpose in his art: "Soyinka may be radical but when it comes to the ideological question he would not be in the same bracket with people like the equally popular Kenyan writer, Ngugi wa Thiong'o, or Senegal's Sembene Ousmane, who are decidedly with the masses."[2] Femi Osofisan once accused him of being a "bourgeois" artist who inevitably projects a tragic view of man and history because of the absence of a socialist realistic consciousness of his society.[3]

This book however argues that both writers' sense of commitment derives from a more sublime perception of civic or social responsibility which in addressing contemporary national issues and the human condition in general, move beyond mere conditioning by contemporary imperatives. Yeats and Soyinka vigorously defend the fact of their commitment in response to critical doubts. Yeats refers constantly to the redefinition in more stridently traditional Irish terms of his Anglo-Irish Protestant heritage, and subsequent identification with the plight of the oppressed majority. He affirms in the manner of all Irish nationalists, "I am an Irishman, am as good as any Englishman. Ireland is, therefore, as good as England. Yet England governs himself; Ireland is governed by England. Can this be right?"[4]

Soyinka on the other hand makes no apologies for the absence of an ideological or socialist superstructure to his work. For him, ideologies are very much systems of thought or speculative goals considered desirable for the health of existing institutions – which are, or have come to be regarded as, ends in themselves. He perceives the role of the writer in Africa as being to be far more preoccupied with the visionary projection of society than with speculative projections of the nature of literature or of any other medium of expression.[5] And he does proclaim his commitment to contemporary issues in his art:

> Art can and should reflect with the "dominant" temper of the age, those vital positive points which, even in the darkest times, are never totally absent. Equally is it necessary that art should expose, reflect, indeed, magnify the decadent, rotted underbelly of a society that has lost its direction, jettisoned all sense of values and is careering down a precipice as fast as the latest artificial boom can take it. – What the writer will not accept is the irrational claim that a work of social criticism must submerge its expression of moral disgust for the anodyne of 'correct' class analysis.[6]

The plays to be analyzed in this study manifest both writers' commitment to the awakening of consciousness to contemporary societal imperatives, but that consciousness is not prescribed by any national boundaries. The upsurge is a sense of communality of all life so that what obtains in one country can speak to citizens of another.

This broader sense of commitment was greatly informed by their respective childhood experiences. Both were born into relatively comfortable, middle-class families, another factor often used to question their sense of commitment to the oppressed majority. Yeats was born in 1865 into two prominent families in Ireland, the Pollexfens of Sligo and the Yeats', who trace their ancestry to James Butler, the sixth Duke of Ormond famous for his exploits at the Battle of the Boyne in 1690. Catholic defeat at the hands of the Protestants at this battle and its yearly celebrative commemoration continues to fuel the sectarian violence in the region. Soyinka was born in 1934 into a middle class Christian family of Abeokuta and was a student of such elitist educational institutions in Nigeria, as Government College, Ibadan and the University of Ibadan, then an affiliate of the University of London.

Both writers' relatively privileged backgrounds rather encouraged, than precluded, an ingrained sense of social justice. They very early on appointed themselves spokespersons for the oppressed majority in their communities, either in the colonial or post-colonial context.

Politicization and Effect

Yeats' politicization was effected, first, through contact with John O'Leary and Maud Gonne, two prominent agitators in the struggle against English colonial rule. O'Leary, the leader of the abortive but politically significant Fenian Rising of 1867 epitomized his ideal of a nationalist and he liked to think of himself as "a nationalist, of the school of John O'Leary". This school was characterized by a combination of militancy and intellectual nationalism. The Dublin Fenians whom Yeats joined for example, were more concerned with the maintenance of "an organization in being for the day when a general uprising would become a political possibility".[7] In the interim, they spearheaded a revival and celebration of Irish culture which they considered a necessary prelude to the insurrection.

Yeats' intense emotional relationship with Maud Gonne prompted his brief membership of the Irish Republican Brotherhood, the precursor of the present day IRA (Irish Republican Army). He also participated in the preparations for the Wolfe Tone centennial in 1898, the purpose of which was to stage the greatest possible mass demonstration against English rule in Ireland. The death in 1891 of Charles Stewart Parnell who, more than any other nationalist brought Irish Home Rule or Independence closer to reality also helped to define for Yeats his role in the course of Irish history. In his acceptance speech on receiving the Nobel Prize for

Literature in 1923 Yeats recalled that with the fall of Parnell, "a disillusioned and embittered Ireland turned from parliamentary politics; an event was conceived and the race began, to be troubled by that event's long gestation."[8] Parnell's death apparently afforded Yeats the singular awareness that the time had come for him to act on two fronts, the political and cultural.

His political activities were directed mainly against the emergent Irish middle class characterized by a new materialism and a misplaced sense of righteousness, members of who were at the helm of Irish affairs. They were the newly affluent Irish Catholic businessmen who enjoyed the full support of the Catholic clergy. William Martin Murphy and Tim Healy were the representative leaders of this new class. Yeats frequently referred to this middle class as the "base" element in Irish society. He had already witnessed the powerful tentacles of this element at work in the Parnell debacle and in the riots over John Millington Synge's *The Playboy of the Western World*.[9] Furthermore, with independence in Ireland they had become what he considered unworthy overseers of the paths towards de-colonization and reconstruction.

His lobbying for election to the Senate of the new Free State in 1923 was pre-eminently driven by his attempts to curb the influence of this middle class and the clerical hierarchy in Ireland. An example of his confrontation with the "national bourgeoisie" is what is often referred to as the great Dublin Lock-out of 1913, when Dublin employers, led by William Martin Murphy tried to starve their workers into submission in order to break the strike led by the Irish Transport and General Workers' Union (ITGWU), under the chairmanship of Jim Larkin. Yeats stood explicitly and vehemently on the side of the workers against the activities of the employers' principal allies, the Police and the Press – which was virtually controlled by William Martin Murphy – and the Clergy.

His intervention was motivated by Murphy's tactic of enlisting clerical aid to prevent the starving children of the Dublin workers from being sent to the homes of English sympathizers, on the grounds that the children's departure constituted a danger to their Catholic faith. Yeats attacked Murphy's perversion of the basic Christian tenet of charity, of "deliberately arousing religious passions to break the organization of the working man."[10] He also vilified the clergy for their role in continuing the starvation of the children under the pretext that their faith was in danger. The poem, "September 1913," succinctly captures his disillusionment with the national bourgeoisie and with their impact upon the national scene:

> What need you, being come to sense,
> But fumble in a greasy till
> And add the half pence to the pence
> And prayer to shivering prayer, until
> You have fried the marrow from the bone
> For men were born to pray and save:
> Romantic Ireland's dead and gone,
> It's with O'Leary in the grave.[11]

In the face of the growing threat to justice and right rule posed by the new class, Yeats redefined his political stand as that of spokesman for the peasant majority, and for the traditional values to which they still clung tenaciously. He also saw himself as a critic not only of English rule in Ireland but also of the new element in Irish society who exhibit the same materialistic and hypocritical tendencies as their English oppressors.

Soyinka's response to socio-political developments in Nigeria was similar to that of Yeats before him, leading him to a position of direct commitment to the awakening national awareness of them without recourse to any political, ideological or even literary straight jacketing:

> There are no binding laws of commitment. – Each individual discovers sooner or later his own level and areas of commitment. If I had a choice in the matter I'd

rather be a writer with no social commitment. That is by
far the most comfortable form of creativity. For reasons
I don't understand and cannot help, I am incapable of
any peace of mind under certain social situations. There
is nothing I can do about it, I can't change. Before one
is a writer, I suppose one is a person.[12]

The individual, moreso the writer must be actively engaged, for it
is the individual, working as part of a social milieu – and this may
be a fluctuating milieu – who raises the consciousness of the community of which he is a part. This active involvement in Soyinka's
case dates from childhood, when contact with real-life activists,
such as Mrs. Funmilayo Ransome-Kuti, who was instrumental to
the success of the Abeokuta Women's Riots, served as the catalyst
for his own future participation in national politics.[13]

Independence and the onset of neo-colonialist tendencies
in the new leadership in Nigeria forced Soyinka to adopt a more
militant stand in relation to the ills of Nigerian society in particular,
and in Black Africa, in general. In a series of newspaper articles, he
launched attacks on the so-called leaders of the new Nigeria and
their latent hypocrisies. For example, the declaration of a State of
Emergency following elections in the Western Region in 1962 led to
his active involvement in the newly-formed Committee of Writers
for Individual Liberty (CWIL), which argued that the declaration
was uncalled for, and that far from reducing post-election tension,
actually exacerbated it.[14] In the wake of the annulment by General
Ibrahim Babangida of the June 12th, 1993 elections, which were
widely believed to have been won by Chief M.K.O. Abiola, Soyinka
resurrected CWIL as the first phase of a never ending grandstanding
with the military authorities in Nigeria. Earlier on, the Biafran
secession and the rumblings of civil war in mid-1966 had seen
him appealing for a truce between the conflicting sides, while
condemning those who were exploiting the chaos and confusion
into which the country had fallen for their personal gains.

He asked for "a sense of the future," suggesting that the impending war "could be no victory for anyone in the conflict, only a repetition of human material wastage and a superficial control that must one day blow up in our faces and blow the country finally to pieces."[15] His attempts to halt the momentum towards civil war included a visit to the Eastern region to try to dissuade the leaders there from embarking upon the costly war; and a move towards recruiting the country's intellectuals, within and outside, "for a pressure group which would work for a ban on the supply of arms to all parts of Nigeria, a Third Force which would utilize the ensuing military stalemate to repudiate and end both the secession of Biafra and the genocide consolidated dictatorship of the Army which made both secession and war inevitable."[16]

The autobiography, *The Man Died*, rather than being the "ego-blender after the event" it has been titled, is a perceptive recounting of his war-time experiences.[17] It captures also the sense of the now endemic manipulation of the Nigerian poor by the privileged few in order to realize their selfserving aims. This was often the topic of conversations with Victor Banjo, the leader of the Biafran incursion into the then Mid-west state of Nigeria:

> Banjo said, 'The nation is not faced even with a choice of two evils, whichever way this sort of war goes, the only results will be the entrenchment of the worst of both evils. The Soviets fought their Civil War gun in hand and political ideology in their heads – But we thrust soldiers into the field with just the slogan, Kill-Yanmirin! or Kill-Hausa! And for whose benefit? The damned bourgeois capitalists who have already begun to lap up the profits of a rising war industry.'[18]

The same sense of commitment characterizes his reaction to socio-political developments on the African continent.

African dictators both living and dead, from Idi Amin of

Uganda, Jean-Bedel Bokassa of the Central African Republic, Marcias Nguema of Equatorial Guinea, to Mobutu Sese Seko of Zaire, and Sani Abacha of Nigeria, have always been the target of his attacks. He succinctly captures their grotesque malevolence in his *A Play of Giants* (1985). He once called Idi Amin "a murderous buffoon" criticizing those who had fallen for his "dictation of revolution"; in 1978 he advocated the shifting of the Organization of African Unity's summit for that year from Kampala to Mozambique, partly in recognition of Samora Machel's more people-friendly government but also to initiate "Amin's total isolation and to serve as a warning to his blood brothers on the continent."[19]

On the national level his constant face-off with the military dictatorships of first General Ibrahim Babangida and later, Sani Abacha led to a self-imposed exile from Nigeria in 1993, notably to America, from where he has continued the struggle, nevertheless.

A Fiery Cultural Nationalism

Contemporaneous with a socio-political consciousness was also its cultural counterpart. This invariably manifested itself initially in both writers' preoccupation dating from childhood with their respective indigenous cultures which they frequently juxtaposed with aspects of the superimposed culture of the colonials, in the bid to comprehend the merits and demerits of each. With maturity came an affirmation of their respective indigenous cultures, and recognition of their utility as the framework for the sensitizing of national consciousness.

Yeats' *Autobiographies* details the sense of wonder he felt upon his first stumbling upon aspects of traditional Irish culture through association with the peasants around his Co. Sligo home:

> One day it was a cobbler with a doleful discourse about a cat "not to be 'dipended' (sic) upon" because it murdered birds. Another time it was a chance meeting with a man who – invited him for a row, and in an afternoon

provided him with two notebooks of "fairy yarns". Still again, it was an encounter with an old man, a local tax-collector fallen unto hard times who drew himself up when reminded of a local legend connected with his people. "Yes, sir," he replied, "I am the last of a line of princes[20]".

In *Essays and Introductions,* he compares the Gaelic speaking peasants listening to songs and epic Irish poems in their cabins with the audiences of Sophocles, Shakespeare and Calderon.[21] Yeats was particularly enamored of the peasants' full-blooded expressiveness and spontaneity, their freedom from the narrow constraints of materialism and their spirituality, all of which he found lacking in the Irish middle class. The most important quality of the peasants to him was however, their continued adherence to traditional Celtic culture. The fact that the majority still used Gaelic as *lingua franca* despite centuries of superimposition of the English language was evidence enough of this adherence. Their belief in the co-existence of the natural with a supernatural world was another. They acknowledged the existence of pagan gods, druids and fairies, who occasionally revealed themselves to humans and exerted a tremendous influence on human life; yet they while still practiced the Catholic Christian faith in one God who created the universe who is omniscient and ubiquitous.

The juxtaposition of pagan beliefs with predominantly Roman Catholic ones can be exemplified by the celebration of the Festival of *Beltaine,* the ancient Celtic spring festival in honor of the regeneration and renewal of all things. In West Clare, it is celebrated as the religious festival of garland Sunday, on the first Sunday of every month of May. The peasants also adhered to a cyclic view of man's history, which posits the concept of regeneration and of all life as being in an eternal state of flux, in contrast with the colonialist concept of the history of man as linear. Another attraction the peasants held for Yeats was their folk art and supernatural lore, an aspect being their traditional music with its half-spoken, half-sung poetic declamation. In *The Celtic Twilight*, he writes of a typical roadside concert in Sligo where the singers sang 'mournful songs of separation, of death and exile," during which some of the men began to dance, and others lilting the measure they dance to.[22]

Yeats steeped himself in the study of these aspects of the Irish peasantry. As his consciousness deepened he began to transcribe a number of them and to cultivate a cult of the peasant which became the framework for Celticism and for the literary revival which it spawned. *Fairy and Folk Tales of the Irish Peasantry* (1888) is basically a collection of charming, quaint tales of the supernatural related to him by the peasants of Sligo. The short sketches of Irish story tellers and their tales of magic and the supernatural in *The Celtic Twilight* (1905) is intended to "create a little world out of the beautiful, pleasant, and significant things of this marred and clumsy world, and to show in a vision something of the face of Ireland to any of my own people who would look where I bid them."[23] Simultaneous with his deliberate cultivation of the cult of the peasant was his contact with traditional Celtic mythology, effected through an intense study of Standish O'Grady's *History of Ireland: Heroic Period* and other works such as Sir James Frazier's *The Golden Bough*, Count d'Arbois de Jubainville's *The Irish Mythological Cycle* and *Celtic Mythology* and John Rhys's *Early Celtic Britain*.

Intense study of the Celtic scholars led to a greater acquaintance with the Celtic mythological cycles dealing with the gods and their relations with men, the legendary hero, Finn MacCumaill, and his son Oisin; the narratives of vision and imaginary journeys, stories of the early Christian saints and of the heroic acts of the epic hero, Cuchulain, the most prominent hero-god of Druidic Ireland and of the men of Ulster. Yeats' study of the Celtic scholars imbued him with a sense of pride in his own tradition and formed the framework for its affirmation. Reviewing O'Grady's *History* in 1895, for example, he comments:

39

It is probable that no Englishman can love these books as they are loved by the many Irishmen who date their first interest in Irish legends and literature from the *History*. There is perhaps, too, something in their tumultuous vehemence, in their delight in sheer immensity, in their commingling of the spirit of man with the spirit of the elements, which belong to the wild Celtic idealism rather than to the careful, practical ways of the Saxon.[24]

The intense study of Celtic mythology spawned an equally intense interest in those features of the Irish landscape connected in the popular imagination with incidents in legend, folk-tale and myth.

Celtologist, John Rhys notes that in the Celtic tradition, every locality had its own divinity, with rivers and mountains, for example, identified with gods and supernatural beings. Yeats' consciousness was stirred by these associations and, as Flannery comments, his earliest "religious sensations – were stimulated by the very skies of Sligo and later by the fairy and other supernatural stories associated with the area; in particular the valley between the mountains of Knocknarea, with its great *cairn* on the summit said to be the grave of Queen Maeve, and Ben Bulben, where Diarmuid and Grania were pursued by Finn, and where the former was fatally wounded by an enchanted boat."[25] These aspects of Ireland and the Irish landscape left indelible impressions that were to manifest themselves later in his art.

A similar sense of curiosity, wonder and pride characterizes Soyinka's contact with his own Yoruba traditional heritage. The autobiographical novels, *Aké: The Years of Childhood* (1981) and *Isara* (1989) poignantly capture his childhood curiosity about aspects of traditional culture, a curiosity exacerbated by parental prohibition of interest in favor of the preferred Christian culture. The traditional Yoruba belief in the supernatural world of gods and demons that exert a tremendous influence on the world of humans fascinated him, and most of his early efforts were directed towards the identification of the manifestations of these supernatural elements. His attraction to his Uncle Sanya for example, stemmed from the fact that he was reputed to be an *oro*, a kind of tree demon which frequently saw him communicating with other wood spirits.[26] The Bookseller's daughter, Bukola, was his first contact with the traditional concept of *Abiku* – which defines the child who is born, dies, is born again and dies in a repetitive cycle:

> (i)t seemed to me that Bukola was one of the denizens
> of that other world where the voice was caught, sieved,
> re-spun and cast back in diminishing copies. Amulets,
> bangles, tiny rattles and dark copper twist rings earthed
> her through ankles, fingers, wrist and waist. She knew
> she was *abiku*. The two tiny cicatrices on her face were
> also part of the many counters to enticements by her
> companions in the other world. Like the *abiku* she was
> privileged, apart. Her parents dared not scold her for
> long or earnestly.[27]

Bukola made an strong impression on him, and the concept she embodied was to recur frequently in his writings and indeed in the writings of subsequent Soyinka disciples, most notably Ben Okri in his Booker Award-winning novel, *The Famished Road*.

The break with the Christian milieu of his parents and a subsequent association with its traditional counterpart were effected through his relationship with his grandfather. The sojourn in Isara in Ijebu-land with his grandfather signaled his acquaintance with the less privileged world of the rural dwellers and their marked bondage to tradition, a trait also characteristic of the Irish peasantry. His grandfather epitomized for him this characteristic. He belonged in the same province of beliefs as the *Ogboni* of Ake:

> (a)s the priest and priestesses of various cults and
> mysteries against whom Wild Christian (his mother)

and her co-religionists sometimes marched on some special week-end of the year, preaching the word of God to them in market places, on the streets, in their homes – their mission was to perpetuate the spirit of the [early] missionaries and bring a few more pagans into the Christian fold.[28]

His grandfather resisted these Christian attempts and was instrumental in turning the young Soyinka from a concept of Ogun as "the pagans' devil who kills people and fights everybody" to one who "protects his own."[29]

Curiosity led Soyinka to further intense study of his traditional heritage. Formal education at Government College and at University College, both at Ibadan, and at Leeds University ensured his adoption of a more systematic study of this heritage, despite the emphasis in both institutions on the Western or colonial literary culture. Exposure to the two traditions facilitated his identification of similarities in the composition of the Greek and Yoruba pantheons as well as his definition of an African consciousness, distinct from a Western or colonial one. His anti Negritudinist stand was taken in the spirit of the definition of this consciousness. Typifying the English speaking West African's brand of nationalism he labels the idealistic postulations of the Negro and the nature of his being forwarded by Senghor and his associates an acceptance of "one of the most commonplace blasphemies of racism, that the Blackman has nothing between his ears," and accused them of proceeding to subvert the power of poetry to glorify this fabricated justification of European cultural domination."[30] In the stead of this idealism, he postulates a Yoruba consciousness as the framework for the African one, a consciousness which can be defined by its own frames of references, in contrast to the affirmation of the pejorative colonial frames of reference practiced by the Negritudinists.

In the essays, "Morality and Aesthetics in the Ritual Archetype" and "The Fourth Stage," the latter being part of a *Festschriften* to

G. Wilson Knight, his mentor at Leeds, Soyinka details the major metaphysical and ontological postulates of the Yoruba world as a means of defining an African world view, as well as arriving at a definitive framework for his dramatic art. For example, he posits that the Yoruba world view operates a cyclic concept of time which "denies periodicity to the existence's of the dead, the living and the unborn", a feature also common to most African metaphysics. In "Yoruba metaphysics no other deity in the pantheon (apart from Ogun) correlates so absolutely through his own history and nature, with the numinous temper of the fourth area of existence which we have labeled the abyss of transition."[31]

Consciousness and affirmation of their respective indigenous or traditional heritage by both writers were obviously a necessary prelude to a literary response. T.S. Eliot recognized this essential correlation between a writer's sense of the past or history and the creative response, describing it as a "nearly indispensable" prerequisite for "anyone who would continue to be a poet beyond his twenty-fifth year"; it entails:

> a perception, not only of the pastness of the past, but of its presence; the historical sense compels a man to write not merely with his own generation in his bones, but with a feeling that the whole of literature of Europe from Homer and within it the whole of the literature of his own country has a simultaneous order. This historical sense, which is a sense of the timeless as well as of the temporal, and of the timeless and of the temporal together, is what makes a writer traditional.[32]

Yeats and Soyinka however, did not merely reproduce the past for its own sake. In keeping with Isidore Okpewho's categorization of approaches to tradition they refined and revised it to conform to their consciousness of national imperatives. The expression in literature often incorporated an apprehension of the immediate, contemporary sociopolitical or national issue, as well as of its personal (particularly with Yeats), universal and metaphysical referents. As Yeats asserts with respect to his own approach:

> I am not very fond of retrospective art. I do not think that the pleasure we get from old methods of looking at things – belongs to the best literature. I do not mean that we should not go to the old ballads and poems for inspiration, but we should search them for new methods of expressing ourselves.[33]

In so doing, Yeats suggests, a dead mythology might be changed to a living one.

His first literary effort in this regard is the long narrative poem, *The Wandering of Oisin* (1889), based upon a translation by Michael Comyn he found in the "Transactions of the Ossianic Society". He found in Comyn's poem, *The Life of Oisin in Tir na Og* an example of the rise and fall of all life. Consciously he searched for the significance of the myth to himself, to his nation, and to the world at large. He realized that in order to find an answer he would have to reshape the story to clarify its meaning.

He therefore modified certain aspects of the myth of Oisin to express his consciousness of himself, of Ireland and of the world. He turned Comyn's account of the "Country of the Young", to which Oisin journeys, into three Islands – the Islands of Dancing, of Victory and of Forgetfulness. On the personal level, the islands represent Yeats' idyllic boyhood at Sligo, his search for and assumption of a distinct Irish identity in West Kensington in London, and his day-dreaming adolescence on Howth. But Yeats suggests that these three stages also exemplify the rise and fall of all life, for they parallel the periods of childhood, of aggressive maturity, and of senility in the lives of all human beings. In terms of national politics the chained lady whom Oisin has to liberate in the Island of Victory bears a strong resemblance to Ireland in English chains;

and the suggestion that the Oisin's battles are "never done" projects the continuous Irish struggle for complete independence.[34] The overall result is a poem which, within the framework of the Irish legend, reaches towards a more complex meaning.

Soyinka's deliberate use of a traditional framework for literary expression has, as has already been suggested, little to do with a mere interest in the indigenous. In the collection of poems titled, *Idanre and Other Poems*, he re-interprets the Ogun myth to express his consciousness of man, nature and society. The title poem 'Idanre' reveals his concern with what he calls "the eternal cycle of Karmas that has become the evil history of man," which he identifies with the god Ogun.[35] Ogun must reenact annually a redemptive pilgrimage to earth. His repetitive destiny is symbolized by the Mobius Strip image, which Soyinka defines as a "mathe magical ring, infinite in self-recreation into independent but linked rings," and which was suggested to him by the loops made by a snake devouring its tail. (This symbol is examined in greater detail in chapter five.) This Mobius ring, as Maduakor suggests, is to Soyinka, "the freest conceivable symbol of human / divine relationships".[36] These relationships are characterized by one common constant: conflict. Conflict can recreate itself into circles of interlinking plagues both in the spheres of divine relationships and in those of man. This is the basis for Soyinka's claim that "in the human context of my society, *Idanre* has made abundant sense," for the bloody events narrated therein anticipated the bloodbath in Nigeria during the Civil War.[37]

The Idea of a Theater

The one medium which for both artists, particularly lends itself to the effective manipulation of indigenous culture to the expression of their consciousness is the theater. Both recognized from the outset the greater audience affect qualities and the potentials for regenerative action incorporated in the form. Yeats turned to the theater in tacit recognition of the fact that "the Irish people are at that precise stage of their history when the imagination, shaped by many stirring events, desires dramatic expression".[38] He recognized the affective and cohesive properties innate in the art form, its power of transforming isolated individuals into the unity of an audience. He felt "most alive," he comments, "when a room full of people share the same lofty emotion."[39] Soyinka also endorses the affective and cohesive properties of the theater thus:

> It is a truism that the theatre is simply but effectively in its operational totality, both performance and audience; and there exists already in this truth a straightforward dynamic of drama which is not to be found in painting, a technique whose only end can be change, not consolidation. – It suggests that theatre is perhaps the most revolutionary art form known to man. [40]

The recourse to the theatrical medium in both cases had metaphysical, as well as aesthetic implications.

It centered on a conception of the medium as ritual, the only means whereby societal or the collective consciousness could be impacted. Both shared a Jungian concept of myth and ritual as the natural effluence of man's yearning for spiritual meaning in life. Both understood ritual to denote the communicative aspect of culturally defined sets of behavior or customs, a much wider interpretation of the term than that by Aristotle or Nietzsche. Both averred that the dramatic performance of a recognizable rite, a rite drawn from the mythical heritage of the community forces the active participation of members of the community in the ritual. Through submergence in the ritual members of the community emerge with a new consciousness of themselves as individuals and as a collective. Both therefore, used the ritual format to express their consciousness of socio-political imperatives, precisely because of its communal or audience affective qualities. Both envisaged the consequent awakening of communal consciousness to be the preliminary step towards change or action.

Yeats' theory of ritual theater was based on a fundamental recognition of the form as the most effective means available to reach at what he calls the *spiritus mundi,* the "common life all men share in the depths of the collective soul," equivalent to the Jungian collective racial unconscious.[41] A play must therefore recede from the surface of life where men are separated from one another by character into the aegis of their archetypes; there, "we can share the same lofty emotion," there, "we are almost completely alive."[42] In the same manner Soyinka avers that ritual theater "aims to reflect through physical and symbolic means the archetypal struggle of the mortal being against exterior forces."[43] This quest for the affirmation of the communal self is "a clue to the deep seated need for creative man to recover archetypal consciousness in the origin of the dramatic medium."[44]

Yeats' Theater

Yeats developed his theory of the theater as a response to the unfolding Irish history, his interest in mysticism and the occult, and his contact with the Japanese Noh dramatic form. His interest in mysticism and the occult has been the subject of controversy between those who are embarrassed by what they perceive to be recourse to a private never never land, and those who construe it as an intricate aspect of his development as a poet and a dramatist. Yeats' mystical and occultist associations were the natural consequences of his identification with the peasant ideal, of his deliberate denial of the rational, materialistic and a-spiritual world of his compeers in favor of the spiritual and mystical world of the Irish peasants.

It was also a response to the ontological uncertainties generated by the philosophical and scientific thoughts of his impressionable years, such as the engendered by Darwin's seminal *The Origin of the Species.* These uncertainties and the subsequent confusion and "fragmentation of thought" they engendered in the modern mind can be defined in terms of T.S. Eliot's "dissociation of sensibility"; for Yeats, it was akin to a "bursting into fragments." Through mysticism and the occult he hoped not only to discover a ritual framework for the expression of his consciousness but also to effect a reconciliation of the contradictions he felt within himself, between man and nature and between the demands of the intellect with those of the imagination.

Yeats was deeply concerned with the hidden significances underlying the appearances in the universe and in human life. He was in all respects, a "religious" man who confronted with what he perceived to be inadequacies of orthodox Christianity and modern science, sought constantly for the "jewel of enlightenment which would make intelligible the burden of the mystery – of all this unintelligible world."[45] His involvement in mysticism was a direct consequence of this search. His membership of the Theosophical Movement of Madame Blavatsky in London brought him into contact for the first time with a systematic approach to the beliefs he had evidenced in the Irish peasantry, which were based on the support of a secret, mystic and ancient wisdom, and on the opposition to materialism. Basically, theosophy postulated three concepts: the existence of an omnipresent, eternal, boundless and immutable principle on which all speculation is impossible; a belief in the fundamental identity of all souls with the Universal Oversoul; and a belief in the "obligatory pilgrimage of every soul through the cycle of Incarnation in accordance with cyclic and karmic law."[46]

Contact with the theosophists strengthened his conviction in the coexistence of the pagan, supernatural world with the natural, from which an increasingly materialistic and rationalistic Ireland was turning away. He incorporated most of the theosophical doctrines in his writings, though he attributed them to more respectable sources as Boehme and Swedenborg to pre-empt the skepticism which he knew these doctrines were likely to generate in Ireland. The theosophical conception of history as cyclical and of a divine incarnation at the beginning of each cycle, proved further validation of the peasants' adherence to such a view of history, and provided the groundwork for his further study and expression of the theory in the light of his readings of Nietzsche, and his postulation of a philosophy of man and civilization in *A Vision* (1927).

The Rosicrucian Order of the Golden Dawn was another mystical group with which Yeats associated. The Order, founded by MacGregor Mathers, presented him with the ritual format upon which he practiced his concept of theater. The activities of the Order centered on a re-birth initiation. The adept symbolically died or killed himself, whereupon he was spiritually re-born as Osiris, Orpheus, Dionysus, Christ or a fourteenth century adept known as Father Christian Rosenkreuz. His rebirth symbolized the alchemist's transmutation of matter into its divine or supernatural counterpart, as well as his own ascent up the Sephirotic tree of life to God. The hermetic students divided their society into ten grades and two orders. They had their oaths, invocations and ceremonial gestures as well as many mysterious symbols. One of such symbols which occurs frequently in Yeats' early writing was that of a rose superimposed on a cross, signifying love and sacrifice, eternity and time and the resolved antinomies. As Morton Seiden suggests, the Hermetic students "looked upon themselves as intermediaries between society and the *Ain Soph Aour,* (an ideal world akin to Nirvana). As a consequence they were ardent political and social reformers and went so far as to even look forward to and to urge a violent world wide revolution."[47]

The Order's emphasis on the rebirth of the individual, achievable through magical training and practice, was especially significant. Yeats worked towards a self-transmutation using his Order name, *Demon est Deus Inversus* (a demon is an inverted god). The attempts to effect a self-transmutation were the first steps towards the attainment of a more general transmutation, in conformity with the true ideal of the adept in the Order, which was "to choose a life which shall bring him in touch with the sorrows of his race rather than accept the *nirvana* open to him, and, like other saviors of the world, to remain manifested as a living link between the supernatural and terrestrial natures."[48] Yeats related the mystical idea of a Christ like figure effecting a spiritual regeneration to the Irish context. In response to his consciousness of the Irish condition he aimed at the recreation of the "rituals of a lost faith," a "ritual in Ireland which would unite the truths of Christianity with the Druidic truths of a more ancient world," in order to effect a spiritual regeneration of his countrymen.[49]

The first step towards the achievement of this objective was to create an Irish mystical order, similar in nature to the Order of the Golden Dawn. This "Order of Celtic Mysteries" was to be headquartered in an unoccupied castle in the middle of Lough Key in Co. Mayo. To this "Castle of Heroes would come the finest men and women of Ireland, for spiritual inspiration and teaching, and they would return, fortified by the natural powers which the Irish mystical, order had concentrated, to act – as living links between the supernal and terrestrial natures."[50] Members of the Order of Celtic Mysteries plunged themselves into a study of Irish Saga material and of the commentaries on that by mythologists and Celtic scholars.

The Order was to use a specifically Celtic symbolism in its rituals for it was through the "means of traditional symbolism" that the writer can "bridge the gap between the mortal and immortal worlds, re-awakening through the magical power of the word a sense of the *Spiritus Mundi* or Great Memory from which all things had sprung."[51] Through a program of rituals and deliberations on the symbolisms, members of the Order were to emerge ready and fortified to effect a spiritual regeneration on the national scale. In writing of the Irish Mystical Order in *Autobiographies* however, Yeats tells us that his attempts to maintain the Order proved futile.[52] But these attempts, though yielding no enduring fruits, provided the foundation for the dramatic expression of his consciousness of the Irish condition.

Yeats first defined his consciousness of, and relationship to Ireland, in terms of a quest for three inter-related concepts known as the three Unities: Unity of Being, Unity of Culture, Unity of Image. He originally derived the concept of Unity of Being from his father, John Butler Yeats who emphasized the maximum development of the personality as the ultimate human goal. Yeats then equated Unity of Being with the fully developed personality, where all parts are subordinated to the whole as in a perfectly proportioned human body.[53] The concept of Unity of Being can best be understood in the context of the 'mask' symbolism, with which Yeats was pre-occupied throughout his life. The symbolism originally derived from his association with the aesthetes of the "decadent" period of the 1890s London, best typified by Oscar Wilde. Like his immersion in mysticism and the occult, he utilized it to try to reconcile the disparate elements and conflicts he felt within.

By means of the mask, Yeats was able to contain and objectify the war of incompatibles that raged in him and to aspire towards the achievement of Unity of Being. The attainment of this Unity of Being for the writer was possible only in the context of a society which had achieved what he termed Unity of Culture. A society achieved Unity of Culture when "its religious, aesthetic and practical life were one", when no social or occupational distinctions existed because all – the prince and the peasant, craftsman and poet, artist and laborers – were of one mind and heart.[54] Unity of Culture was, in turn, defined and evoked by Unity of Image. The writer, as a creator of images, provided the means whereby society attained Unity of Culture, either through the incorporation into his creative output of the myths and rituals of his race or nation or through his revisions of that society's inherited traditions.

Yeats therefore, had a sense of the onerous responsibility of the writer to his society, as the custodian, as well as the creator of culture. Unity of Being thus, was possible only in societies where unity of minds had been achieved through the images created and sanctified by the writer. History abounds with examples of such societies; Renaissance Italy for one, and Elizabethan England. Most significant of all was the Athenian society in ancient Greece, where "civilization rose to its highest mark."[55] Yeats was particularly enamored of the theater of Dionysus on the slopes of the Acropolis, the center of the life of the Athenian community. There, the myths and rituals of the Athenians were transformed into art forms in order to raise their consciousness, and to evoke amongst them a powerful sense of communal identity. He aimed at the creation of an Irish equivalent of the theater of Dionysus in which the people would watch the "sacred drama of their own history, with every spectator finding self and neighbor, finding all the world there as we find the sun in the bright spot under the looking glass."[56]

His leadership role in the Irish dramatic movement, particularly in the foundation of the Irish Literary Theater and the famous Abbey Theater, was assumed with these objectives in mind. During the early years of the Abbey he practiced his concept of theater. Although the ritual form is incidental to his early plays, they exhibit an underlying metaphysical pattern developed in the later ones, whereby the external and internal conflicts of the characters are resolved only through a material or psychic change that leads them to a spiritual re-birth. Three main aspects of his consciousness of Irish life figure prominently in these plays: the Irish landscape, the Irish peasantry and traditional Irish mythology. All of his early plays are deeply imbued with a feeling for the Irish landscape, the historical place names of Ireland and the heroic legends and folklore associated with them, in the hope that he might "help the imaginations that are most keen and subtle to think of Ireland as a sacred land."[57]

His cultivation of the cult of the Irish peasant and his belief that they were much closer to the attainment of Unity of Being than any other class meant that they provided the ultimate sources for the plots, themes and characters of his plays. The emphasis on the Irish peasantry formed the basis for his celebration of the Irish way of life in response to British cultural imperialism in such plays as *The Land of Heart's Desire* (1894), *The Pot of Broth* (1904) and *Cathleen Ni Houlihan* (1902). Traditional Celtic mythology also formed the source for the material of most of his plays, but he continually refined the mythological framework to reflect his immediate artistic and personal concerns. The Cuchulain cycle of plays, for example centers on the exploits of the Irish mythical hero, Cuchulain. He is the hero of the ancient Gaelic epic, the *Tain Bo Cuailgne* (The Cattle-Raid at Cooley) which details Cuchulain's brave defense of Ulster against foreign forces attempting to capture the famed Brown Bull of Cooley. The legend is told in the context of an agrarian society where valor and honor are measured in terms of cattle heads and cattle raids. Yeats' symbol for Cuchulain is the hawk, a solar bird with the same attributes as the eagle, such as power, royalty, nobility as well as courage. Like the eagle, the hawk is reputed to be able to fly up to the sun and boldly confronted its glare.

Cuchulain's battles take place in the context of a feud between his King, Conchubar Mac Nessa, high king of Ulster and Maeve, the wife of Ailill, the King of Connaught. The main story deals with the consequences of Maeve's attempts to steal the Brown Bull of Cooley and Cuchulain's bravery and wit in preventing her from achieving her aims. The epic also records his heroic deeds elsewhere, particularly against the armies of Aoife, a Scottish warrior queen and his successful wooing and marriage of the unapproachable Emer. Juxtaposed with his heroic exploits, however, are his anti heroic propensities, the result of over weaning pride; his penchant for wine and women also compelled him to a number of destructive acts, as will soon be seen in some of the plays discussed.

With the advent of Irish cultural nationalism, Yeats ensured that Cuchulain assumed a symbolic significance to the nationalist movement.[58] His heroic exploits become the basis for the propagation and celebration of the Celtic ideal undertaken by him and his colleagues at the Abbey Theater. Yeats modifies these exploits to reflect his concern with the increasing merchant mentality in Irish society in *On Baile's Strand* (1904) and to dramatize his consciousness of man and his tragic destiny in *At the Hawk's Well* (1917). The symbolism and allegory of Irish supernatural lore also feature prominently in his plays, as a means of communicating his belief in the "war of the spiritual with the natural order," central to his conception of the theater. He modifies or re-charges them to make them more powerful and socially relevant, and thus usher in a Unity of Culture and a Unity of Being in Ireland.

Consequently, early plays like *The Countess Cathleen* (1892), The *Shadowy Waters* (1911) and *The Land of Heart's Desire* (1908) reflect the influence of the supernatural world upon the natural which Yeats hoped would reawaken Ireland's sense of her ancient holiness. The bardic tradition of the half-spoken, half-sung poetic declamation in the folk music of the peasantry also features in his plays. He utilizes them for a number of purposes: to intensify the mood of serious passages in *The King's Threshold* (1904), *Deirdre* (1907) and *The Resurrection* (1931); to serve as ironic counterpoints to the heroic figures and lofty poetic diction of such plays as *On Baile's Strand* (1904) and *The Death of Cuchulian* (1939), and to express thematic ideas without being overtly didactic as in the lyrics of all the dance plays.

Yeats' ideas for the Irish national theater conflicted not only with those of political nationalists who comprised the majority of Irish audiences, but also with those of the other Abbey playwrights, notably Lennox Robinson, Padraic Column and T.C. Murray. The trio, as mentioned in the previous chapter, were strongly influenced by Ibsenism and the realistic movement and advocated a concern with realistic social issues such as the problems attendant upon urbanization or industrialization. Yeats however, persisted in his role as the guardian and creator of tradition. However, the increasing popularity of the realists amongst Abbey audiences served to convince him of the need for a definitive ritual format and a new audience for his drama. As David Clark contends, Yeats considered his "man of action" period in the Abbey to "have been one in which he served strange gods, a period of illusion from which he retired knowing that its chief value was that it taught him that his role was not the management of men but the lonely perfecting of an artifact".[59] He turned to the Japanese Noh theater, to which he was introduced by Ezra Pound, the literary executor of the Fennellosa manuscripts which had introduced the unique drama to the West.

"Noh" means accomplishment, and Noh plays were the rituals of the Japanese warrior class. Yeats was particularly drawn to the fact that the Noh plays were for the select few, that they employed traditional mythology and symbolism and that they were filled with spirits and masks:

> The art of allusion is at the root of the Noh. These plays or eclogues were made only for the allusion. In the Noh we find an art based upon the god-dance, or upon some local legend or some spiritual apparition or on *gestes* of war and feats of history; an art of splendid posture, of dancing and chanting, and of acting that is not mimetic. – It is a symbolic stage, a drama of masks.[60]

The crises in these plays usually occurred when a character who appeared to be an ordinary mortal was suddenly revealed to be a god or a spirit. The Noh play is a purely ritual experience in which a unified vision of universal order is suggested through a parallel cycle of emotional responses arising directly from the presentation. Human experience is raised to the level of a spiritual or heroic ideal, and, rather than merely analyzing psychological or social problems, a cycle of Noh plays outlines an experience which incorporates a universal world view.

The Noh form afforded Yeats the means to effectively actualize his conception of drama as a sacred ritual. He modified the major principles of the form to emerge with a composite which bears the stamp of his individuality. Irish mythology replaced the

Japanese one in his bid to relate the concepts of the Noh to the Irish environment. In the essay, "Certain Noble Plays of Japan," Yeats defines his particular attraction to the quality of the Noh art form which is "the meeting of ghost, god or goddess at some holy place or much legended tomb, which reminds me at times of our own Irish legends beliefs."[61] Two striking aspects of the Noh which Yeats modified and incorporated in his plays are the mask and the dance. The mask and the dance in the Noh play have properties similar in nature to that found in African traditional drama.

The mask is used as a distancing and universalizing technique. An actor becomes a living embodiment of the character he represents when he assumes a mask; his entire body and spirit take on the character of the role as though the mask had a life of its own. Through the mask, he is able to suggest ideality, the archetypal rather than the individual character. The dance on the other hand embodies an idealized image of both the experience felt or aroused on the stage and the reaction. It often occurs at the ritual climax of the play, reflecting the particular idea or the entire quality of the play. When poetry alone ceases to be effective as an expression of intense emotion in the Noh play, the protagonist dances, projecting feeling beyond logic and conscious communication.[62] Yeats wrote a total of "Four Plays for Dancers," each a ritual based on a Japanese original: *At the Hawk's Well* (1917), *The Dreaming of the Bones* (1919), *The Only Jealousy of Emer* (1919), and *The Cat and Moon* (1926).

Soyinka's Theater

In formulating a ritual concept of a theater, Soyinka, like Yeats, immersed himself in the traditional milieu of his people. He did not, however, undertake the quest for a ritual form that led to his Irish counterpart's interest in the occult, mysticism and the Japanese Noh drama, since the African dramatic milieu within which he was working obviously incorporated the traditional ritual framework. Rather, he evolved a ritual theory of the theater which reflected his individual exposure and comprehension of the admixture of western and traditional concepts of the medium. His ritual theory of theater also had metaphysical origins and implications. He agreed with the common notion that human beings' apprehension and fear of the cosmic vastness which surrounds life creates the need for ritual, for a challenger, a representative to act periodically on behalf of the community. Ritual drama then is basically a "cleansing, binding communal and recreative force," and its setting is the cosmic entirety.[63]

Ritual is also the drama of the passage-rites of the hero gods, of their ordeal, death and re-birth, the re-enactments of which are projections of humans' conflict with forces which challenge their efforts to harmonize with the environment. The Yoruba world view, like its Celtic counterpart, operates a cyclic consciousness and postulates three major areas of existence – the world of the dead, the living and the unborn – all three being in a state of eternal flux. The world of the unborn "is as evidently older than the world of the living as the world of the living is older than the ancestor world.[64] A less well-known fourth mediatory world is the area of transition – "the chthonic realm, the area of the really dark forces, the really dark spirits, and it is also the area of stress of the human will."[65]

Traditional Yoruba world view also postulates the coexistence of the gods with humanity in these multiples worlds, an ontological postulate reminiscent of the traditional Celtic idea of the co-existence of the natural and spiritual orders, which Yeats capitalized on in his plays. Since ritual is concerned with the rites of passage of the hero gods, Soyinka elaborates on the rites of passage of three major deities of the Yoruba pantheon – Sango, Obatala and Ogun and especially that of Ogun – to arrive at an essentially ritual theory of theater which defines the experience of drama in the context of its audience-effective potentialities. The pantheon as earlier indicated, originated from one solitary being, Orishanla, defined as the primogenitor of both god and humans. His slave Atowoda, in an unspecified act of jealousy and rebellion rolled a huge boulder onto Orishanla, disintegrating him into an unspecified number of fragments. According to this creation myth the resulting multiple god-head initiated a division of labor among the gods.

The shard of the original primogenitor which contained the creative flint passed into Ogun, the Yoruba god of iron and war; hence, his association with artistic creativity and technological proficiency. Soyinka's symbol for Ogun is the snake, a complex polyvalent and universal symbol characterized by the contraries of male and female, life and death, solar and lunar, light and darkness, good and evil, wisdom and blind passion, etc. Ogun is the tutelary deity of hunters, blacksmiths, goldsmiths, barbers, butchers, mechanics, lorry and taxi drivers, indeed all workers in iron and steel, the minerals associated with him. Practitioners of the above-named professions pay homage to Ogun before embarking on duty, for protection against accidents and for success in their duties. He stands for absolute justice also, and is often invoked during the signing of treaties or pacts. Dawn is his particular hour and among the offerings made to him are palm wine, dogs and roast yams.

The gods, the fragments from the primogenitor, needed to come in contact with humanity for two reasons: to justify their existence by drinking at the fount of mortality and achieving "completeness," (Yeats' unity of being) and to inspect humanity and see if the world peopled by the shards from the common ancestor was indeed thriving. This contact however, necessitated traveling through a deep chasm of existential chaos, the abyss of transition, which had become impassable. One of the gods, Orunmila tried to cut his way through this abyss but his machete bent because it was made from lead. Ogun however, with his technical instruments "forged from the ore of mountain wombs, cleared and cut a path through the primordial jungle, plunged into the abyss and called upon the others to follow."[66] He is, thus, identified with this transitional abyss known as the fourth area of existence, where the inter-transmutation of essence, ideal and materiality occurs. For his singular act of courage he is the one deity appealed to for help in clearing the way or for removing the barriers in one's life.

Upon arrival on earth the gods went their various ways. Ogun came to the town of Ire, where he was well received, later returning its hospitality by coming to its aid against an enemy. After persistent pleas by the elders of Ire to accept the crown of leadership, Ogun finally consented; the festivities marking his kinship of Ire were however, marred by the machinations of Esu, a trickster god, who left a gourd of delicious palm wine for Ogun, knowing his predilection for it. Ogun performed more creditably than ever in the subsequent campaign against the town's enemies, but in the confusion generated by drunkenness, he slaughtered friend and foe alike, the destructive complement to his creativity manifesting itself fully.

The rites of passage of the god Ogun elaborate Soyinka's conception of ritual theater, because the god encapsulates the Yoruba cosmogony's "coming into being in his own rites of passage."[67] He is the key to the understanding of Yoruba metaphysics essentially because of his correlation with the numinous temper of that fourth area of existence, the abyss of transition. Soyinka avers that his leading the other gods through the primordial chaos of this abyss, although essentially a stress of the individual will was still a communal one, one which enabled the other goods to effect their aims. This communal factor is of supreme importance in the enactment of the Ogun rites of passage.

The actor in the ritual becomes the "unresisting mouthpiece of the god, uttering visions symbolic of the transitional gulf." He prepares himself mentally and physically for his disintegration and re-assembly within the universal womb of origin. He harnesses his will and disintegrates into this womb, the transitional chaos. He re-assembles himself, returning from the "hinterland of transition," communicating a new strength for action.[68] His disintegration and re-assembly in the abyss of transition is an act taken on behalf of the community of which he is a part. Members of this community are what Soyinka calls the "communicant chorus," since their collective consciousness incorporates the essence of that transitional abyss. This results in their active, mystical participation in the emotions associated with the protagonist actor's disintegration and re-assembly primarily through the interjection of poetry, music and dance, the integral qualities of ritual. Like the protagonist-actor, the community emerges from the ritual experience "charged with a new strength for action because of the protagonist's Promethean raid on the durable resources of the transitional realm."[69]

In his plays therefore, Soyinka concerns himself with the re-creation of that ritual experience. It is the experience which informs the expression in the dramatic medium, of his consciousness of contemporary society:

> In the arena of the living, when man is stripped of excrescences, when disasters and conflicts, (the material of drama) have crushed and robbed him of self consciousness and pretensions, he stands in present reality at the spiritual edge of this gulf (of transition), he has nothing left in physical existence which successfully impresses upon his spiritual or psychic perception. It is at such moments that transitional memory takes over and intimations rack him of that intense parallel of his own progress through the gulf of transition, of the dissolution of himself and his struggle and triumph over sublimation through the agency of the will.[70]

The traditional ritual of self-sacrifice taken on behalf of the community prefigures in the need for regenerative action in contemporary society in a number of his plays: for the selfless purgation of societal ills in *The Strong Breed* (1964) and in *The Bacchae of Euripides: A Communion Rite* (1973) where Soyinka re-interprets the Dionysian myth which informs the original Greek play in terms of the Ogun rites of passage to comment on post-colonial Africa. In *The Bacchae* the transference of the question of sacrifice from the slaves to the king Soyinka suggests that post-colonial African leadership needs to see their role as that of sacrifice on behalf of the people, for by drinking the king's blood, the community as a whole partakes of his power and all are revitalized and unified.

Ritual Theater and Tragedy: The Nietzschean Nexus

The idea of theater as ritual as advocated and practiced by Yeats and Soyinka is also essentially, a theory of theater as tragedy. Both reinterpret Aristotilean and Nietzschean concepts of the form in conformity with their vision of theater as a change-inducing vehicle. In their plays to be considered shortly they both transmute the tragic process from its previous associations with the individual and psychological processes to the much broader realm of communal or social process, where it becomes the most revolutionary form available for impacting upon human consciousness. Their reinterpretations tally with Raymond William's observation of the modem tragic tendency to connect "revolution and tragedy, connections lived and known."[71]

In the *Poetics* Aristotle, the father of tragedy defined the form as "the imitation of an action that is serious, having magnitude and complete in itself," in the medium of poetic language and in the manner of dramatic rather than narrative presentation, wherewith to accomplish the catharsis of such emotions as pity and terror, which finds its origins in the Dionysian dithyramb. In *The Birth of Tragedy* Nietzsche extends Aristotle's peroration on the form to postulate a theory which emphasizes the relationship between ritual and individual and metaphysical conflicts, and its influence on the audience member. Nietzsche asserts that tragedy "arose from the tragic chorus" of the Dionysian festivals; the most important feature of the chorus in his estimation was the fact that it was originally composed of satyrs with their "Dionysian wisdom of tragedy," a wisdom not cerebral but intuitive; "the Greek man of culture felt himself nullified in the presence of the satiric chorus, the state and society, and, quite generally, the gulfs between man and man give way to an overwhelming feeling of unity leading back to the very heart of nature."[72]

Nietzsche thus links tragedy with Dionysus, whose promotion of "intoxicated ecstasy" combines with Apollo's "dream inspiration" to provide the revelation of primordial oneness in a "symbolical dream image."[73] Incited to active contemplation and participation by Dionysian music, song and dance, the Greek spectator is drawn into empathy with the sufferings of Dionysus, who then emerges in the masked, statue-like dimensions of the actor. Tragedy thus, affords the spectator a surrender of individuality and a way of entering into another character. Magic transformation is the presupposition of all dramatic art. In this magic transformation, the Dionysian reveler sees himself as a satyr, and as a satyr, in turn he sees the god, which means that in his metamorphosis he beholds another vision outside himself, as the Apollonian complement of his own state.[74]

Like Nietzsche, Yeats and Soyinka place tragic ritual squarely in the metaphysical framework of man and his relationship with his universe.

Terror for Yeats is a necessary element of tragedy. It is "continually evoked by asking the ancient questions: Is there reality anywhere? Is there a god? Is there a soul?"[75] For Soyinka, tragedy is "the key to the human paradox, to man's experience of being and non-being, his dubiousness as essence and matter, intimations of transience and eternity, and the harrowing drives between uniqueness and Oneness."[76] Both also shared Nietzsche's view of tragic art as lifting one beyond the realm of self-conscious ego into the timeless, transparent world of primordial being. The tragic hero in their rituals transcends the self through an act of the will to define and resolve man's metaphysical situation. The hero in both cases is drawn from the national mythological heritage. He is defined primarily in terms of the Nietzschean superman or *Ubermensch*, one who is the sovereign creator of his own values, self-possessed, self-affirming, self-revering, an embracer of all the contraries within himself and of the hubristic qualities which distinguish him from other men.

This hero invariably also embodies Dionysian and Apollonian virtues; he is Dionysian in the Nietzschean sense that he encapsulates an urge to unity, a reaching out beyond personality, the everyday, society, reality, across the abyss of transitoriness – an ecstatic affirmation of the total character of life – the great pantheistic sharing of joy and sorrow that sanctifies and calls good even the most terrible and questionable qualities of life; the eternal will to procreation, to fruitfulness, to recurrence; the feeling of the necessary unity of creation and destruction.[77]

He is Apollonian in the sense of the "urge to perfect self-sufficiency – the highest form of self-affirmation in a cool, noble, severe beauty."[78] Yeats and Soyinka however, show a marked preference for the Dionysian qualities of the tragic hero as outlined above. The element of hubris is posited as being innate to the tragic hero, being the factor which defines his plunge into or a reaching out across the abyss of transitoriness, in which he suffers or disintegrates willingly to bridge the gulf between man and the supernatural, and become superhuman

By actively participating in the ritual drama of hero gods already familiar to them, in the sense that they are communal archetypes, the audience submerge themselves into the collective consciousness from which they individually emerge with a new sense of self as individuals and as a community. It is within this audience effect mechanism that the change inducing or revolutionary potentials of the tragic ritual lie. The plays analyzed in the following pages are essentially both artists' adaptations of the dance of passage of traditional Irish and Nigerian tragic heroes to the expression of their consciousness of contemporary socio-political realities, in the belief that individual and societal awareness and submergence in the tragic ritual leads to a broader communal or national awareness of these realities.

Yeats' Idea of Tragic Theater

Yeats does not predicate his definition of the tragic process on the rites of passage of a specific tragic hero, as does Soyinka. He, rather, generalizes the process, and then refers to specific examples within his mythological heritage. He defines tragic art as "a passionate art, the drowner of dykes, the confounder of understanding (which) moves us by to reverie, by alluring us almost to the intensity of trance."[79] In this state of reverie or trance, the audience-member is enabled to submerge himself in the suffering and resolution of the tragic hero. The suffering of the tragic hero, as he tries to bridge the gulf between humans and nature is essentially an affirmation of the will, the *hubristic* streak; the tragic hero chooses and executes his fateful action entirely of his own volition and not at the behest of others. The essential thing that happens to the hero, as to the great writer, is that he moves beyond the individual will to a higher apprehension. As Yeats puts it, "the heroes of Shakespeare convey to us – the sudden enlargement of their vision, their ecstasy at the approach of death."[80] He then defines the audience-member's experience of this suffering and resolution in terms of two closely-related concepts, tragic pleasure and tragic ecstasy.

Tragic pleasure is the actual state of reverie or trance, "the twilight between sleep and waking, this bout of fencing, alike on the stage and in the mind, between man and phantom."[81] Poetry, music and dance play a significant role in the momentum towards this reverie. They engender the prerequisite mood for tragic ecstasy, the moment of the audience's empathy with the actions of the tragic hero, their submergence into a communal consciousness from which they emerge with a new sense of self and community. With tragic ecstasy, the audience loses a sense of everyday reality; and the protagonist actor to them loses his humanity and becomes a symbol of one perfection with the hero: "Ecstasy – is the end of art – that mood awakened before an ever-changing mind of what is permanent in the world or by the arousing of that mind itself into the very delicate and fastidious mood habitual with it when it is seeking those permanent and recurring things."[82] Yeats' plays are infused with this experience of this tragic ecstasy.

The Dionysian/Apollonian qualities of over-reaching the self, strength of will, the unity of creativity and destruction are hallmarks of such mythical heroes as Seanchan and Cuchulain. In *The King's Threshold* (1903–4), Seanchan's self-imposed starvation is tantamount to a conscious, active choosing of death in the manner of the Nietzschean hero. The Youngest Pupil, recognizing his mentor's revolutionary attitude to death as something willed rather than inflicted announces that, "The ancient right is gone, the new remains/And that is death." Seanchean finds joy not only in death but also in the transmutation of values which would follow, beginning with the apocalyptic destruction of mediocrity.[83] The effect is to induce audiences into translating aspects of Seanchean's ritual to their environment, wherewith they relate it with the issues of hunger strike and death in the political protests against colonial rule endemic to early twentieth century Ireland, and to the need for a negation of the culture of mediocrity which defines Irish society. In the plays to follow Cuchulain, like Seanchean, is resolutely disdainful of political expediency and societal expectations. He pursues his heroic destiny, with all the tragic isolation from other men that this commitment entails.

Soyinka's Idea of a Tragic Theater

Soyinka squares his consideration of tragedy in the rites of passage of Ogun, his favorite god in the Yoruba pantheon. Juxtaposing the orthodox creation essence of Obatala with the revolutionary spirit of Ogun, he avers that the journey to "the heart of Yoruba tragic art" belongs to the "mysteries of Ogun and the choric ecstasy of revelers."[84] Like Seanchean and Cuchulain, Ogun embodies both Apollonian individualism and self-sufficiency and Dionysian disintegration within the abyss of transitoriness, the essence of recurrence of all things and the unity of creation and destruction. Soyinka however, expands Ogun's Dionysian attributes to inculcate a Promethean will to challenge: "Ogun is the embodiment of Will and the Will is the paradoxical truth of destructiveness and creativeness in acting man."[85] The will to challenge is responsible for "the channeling of ritual anguish into a creative purpose," which by paralleling his own experience with that of god, "releases man from a totality destructive despair, releasing from within him the most energetic, deeply combative inventions which, without usurping the territory of the infernal gulf, bridge them with visionary hopes."[86]

The infernal gulf is the abyss or gulf of transition: Soyinka's theory of tragedy like Ogun, plunges straight into this realm. The tragic spirit obtains in the anguish of severance, the fragmentation of essence from self which Ogun and his colleagues experienced in their bid to forge contact with humanity, the achievement of which posits the Yoruba metaphysics of accommodation and resolution. In the performance of the rites of passage of the god the protagonist actor reaches out to the chaotic, transitional gulf, "through areas of terror and blind energies into a ritual empathy with the god – who once preceded him in parallel awareness of their incompletion."[87] The ritual anguish he experiences in the inchoate matrix parallels that of Ogun eons earlier; and so is the creative purpose which releases him from a totally destructive despair and which enables him to transmit the essence of the gulf through song and dance. The protagonist actor becomes a mouthpiece of the chthonic forces of the matrix and his somnambulist improvisations, a simultaneity of musical and poetic forms are not mere representations of the ancestor, recognition of the living or unborn, but of the no man's land of transition between and around these temporal definitions of experience."[88]

The participant audience in the Ogun ritual understand this music for it is "filled with archetypes" from their collective mythical heritage. In experiencing (not just witnessing) the tragic rites of the god, they lose their sense as individuals into a communal consciousness, and parallel it with that of the god. Through submergence into the mythic consciousness they overcome the sense of despair over the loss of individual identity, the fragmentation of essence from self into a community, and recreate a new self through poetry and dance, both "celebrative aspects of the resolved crisis of their god."[89]

Chapter three
The Early Plays:
The Quest for a Ritual Format

The violent wrenching of the national psyche by colonialism, and the subsequent, often bloody struggles by colonized peoples to overcome and define their identities are thematic drivers for both Yeats' and Soyinka's earliest plays. Soyinka was commissioned by the Nigerian government to write A *Dance of the Forests* (1960) and to stage it as part of a concerted nationwide effort to define a national identity. This chapter aims to compare Soyinka's response to the colonial experience with Yeats' by analyzing three plays, *A Dance of the Forests*, *The Countess Cathleen* (1899) and *Cathleen ni Houlihan* (1902).

The Primacy of National Landscape
National landscape, in its physical as well as its cultural, specifically mythological, connotations, forms the framework within which both artists assess and prophesy on the consequences of the colonial experience on their respective societies. Soyinka's use of national landscape in *A Dance of the Forests* conforms with Yeats' argument

in *Essays and Introductions* that "a writer should hold as in a mirror, the colors of his own climate and scenery in their right proportion".[1] In *The Countess Cathleen* and *Cathleen ni Houlihan,* Yeats projects a rural Irish physical landscape, which he infuses with a romantic, almost prelapsarian quality. He evokes and celebrates a sense of the mystical quality of Ireland, her 'other worldliness' which he infers has been contaminated by British colonialism. In *A Dance of the Forests,* Soyinka projects a forest where the gods and men assemble to celebrate the Gathering of the Tribes, Soyinka's euphemism for Nigerian Independence. The physical forest, in traditional Yoruba world view, is the repository of the unknown, of the supernatural and the cosmic entity which humanity holds in awe and with which we commune through intermittent ritual performances.

Complementing a stark physical landscape in each play is a mythological counterpart. *The Countess Cathleen* is based on a traditional Irish story which Yeats came across while compiling his *Fairy and Folk Tales of the Irish Peasantry* (1888). He defined the story as an example of one of life's paradigms which, though rare, is repetitive – that of self-sacrifice for the collective good, particularly when faced with a Faustian choice. It details the arrival to a poverty stricken Ireland of two demon merchants who flaunt their wealth, buying up the souls of the poor and needy. The leader of the peasants', the Countess Kitty O'Connor, sells all her treasures, retaining only her castle and its surrounding pastures to save her subjects. The merchants are not satisfied, however, and they continue with their merchandising, forcing her rural subjects to choose between starvation to death and eternal service to the devil. Following a night of anguish caused by indecision the Countess decides to sell her own soul for the highest price she can get. Three days later she is found dead but the sin of the sale of her soul to the devil, entered into out of charity, is nullified by God.[2]

Cathleen ni Houlihan, is based on the traditional conception of Ireland as the *Shan Van Vocht,* the poor but dignified old woman struggling to regain her stolen lands, popular in peasant imagination. The image, as Flannery notes, was,

> real enough in terms of Ireland's history of conquest and suffering; but it was transformed into mythology by the Irish poets of the eighteenth century, those last straggling descendants of classical bards of ancient Ireland who created a new poetic form, the *aisling* in order to express their almost invarying cry of agony at the destruction of Gaelic civilization and all that is implied for their own formerly honored way of life and art.[3]

A *Dance of the Forests* is Soyinka's first conscious attempt at dramatizing what is to be his enduring preoccupation with the metaphysical and ontological beliefs of the Yoruba people. To celebrate the Gathering of the Tribes members of the new community call upon Forest Head, an omniscient, supreme being with the same attributes as the Christian Creator God, to send them worthy ancestors to lend pomp and pageantry to the occasion. Through the agency of Aroni, however, Forest Head sends them the Dead Man and the Dead Woman instead, whose contact with three human protagonists, Demoke, Rola and Adenebi sets in motion the train of events by which the community, and by extension the nation, is confronted with the eternally recurring truths of its pasts, present and future existence. A more thorough examination of the plays will bear out the tentative nature of dramatic technique and vision, as both artists resort to landscape in its physical and less subtle cultural connotations to express the colonial stimulus on their consciousness.

In *The Countess Cathleen*, Aleel admonishes Oona for her insensitivity to the Countess' disquiet and warns her: "although you live unto a hundred years / and wash the feet of the beggars and give alms / And climb Cro-Patrick, you shall not be pardoned."[4] Croagh Patrick, the mountain to which he refers is in south-west County Mayo, and is one of the traditional centers of pilgrimage from which St. Patrick the Irish patron saint who, reputedly brought Christianity to Ireland, is said to have banished snakes from Ireland, leaving the country a snake free isle. The evocation of the mountain and its sacred associations highlights the concept of the spirituality of Ireland which Yeats deliberately juxtaposes with the materialism of the demon merchants, the obvious cause of the Countess's disquiet. In the same manner, the reference to Killala in *Cathleen ni Houlihan* is intended to stir up memories of past Irish successes in the struggle for nationalism.

Killala is the port in County Mayo where a French expeditionary force of about a thousand soldiers landed in August 1798, the year of revolutions in Europe. They were joined by peasant forces armed with makeshift weaponry; together they marched inland to Castlebar where they defeated a division of British troops. 1798 was also the year of the Wolfe Tone rebellion which was greatly influenced by the *egalite, liberte et fraternite* tenets of the French Revolution, as well as by Thomas Paine's Rights of Man declaration in the American revolution. The evocation of memories associated with Killala suggests Yeats' intention to effect a transposition of the spirit of the historical struggle to his contemporary world.

Against this physical landscape he projects two peasant families who basically refine the spirituality and edenic qualities of the landscape. In each of the two plays under consideration he emphasizes the peasant families' simplicity, humility and a-materialism, as well as their close harmony with nature. These simple peasants believe that their world is peopled by other beings not necessarily human in form. In *The Countess Cathleen,* for example, Teigue Rua describes the demon merchants as "two birds – if you call them birds – / I could not see them rightly for the leaves – But they've the shape and color of horned owls / And I am half certain they've a human face."[5] In the Introduction to the play, Yeats avers that 'horned owls' are associated with evil in popular Celtic belief.

A miniscule stretch of the imagination will also associate the image with the Christian conception of Satan as a "horned" being.

The simplicity and dignity of the Rua family is in stark contrast with the lavish wealth of the demon merchants. Mary Rua continues to grind her 'quern', a traditional Irish handmill, while Teigue Rua brings in the turf or Irish peat, to keep the hearth fire going. The light and warmth of the peasant cottage contrasts with the cold and darkness of the woods from which the demon merchants emerge. The warm, innocent nature of the Rua family is reflected in their willingness to open their doors to any stranger in need. True to nature the invaders recognized and exploited this trusting and friendly nature:

> SHEMUS [*at door*]: Whatever you are that walk the
> woods at night,
> So be it that you have not shouldered up
> Out of a grave for I'll have nothing human
> And have free hands, a friendly trick of speech,
> I welcome you. Come, sit beside the fire.
> What matter if your head's below your arms
> Or you've a horse's tail to whip your flank
> Feathers instead of hair, that's all but nothing.
> Come share what bread and meat is in the house.
> And stretch your heels and warm them in the
> ashes.[6]

Rather than accepting the invitation in good faith, however, the demon-merchants subvert it to perpetuate a system of economic exploitation.

They are the agents of the "Master of all Merchants" and are responsible for the famine which has struck the land. Yeats' association of English colonialism with the ultimate evil, Satan, is a theatrically effective means of arousing nationalist sentiments against the prevailing status quo in the Ireland of the time. The famine which the demon merchants perpetuate is intended to recall its historical counterpart and is to be seen as a direct consequence of English colonialism. Having instituted an exploitative regime, the demon merchants deceive the peasants into selling their souls to the devil for money. They force them to exchange their innate spiritual qualities for their materialism:

> OLD WOMAN: God bless you, Sir [*She screams*].
> O Sir, a pain went through me!
>
> FIRST MERCHANT: The name is like a fire to all damned souls.
>
> MIDDLE-AGED MAN: Give me my soul again.
>
> WOMAN: [*Going On her knees and clinging to the merchant*]. And take this money too, and give me mine.
>
> SECOND MERCHANT: Bear, bastards, drink or follow some wild fancy
> For crying out and sighs are the soul's work.
> And you have none.
> [*Throws the woman off*] [7]

The Gillane family in *Cathleen ni Houlihan* exhibit the same simplicity and warmth as the Rua family. As with the traditional *aisling* Yeats subverts characterization to the message. His technique is to individuate each member of the family by his or her particular singularly mundane thought or need, deriving from the preparations for the wedding of Michael and Delia. Peter Gillane is preoccupied with the size of his son's dowry. Bridget, his wife, deliberates on the various domestic uses to which the dowry will be put. Patrick dreams of the greyhound pup which Delia promised to give him, while Michael dreams of Delia and of their impending marriage. Punctuating Yeats' stereotyping of the Irish peasantry are subtle yet evocative references to aspects of their life. Peter for example, mistakenly attributes the cheering off-stage signaling the landing at Killala to that of a hurling match. Hurling is a traditional game similar in nature to hockey; it was one of the games revived and encouraged by the Gaelic Athletic Association (GAA) as part of the struggle for cultural nationalism.

Given the innocence and honesty of the Gillane family their sense of shock at the plight of the Old Woman who suddenly enters their lives is hardly surprising. She complains of unwanted strangers who have taken her land from her and turned her out of her own house:

> BRIDGET: What was it put you wandering?
>
> OLD WOMAN: Too many strangers in the house.
>
> BRIDGET: Indeed, you look as if you'd had your share of trouble.
>
> OLD WOMAN: I have had trouble indeed.
>
> BRIDGET: What was it put the trouble on you?
>
> OLD WOMAN: My land that was taken from me.
>
> PETER: Was it much land they took from you?
>
> OLD WOMAN: My four beautiful green fields.[8]

The unwanted strangers are of course, the English colonialists. Yeats evokes a sense of their total unscrupulousness not only in the fact of theft but also in their choice of victim, a defenceless old woman. The four green fields refer to the four provinces of Ireland, Ulster, Munster, Leinster and Connaught. Green itself is an archetype representing Ireland and it is the color which dominates the Irish landscape during national day celebrations, also the feast of St. Patrick's Day, celebrated every 17th March. Yeats therefore suggests that colonialism is evil and obviates the need for revocative action.

Soyinka adopts a similar approach in A *Dance of the Forests*.

The physical landscape of the forest is a microcosm of the larger Yoruba metaphysical landscape within which Soyinka dramatizes a number of sociopolitical and ontological facts made more pressing by independence from colonial rule. The reactions of the three human protagonists, Demoke, Rola, and Adenebi, to the Dead Man and the Dead Woman suggest their culpability in a series of crimes with which Soyinka, working through Forest Head and Aroni, confronts them. Adenebi describes the wandering couple as "two mad creatures" who were "very unpleasant looking" and who "seemed to follow us all over the place," making him feel like vomiting".[9] His description encapsulates what the Dead Couple come to represent in the play: they are the guilty consciences of the three protagonists who are "unpleasant looking", following them everywhere, pricking their consciences continually and eventually forcing them to "vomit" and acknowledge their crimes.

Adenebi's near romantic conception of the threshold of independence on which the nation stands is a convenient camouflage for his implication in a particularly ignominious crime. In characteristic politicians' rhetoric, he speaks of "the era of greatness" and of ancestors who will be "our historical link for the season of rejoicing. Warriors, Sages, Conquerors, Builders, Philosophers, Mystics. Let us assemble them round the totem of the nation and we will drink to their resurrected glory."[10] His *double entendre* and his refusal to boldly confront the Dead couple suggest his affinity with those Africans who would glorify even the negative aspects of African history in response to colonialism and independence, rather than sifting through that past to derive stable norms for the present and for the future. Soyinka's well-known diatribes against the Negritudinists were based on a similar disdain for their blind celebration of the African and his past.

Adenebi's culpability in the deaths of the sixty-five victims of "The Incinerator," a decrepit lorry which, though officially certified safe, overturned and burst into flames on its way to the Gathering of the Tribes is not in doubt, despite his feigned concern for its victims. Disguised as Obaneji, Forest Head indirectly confronts him with his part in this crime:

> OBANEJI: Please ... it is only for the records.
>
> ADENEBI: Then to hell with your records. Have you no feelings for those who died? Are you just an insensitive human block?
>
> OBANEJI: I didn't kill them. And any way, we have our different views. The world must go on. After all, what are a mere sixty-five souls burnt to death? Nothing. Your bribe-taker was only a small-time murderer; he wasn't even cold-blooded. He doesn't interest me very much. I shall be writing his name in small print.[11]

What interests Obaneji is the larger, archetypal significance of Adenebi and his type, which Soyinka forcefully brings to bear in the flashback to the Court of Mata Kharibu.

The flashback to the Court of Mata Kharibu is a structurally significant device that Soyinka uses to demystify the past that Adenebi has just glorified. Soyinka dramatizes a particularly ignominious section of that history, the African's culpability in the decimation and enslavement of fellow Africans for which the white colonialist has always been held solely responsible, an abnegation of cultural archetype which recalls Yambo Ouologuem's *Bound to Violence*, and Ayi Kwei Armah's *Two Thousand Seasons*. As the Court Historian in the flashback, Adenebi is the cold-blooded advocate of war and wanton wastage of human lives:

> COURT HISTORIAN: War is the only consistency that past ages afford us. It is the legacy which new nations seek to perpetuate.
> Patriots are grateful for wars.

> Soldiers have never questioned bloodshed.
> The cause is always the accident your Majesty,
> And war is the Destiny.[12]

The fact of war as a repetitive evil which nations seek to perpetuate is fundamental to Soyinka's scheme. In demonstrating its past referents the Court Historian flamboyantly encourages Mata Kharibu to embark on a war even on the flimsy pretext of a woman's trousseau. This contrasts with the Warrior's condemnation of it and his courageous *non serviam* attitude towards Mata Kharibu.

In response to the Warrior's moral stand; he refers to the Trojan wars which he claims were fought on a pretext analogous to that in the play:

WARRIOR: I am no traitor!

HISTORIAN: I have here the whole history of Troy.
If you were not the swillage of pigs and could
read the writings of wiser men, I would show
you the magnificence of the destruction of
a beautiful city. I would reveal to you the
attainments of men which lifted mankind to
the ranks of gods and demi-gods. And who was
the inspiration for this divine carnage? Helen
of Troy, a woman whose honor became as rare a
conception as her beauty. Would Troy, if it were
standing today, lay claim to preservation in the
annals of history if a thousand valiant Greeks
had not been slaughtered before its gates, and a
hundred thousand soldiers within her walls? Do
you a mere cog in the wheel of Destiny, cover
your face and whine like a thing that is unfit to
lick a soldier's boots, you, a Captain –
Your Majesty, I am only the Court Historian and

78

> I crave your august indulgence for any excess
> of zeal. But history has always revealed that
> the soldier who will not fight has the blood
> of slaves in him. For the sake of your humble
> subjects, this renegade must be treated as a
> slave.[13]

Helen of Troy was, of course, the legendary cause of Greece's nine-year siege of Troy which was undertaken primarily on the question of regaining lost honor. In this play, however, the dishonored king no longer considers Madame Tortoise worth fighting for. But Mata Kharibu is spurred on by the rhetoric of the Court Historian and insists upon war for the sheer pleasure of the carnage involved. The Warrior's refusal to participate in such carnage earns him certain death. In keeping with Court Historian's recommendation he is condemned as a "moral termite" and sold to slavery and violent death; his anguished soul is made to wander in the under streams of the world for centuries, because its body was not properly buried.

Madame Tortoise relishes the idea of bloodshed and wanton destruction on her behalf and rightly envisages war as the defining moment of life in the Court. She is, therefore, perplexed by the Warrior's *non serviam* stance:

MADAME TORTOISE: [*Jerks up his head suddenly laughing*]: You are the one that will not fight for me

WARRIOR: Madame, I beg you to keep your distance. Restraint is a difficult exercise for a man condemned to dishonor.

MADAME TORTOISE: Restraint ha! That is virtue lacked by your soldiers or did you know that?

WARRIOR: I did not mean that kind of restraint. Madame, I know what havoc you have wreaked

among my men, and we now face the final
destruction of a good band of loyal men.
Somehow, I do not hate you. But, I do know
the power of blood on the brain. I beg you to
keep beyond my hands.[14]

The Warrior's stoicism prompts Madame Tortoise to order his
castration before imprisonment in the slave ship, in spite of his
pregnant wife's persistent pleas for mercy.

Back to the present, it is Rola who embodies Madame
Tortoise's attributes. She is a prostitute who revels in her proficiency
in prostitution and makes no apologies for the numerous young
men whose ruinations are directly attributable to her:

ADENEBI: Men! Some of them were hardly grown up.
We heard you liked them young, really young.

ROLA: I regret nothing. You men are conceited
fools. Nothing was ever done on my account.
Nothing. What you do is boost yourselves all
the time. By every action. When that one killed
the other, was it on my account? When he
killed himself, could he claim he did it for me?
He was only big with himself, so leave me out
of it.[15]

She repudiates the Dead Man's request for help, taunting his man-
hood, a repetition in the present of Madame Tortoise's deathly
sentence in the Court of Mata Kharibu.

Madame Tortoise is ironically, the inspiration for Demoke's
totem. "Madame Tortoise is the totem – most of it anyway. In
fact you might almost say she dominated my thoughts." Demoke
claims. The totem was commissioned by the elders in the community to commemorate the Gathering of the Tribes. Demoke

carved it out from the tallest tree in the Forest, the *Araba*, the sacred tree of Fshuoro, the god in the Yoruba pantheon most often imbued with the trickster trait. The fact that Oremole, Eshuoro's bondsman, was killed in the process indicates that the totem was doomed right from the start. By acknowledging the inspiration of Madame Tortoise, Demoke unwittingly suggests that the totem symbolizes many of her negative attributes. Thus, as members of the new community dance around it, they unwittingly commune with the spirit of cruelty, lust and violence it embodies and which become pre-eminent in the new post-independent Nigeria.

Demoke is arguably the most significant of the three protagonists. He is the creative artist, the sensitive member in the community; his characterization signals the importance which his ilk assume in subsequent Soyinka plays. As an artist in service to the community his intention was to design the totem to prick the conscience of the community. However, the circumstances surrounding its creation and their consequences force certain truths and realities upon him and upon the community. Demoke is the only one of the three human protagonists who is not repelled by the Dead Couple. Rather, he is anxious to question them for he is tormented with guilt over his role in Oremole's death:

[*Demoke rises sharply. Goes to the Dead Man*]

DEMOKE: Are you the one who fell from the tree?

ROLA: Use your eyes. He cannot be. Come away, for heaven's sake.

DEMOKE: Did you meet? Does he accuse me?

DEAD MAN: I always did want to come here. This is my home. I have always yearned to come back. – When I died, I fell in the under streams and the great summons found me ready. I traveled the under streams beneath the great oceans. I traveled the under streams beneath the great seas; I flowed through the hardened Crust of this oldest of the original vomits of Forest Father –

DEMOKE: And did you meet Oremole the bonded carver? Does he accuse me?[16]

Demoke the artist, the "son and son to carvers", the "master of wood and shaper of iron" is also is a servant of Ogun, and as such manifests the god's dual, contradictory qualities of creativity and destruction. As an artist he functions initially not in the service of the community but of himself. He carves the *araba* tree, the sacred tree of a god of the community. In terms of the values of the community and of the gods they worship, he has committed a damnable affront. Oremole, acting both out of a sense of communal values and as a servant of Eshuoro, had protested Demoke's desecration of the *araba* only to fuel the latter's envy. Demoke pushed Oremole down from the tree to his death. The re-appearance of the Dead Man and Dead Woman externalizes the inner torture he had being going through as a result of his impetuous act of envy.

In the flashback to the Court of Mata Kharibu he is the Court Poet. His parallel act of violence in Kharibu's court prefigures his murder of Oremole: his apprentice falls off a roof-top and breaks his arm while attempting to recover the queen's canary. Significantly, as the Court Poet, he can look into and confront Madame Tortoise with her cruelty:

MADAME TORTOISE: You have not told me. Where is your pupil?

COURT POET: Being a good pupil, Madame, he has just learned a new lesson.

MADAME TORTOISE: I am waiting to learn too, poet. What lesson was this?

COURT POET: In short, Madame, he was too eager,
and he fell.

MADAME TORTOISE: How fell? What do you mean?
Is he dead?

COURT POET: No, Madame. Only a mild fall. He
broke an arm.
[*They stare each other in the eye*][17]

Demoke's creativity and questioning spirit form the focus of the conflict between Ogun and Eshuoro, a dramatic counterpoint to conflict on the human level.

The gods who both define themselves in terms of humans and exert a tremendous influence on them, are equally culpable of heinous crimes and are shown to manipulate humans for their churlish aims. Ogun and Eshuoro want to figure prominently in the new nation; both thus, resort to various devious means to achieve this aim. Demoke's desecration of the *araba* tree and murder of Oremole is part of Ogun's strategy against Eshuoro, for it is under Ogun's *possession* that Demoke commits these crimes. In response Eshuoro, Soyinka's composite of *Esu* (chance) and *Oro* (the bestial in humanity), declares war on Ogun, on his acolyte, and on the new community whose cause they appear to champion:

ESHUORO: This great assemblage of theirs is an
affront. And I have suffered the biggest insult
any son of Forest Head has ever experienced
from the hands of a human insect.

MURETE: Ask for justice from Forest Head.

ESHUORO: Am I his son or am I not? I have told
him. I have asked that he pass judgment for my
limbs that were hacked off piece by piece. For
my eyes that were gouged out and my roots

disrespectfully made naked to the world. For
the desecration of my forest body.

MURETE: What are you talking about? Is it still about
the woodcutter who chopped off your top?

ESHUORO: Have you not been to the town center?
Have you not seen this new thing he made
from me? The beacon for the gathering of the
tribes. Have you not seen the center-piece of
their vulgarity?

MURETE: What?

ESHUORO: The totem, blind fool, drunk fool,
insensitive fool. The totem, my final insult.
The final taunt from the human pigs. The tree
that is marked down for Oro, the tree from
which my follower fell to his death, foully or by
accident, I have still to discover when we meet
at the next wailing. But my body was stripped
by the impious hands of Demoke, Ogun's
favored slave of the forge. My head was hacked
off by his axe. Trammeled, sweated on, bled
on, my body's shame pointed at the sky by the
adze of Demoke; will I let this day pass without
vengeance claiming blood for sap?[18]

Eshuoro moves to actualize his scheme of revenge against Demoke,
Ogun and the new nation they appear to champion in the
Welcoming of the Dead; this is the actual dance of the forests.

In dramatizing this, Soyinka manipulates features from
traditional or festival theater in his bid to confront the new nation with the "mirror of original nakedness." The "dance" and
the "mask" are two traditional theater motifs which he employs
to great advantage in the prophecies of apocalyptic doom for the
new nation and for humanity, doomsday projections inspired in

the main by Eshuoro. The delivery of the Half-child upon Forest Head's orders is the powerful catalyst that sets the ritual dance in motion. Forest Head orders the delivery so that "the tongue of the unborn, stilled for generations, be loosened". The Half-Child is an *abiku*, Soyinka's personification of the traditional Yoruba idea of malevolent interference in the development of a foetus thus, leading to either an unnatural duration of the pregnancy or to the birth of a child whose constant deaths and rebirths keep his parents in a permanent state of anguish. In the play the *abiku* becomes a symbol for newly independent Nigeria and, as such, suggests that the new nation will experience the uncertainties of identity as well as of direction as its traditional counterpart.

The birth of the *abiku* presents Eshuoro with the working tools with which he plans to actualize his vengeful scheme. As the Figure in Red, he first involves the Half-Child in a game of *sesan, a* traditional Yoruba game which takes the form of getting tiny steel balls into a number of holes carved out on a rectangular board. The game itself is symbolic of the tussle for the survival of the Half-Child in face of the spirit of death represented by the Figure in Red. The Half-Child's sense of doom is echoed in his lament:

> HALF-CHILD: I who yet await a mother.
>   Feel this dread,
>   Feed this dread,
>   I who flee from womb
>   To branded womb, cry it now
>   I'll be born dead
>   I'll be born dead.[19]

His sense of foreboding re-echoes in the utterances of the spirits summoned by the Interpreter on the orders of Forest Head. These spirits possess the three protagonists.

The Spirit of the Palm forecasts the perverse exploitation of natural resources by man to further his proclivities for war and bloodshed and is chorused in turn by the Spirit of the Dark, the Spirit of Precious Stones, the Pachyderms, the Spirit of the Rivers, the Chorus of the Waters, the Spirit of the Sun and the Spirit of the Volcanoes. They all forecast apocalyptic-doom for the new nation and for man. Indeed the Interpreter who summoned them is later revealed to be Eshuoro's jester. The Ant Leader and his various adjutants characterized by one complaint or the other also further Eshuoro's scheme. They represent the downtrodden and exploited majority, the "legion of the world / Smitten, for the good to come". The Ant Leader adds his own refrain to the chorus of doom for the future: after the scourge of silent suffering, there will be blind retaliation. The prophecies of apocalyptic doom for the new nation and for mankind crescendo with those of the Three Triplets. The Triplets outline three phases through which the community will pass on its journey to the dark future.

The First Triplet, the End that will justify the Means, corresponds to the present world of the living where man will always justify his destructive propensities. The Second Triplet, an over-blown head, is "the Greater Cause, standing ever ready, excusing the crimes of today for tomorrow's mirage."[20] He embodies the immediate future when leadership (the head) in the community would have swollen beyond all moral bounds with a sense of its own importance. The Third Triplet, fanged and bloody, is posterity; it corresponds to the real future when the new community would be plunged into intractable, internecine strife.

The course of Nigerian, and indeed African, history in the years following independence appears to have borne out the prophecies of the Triplets. Leadership has been characterized by dictators, military and civilian, with little sense of obligation to the masses and who believe in lifetime iron rule. The Nigerian Civil War (1967 to 1970) and the recent civil crises in the Sudan, Somalia, Angola, Rwanda and Burundi attest to the internecine strife prophesied by the Third Triplet, the "milk on which it has been nourished". The *ampe* dance that the Interpreter dances with each of the Triplets signals the relationship between them and Eshuoro, and their significance to the latter's scheme of vengeance.

Sacrifice and Regeneration

Soyinka is more than merely concerned with bringing the fact of evil as repetitive and cyclical. He proffers the idea of hope for regeneration, for a kink in the vicious cycle which is defines life on earth. His technique in this regard recalls that of Yeats, as this spirit of hope obtains in individual as opposed to collective will. It befalls the most sensitive member of the community, whose self-sacrifice on behalf of the community becomes the example which the rest of the community is enjoined to follow. Soyinka develops the cue from Yeats and defines the creative artist, in this case Demoke, as the sensitive member in his community.

These sensitive individuals who mediate on their community's behalf in the plays initially experience a Dionysian agony resulting from their being torn between self preservation and self sacrifice on behalf of the community. All invariably, pursue the latter line of action and the choice they make, although tragic, is primarily an affirmation of the human will. The Countess Cathleen in Yeats' play of the same name is the prototype of such individuals. She embodies many of the noble, enduring qualities of the peasantry which Yeats celebrates. She is also an aristocrat, not in the contemporary colonial snobbish sense of the term but, as Dorothy Wellesley testifies, in the "proud and heroic" sense.[21] Yeats often projected and celebrated an aristocratic ideal simultaneous with a peasant one and often averred that the two classes in Irish society were closer to the possession of the elusive Unity of Being, by virtue of their tenacious practice of the proud and heroic lifestyle.

In *Essays and Introductions,* for example, he observes that Irish myths and legends were different from those of all other European countries because they had "perhaps the unquestioned belief of peasant and noble alike."[22] And because they shared Unity of Image, Yeats argues that they also shared Unity of Culture and that through this they were closer to the attainment of the Unity of Being, ideally known by the artist than by the middle class element in Irish society. Given these facts, the empathetic relationship between Cathleen and her subjects is hardly surprising.

Cathleen's "goodness of heart" influences her decision to act to save her peasant subjects. Initially, she vacillates between self negation on behalf of the community and self affirmation and apotheosis through escape to the land of the gods. Aleel the poet, plays a prominent role in the latter aspect of her vacillation. He epitomizes the subjective world of the gods, of dreams, beauty and art which contrasts with the harsh realities of life. His language highlights the surrealism of this world:

> ALEEL: I was asleep in my bed, and while I slept
> My dream became a fire; and in the fire
> One walked and he had birds about his head.

> CATHLEEN: I have heard that one of the old gods
> walked so.

> ALEEL: It may be that he is angelical;
> And, lady he bids me call you from these woods
> And you must bring but your old foster mother,
> And some few serving-men, and live in the hills,
> Among the sounds of music and light
> Of waters, till the evil days are done.
> For here some terrible death is waiting you,
> Some unimagined evil, some great darkness
> That fable has not dreamt of nor sun nor moon
> Scattered.[23]

A part of Cathleen belongs to this subjective world of dreams which Aleel conjures for her: "He bids me go / Where none of mortal creatures but the swan / Dabbles, and there you would pluck the harp, when the trees / Had made a heavy shadow about our door, / And talk among the rustling of the reeds, / When night hunted the foolish sun away / With stillness and pale tapers."[24]

But she is pulled in the opposite direction by a sense of responsibility to her peasant subjects under the terrible yoke of the demon merchants. The conflict resulting from her pull to the two wildly differing worlds induces in her a state of trance where she sees her ultimate destiny in a vision. She realizes that the world of dreams represented by Aleel is lost to her, irrevocably. She perceives her primary duty as a participant in the universal scheme of things to be in the objective world, towards her peasant subjects. This epiphany inaugurates Yeats famous dichotomy of the life of man into the subjective and the objective, which he elaborates in *Per Amica Silentia Lunae* and in *A Vision*.

The subjective goal is briefly, to attain heroism or immortality through service to the self; while the objective goal is to achieve same through service or self sacrifice to others. Cathleen's avowed faith in the Virgin Mary and in Christ's teachings is symbolic evidence of this new consciousness of self and duty. She rejects Aleel's tempting offer, in spite of herself, for she has sworn "By her whose heart the seven sorrows have pierced, / To pray before this altar until my heart / Has grown to Heaven like a tree, and there / Rustled its leaves, till Heaven has saved my people."[25] She embarks on a battle of wills with the merchants who have made the acquisition of her soul their primary objective.

In response to further acquisitions of peasant souls and properties by the merchants she re-affirms her faith in "Him who does not forsake the world, / But stands before it modeling in the clay / And molding there His image. Age by age."[26] She assumes the mantle of an avenging messiah, out to halt the armies of the Devil in their eternal nefarious activity against the most precious creation of the Creator, molded in His own very image. The very powerful image of a female Christ invoked in the passages recalls the goddess Hibernia, the pagan goddess of Ireland in her various battles against Britannia, her English counterpart. To Yeats' countrymen with generations of deep devotion and practice of Roman Catholicism, side by side with their belief in the *Fianna*, the image is a rousing call for action against British colonialism.

Faith prompts Cathleen's agreement to a Faustian pact with the merchants:

> CATHLEEN: The people starve, therefore, the people
> go
> Thronging to you. I hear a cry from them
> And it is in my ears by night and day,
> And I would have given hundred crowns
> That I may feed them till the dearth go by.
>
> FIRST MERCHANT: It may be the soul's worth it.
>
> CATHLEEN: There is more: The souls that you have
> bought must be set free.
>
> FIRST MERCHANT: We know of but one soul that's
> worth the price.
>
> CATHLEEN: Being my own it seems a priceless thing.
>
> SECOND MERCHANT: You offer us –
>
> CATHLEEN: I offer my own soul.[27]

She offers her own soul on the pain of death and the victory of the merchants. This death is foreshadowed in the images of darkness and destruction drawn from Irish mythology with which Aleel heralds this triumph of evil.

> ALEEL: The brazen door stands wide and Balor comes
> Borne in his heavy car, and demons have lifted
> The age-weary eyelids from the eyes that of old
> Turned gods to stone. Barach the traitor, comes
> And the lascivious race, Cailitin,
> That cast a druid weakness and decay

Over Sualtim's and old Dectora's child;
And that great king Hell first took hold upon
When he killed Naoise and broke Deirdre's heart;
And all their heads are twisted to one side
For when they lived they warred on beauty and
   peace
With obstinate crafty, sidelong bitterness.[28]

Balor is the leader of the hosts of darkness at the great Irish legendary battle between good and evil, life and death, light and darkness, which was fought on the strands of Moytura, near Sligo, Yeats' own county. Cailitin is the wizard significant in the Ulster Cycle of Irish legends who used his magical artistry to war on Cuchulain, son of Saultim and Dectora. The "great king that Hell first took hold upon," Conchubar, pursued Deirdre and her lover Naoise and finally killed the latter by treachery. He is also held responsible for Cuchulain's death by drowning, a factor which Yeats capitalizes upon in his plays concerning the rites of passage of the tragic hero-god. His association with the evil that has beset the land following Cathleen's faustian pact with the demon merchants is proleptic of the wider role he plays in the destruction of the heroic spirit in *On Bailes's Strand.*

The triumph of evil, though overwhelming, is only temporary. Man's innate nobility endures and eventually overcomes the external forces that threaten to subdue it. Yeats prophesies the ultimate triumph of Irish nationalism over English colonialism. By selling her soul to the merchants in exchange for an end to the plight of her peasant subjects, Cathleen shows herself immensely superior to the merchants who are allegedly gods in their own realms. The Supreme God recognizes this fact and, through the medium of a visionary light, he nullifies the Faustian pact, endorsing Cathleen's self-sacrifice. Christ Himself, in John 15:13, avers "Greater love hath no man than this, that a man lay down his life for his friends." The materialization of the Angels and the mystical, visionary quality of the scene suggests heavenly communion with the Irish peasantry. That God is actually on the side of the Countess and her peasant subjects constitutes the ultimate indictment of English colonialism.

In *Cathleen ni Houlihan,* Michael Gillane chooses self sacrifice on behalf of his community and by implication Ireland. More than the other members of the family, he is particularly sensitive to the Old Woman's plight and her story of injustices suffered at the hands of unwanted strangers. He ferrets out from her further instances of injustices, leading her to recognize in him a potential ally, somebody who "would die for love of me", like the nationalist heroes she recites to him, worthy examples of past attempts to rout the forces of English colonialism:

> MICHAEL: Were they neighbors of your own, Ma'am?
>
> OLD WOMAN: Come here beside me and I'll tell you about them. [*Michael sits down beside her on the hearth*] There was a red man of the O'Donnells from the north, and a man of the O'Sullivans from the south, and there was one Brian who lost his life at Clontarf by the sea, and there were a great many in the West, some that died hundreds of years ago, and there are some that will die tomorrow.[29]

The "Red man of the O'Donnells" for example, refers to "Red" Hugh O'Donnell (1571–1602), a Gaelic king who escaped from English imprisonment in Dublin Castle, participated in the resounding defeat of the British forces at the Battle of the Yellow Ford on Blackwater, went to Spain to enlist further aid against the British, but was poisoned there. The Old Woman is on a recruitment drive for young heroes like Hugh O'Donnell who will be ready to die for her.

Her memories incite Michael's enthusiasm. He urges her to elaborate on her dreams, her hopes; her "hope of getting my beautiful green fields back again; the hope of putting the strangers out my house," essentially manifest the nationalists' hope of liberating Ireland from the shackles of English colonial rule. Volunteers in this regard would have to pay dearly for their decision, but they would think such payment worthy of the cause. Michael is totally aware of the implications of deciding to fight on her behalf, against which is set the option of marriage to Delia and subsequent normal, family life. His vacillation between the two options generates the dramatic tension in the play. He is in a state of trance, "he has the look of a man that has got the touch," and vacillates between moving into the inner room, and consequently towards Delia and family life, and going outside to the voice of the Old Woman and towards certain death on behalf of Ireland. Delia only exacerbates his inner conflict:

> DELIA: Michael, Michael! You won't leave me!
>   You won't join the French, and we going to be
>   married!
>   [*She puts her arms about him, he turns towards her as
>   if to yield.*]
>   [*Old Woman's voice outside*].
>   They shall be speaking forever.
>   The people shall hear them forever.[30]

Michael "breaks away from Delia" and "rushes out, to follow the Old Woman's voice." The triumph of the Old Woman is a triumph of Ireland. The image of a victorious Hibernia is extended in her sudden transformation from an aged, down-trodden woman to a young beautiful girl who had the "walk of a queen," with which the play ends.

In *A Dance of the Forests,* Demoke undergoes a similar anguish of vacillation and final decision with enormous implications for the nation as the Countess Cathleen and Michael Gillane. The action of the Soyinka play is geared towards this precise moment, the Welcoming of the Dead when, having been handed the Half-Child, Demoke is to decide on a course of action pregnant with consequences for Nigeria, in particular, and for humanity in general. The tension is a dramatic rendition of the Ogunnian abyss of transition. As Ogun's acolyte, Demoke is the protagonist actor in the re-enactment of the rites of passage, a task he undertakes on behalf of the community. Soyinka's scheme has been to awaken Demoke, to the mirror of original nakedness, to the fact that he is both creative and destructive, as shown in his carving of the totem and his desecration of the *araba* tree and murder of Oremola respectively.

The masking of the protagonists upon the orders of Forest Head is mandated by the extraterrestrial nature of the dance of the spirits, which encapsulates the spirit of the fearful abyss, the chthonic realm that beckons Demoke's jump and passage. Demoke begins to move around in a slowly widening circle, chorusing Forest Head's order to Aroni; "Aroni, relieve this woman of her burden and let the tongue of the unborn, stilled for generations, be loosened."[31] The Dance of the Half-Child, its being tossed between the conflicting forces of Demoke and Ogun on one hand, and Eshuoro, the Interpreter and the Third Triplet on the other, is the catalyst which awakens Demoke to the whole meaning of Forest Head's scheme.

The Interpreter throws off his mask and reveals himself as Eshuoro's Jester. He draws the child into a game of *ampe*. When the Half-Child is totally disarmed by the Jester, Eshuoro picks him up suddenly and throws him towards the Third Triplet who makes to catch him on the point of two knives as in the dance of the child acrobats. Rola screams, the child is tossed up by the Third Triplet who again goes through the same motion, the other two Triplets continuing the furious *ampe* round him and yelling at the top of their voices. Demoke, Rola and Adenebi again, cluster together.

The Half-Child is now tossed back to Eshuoro, and suddenly Demoke dashes forward to intercept. Eshuoro laughs, pretends to throw the child back, Demoke dashes off only to find that he still retains the child: "They keep up this game for a brief period, with Demoke running between them, until Ogun appears behind the Interpreter, pulls him aside just as the child is thrown towards him, makes the catch himself passing it instantly to Demoke who has come running as before."[32] With a new sense of purpose, Demoke intercepts the Half-Child and plunges into the abyss of transition, thereby actively participating in the dance of the forest spirits.

He is initially overwhelmed by the depth and darkness of the abyss; he momentarily flounders about and hesitates, as he decides to whom to return the Half-Child. He, however, becomes aware of the fact that he is holding a "doomed thing" in his hands, that he "cannot reverse the deed that was begun many lives ago" and returns the child to the Dead Woman.[33] It is already doomed, dating from its genesis in the Court of Mata Kharibu in the past to the present conflicts between gods and between man for it. It must, therefore, be returned to its mother and await a more auspicious conditions to be reborn. Eshuoro's "loud yell of triumph," and the "glee of the Triplets" arise from their realization of the fact that Demoke has failed. Eshuoro's Jester clamps a sacrificial basket on Demoke's head, and he is made to climb the totem until he can no longer be seen. Eshuoro and his Jester set fire to it. Demoke falls but is caught by Ogun. His fall from the totem constitutes the moment of transition, when he stands as "it were beside himself, observant, understanding, creating."[34] Ogun lays him down gently as dawn breaks, leaving his gun and his cutlass beside his chastened acolyte:

OLD MAN: Demoke, we made sacrifice and
demanded the path of expiation…

DEMOKE: Expiation? We three who lived through
many lives in this one night, have we not done

enough? Have we not felt enough for the
memory of our remaining lives?

OLD MAN: What manner of a night was it? Can
you tell us that? In this wilderness, was there a
kernel of light? [*Rola comes forward. She looks
chastened*]

AGBOREKO: I did not think to find her still alive, this
one who outlasts them all. Madame Tortoise....

DEMOKE: Not any more. It was the same lightning
that seared us through the head.[35]

The new awakening he attains as a result of the lightning is proffered as the necessary preliminary to making independence work
for the nation.

Chapter four
Cuchulain and Ogun: The Dance of the Mythical Heroes

Soyinka's most enduring plays are arguably those based purely on the rites of passage of Ogun, the Yoruba god of iron and war. The ritual format in these plays reflects an exegesis of ritual theater as one where the stage becomes the "affective, rational and intuitive milieu of the total communal experience, historic, race-formative, and cosmogonic."[1] Soyinka's dramatization of the Ogun rituals recall that Yeats' with respect to Cuchulain, the hero-god of the ancient Gaelic epic, the *Tain Bo Cualinge*.

One common denominator between the two gods was that they, undertook processes of transition into mortality of their own accord, and came to live amongst men. Both manifested a multiplicity of heroic and destructive characteristics, and are significant national symbols in that they are the inspirations behind communal or individual undertakings. Yeats and Soyinka interpret the mythical heroes in terms of the Nietzschean *Ubermensch*, as sovereign creators of their own values, self-possessed, self-affirming, self-revering, and embracers of all the contraries within themselves.

They are projected as the quintessential tragic heroes. This chapter examines four seminal plays by the two artists, Yeats' *At the Hawk's Well* (1917), *On Baile's Strand* (1904); Soyinka's *The Road* (1965), and the *Death and the King's Horseman* (1975), to derive fundamental constructs pertaining to their use of the dance of their hero gods to express their consciousness and reaction to certain contemporary social factors.

In *On Baile's Strand* Yeats dramatizes the ascendancy of the materialist mentality he so despised and often referred to as the "base" element of contemporary Irish society. As suggested by its title, the primary framework for Wole Soyinka's *The Road* is adverse road conditions in Nigeria, arguably the number one cause of deaths in the country. The play is seminal in Soyinka's protracted preoccupation with this fact of national life; prior to the play, he had published a group of poems, titled "Poems of the Road", in his collection, *Idanre and Other Poems*. One of the poems, "Death in the Dawn," was inspired by Soyinka's own narrow escape from death in a road accident: what had assuaged Ogun's thirst for blood on that occasion was the blood of "dawn's lone trumpeter," a cockerel.[2] *A Dance of the Forests* had also hinted at his abiding concern with road conditions where deplorable road conditions, as well as the corrupt government official whom Obaneji indicts, claimed the lives of sixty-five victims of the lorry, aptly called the "Incinerator."

In an article in the now defunct newspaper, the *Daily Express* titled, "Bad Roads, Bad Users, Bad Deaths", Soyinka raged against those "responsible for road maintenance, road signs and road engineering because of the hazards they posed to Nigerian motorists."[3] He was moreover, "incensed by the hypocrisy of politicians who delivered self righteous speeches on international issues but who failed to help the victims of road accidents."[4] It was this malevolent force which the road has come to symbolize in national life that informed his decision in 1988 to accept the post of Chairman of the Federal Road Safety Corps (FRSC), which the Babangida

Administration offered him. The sycophantic and turncoat reasons which critics of his decision cited have proved untenable, especially in the face of his resignation from the appointment in December, 1991, and his subsequent face-off with the military authorities.

The ritual framework which both artists employ to dramatize the rites of passage of their favorite hero gods intuitively enables derivation of eternal, universal truths about the nature of being. *At the Hawk's Well* impresses the truism that, despite man's heroic exploits, his destiny is ultimately tragic. *On Baile's Strand* trails the deterioration of the history of man from a golden age of Cuchulains dancing with Shape-Changers on the shores of Ireland, to a leaden, materialistic world of Blind men leading other blind men, engineering thefts from untended ovens, and of Conchubars subverting the individual spirit by all means. From age to age, heroic and imaginative man declines; what the future portends for its Cuchulains is foreshadowed in the cozened Fool.

Civilization for Yeats, at the time of composition of the play, was riding the downward arc of the cycle of life. These impressions are borne out further by a statement of his in "First Principles", an essay published in the journal, *Samhain* in 1904, just as he was about to embark on his crucial revisions of the play. In the essay he projects civilization in human form which comes briefly into beauty and strength, and weaving from that beauty and strength, even as they imperceptibly wane, a kind of order, "until in the end it lies there with its limbs straightened out and a clean-cloth folded upon it."[5] The play reflects Yeats' meditations on the pessimistic theory of history to emerge in *A Vision*, and in his later plays and poems.

Soyinka's *The Road* can be interpreted in the more existential terms of our perennial concern with the exigencies of mortal life, our attempts to come to terms with primordial origins and with the fact of death. In so doing, we reach out to the supernatural world which gods and spirits inhabit, because physical forces alone do not sufficiently explain the ultimate value of our existence. Ritual is the most effective narrative medium for man's attempts to reconcile with himself and his environment, for "dramatic or tragic rites of the gods are engaged with the more profound, more elusive phenomenon of being and non-being."[6] Soyinka's strategy in his dramatization of the rites of passage of the hero-god concerned differs from that of Yeats. In both *At the Hawk's Well* and *On Baile's Strand*, Yeats presents Cuchulain, the hero-god himself in his own rites of passage. *The Road* and *Death and the King's Horseman* on the other hand, dramatize attempts at the reenactments of Ogun's passage to transition on the part of two acolyte actors, Professor and Elesin Oba. Similarities persist however, between the three protagonists; Cuchulain, Professor and Elesin Oba, the varying dramatic strategies notwithstanding.

At the Hawk's Well

In *At the Hawk's Well,* Yeats revises or creates a ritual of Cuchulain's transition to a tragic, heroic mortality. There is no foundation in the myths about Cuchulain for the story in the play.[7] Although Yeats based his treatment of the Cuchulain myth on Lady Gregory's *Cuchulain of Muiirthemne,* he followed his artistic instincts and ignored altogether the story of the great Cattle Raid of Cooley. Instead, he centers his treatment on Cuchulain's slaughter of his own son and his subsequent fight with the sea. In this play, he devises a situation similar to that found in the Noh plays, where the "adventure itself is often the meeting with a ghost, or god or goddess at some holy place or much legended tomb."[8] The action takes place in the depths of the mind of the audience and appeals directly to the *spiritus mundi,* the collective racial unconscious, in keeping with Yeats' intention that all Irishmen come together under the aegis of their archetypes, and share in the lofty emotion of Cuchulain's tragic heroism. As such, it is a powerfully concentrated play progressing, not by adding one event to another, but as Donoghue argues, "by releasing a cadence of energy, so that the fall of the cadence coincides with the end of the play."[9]

The play begins with Cuchulain on a quest for immortality which brings him to a barren landscape. He is introduced to us via archetypal images long associated with him:

> I call to the eye of the mind
> A well long choked up and dry
> And boughs long stripped by the wind,
> And I call to mind's eye
>
> Pallor of an ivory face,
> Its lofty dissolute air;
> A man climbing up to a place
> The salt sea wind has swept bare.[10]

The "ivory face" refers to Cuchulain's pale, sun-like features, who, although masked in keeping with the dictates of the Noh theater, will "appear like an image seen in reverie by an Orphic worshipper."[11] The word "dissolute" refers to the chaos and confusion prior to the self definition that result from Cuchulain's quest for immortality. His ascent to the barren well suggests a reaching for that which will define him, and his future.

The symbolism of the well has been exegetized in a number of ways: T.R. Henn associates it with sexual virility,[12] while Peter Ure claims that it is "the one precious and mysterious gift that will release Cuchulain and the Old Man, the one from the toils of old age, and the other from the bitter entanglements of the heroic fate."[13] However, Wilson's interpretation of the symbolism of the well in *Yeat's Iconography* seems more relevant to Yeats' intentions in the play. Wilson sees the well primarily as an archetypal symbol of life and makes a distinction between the full well, which is an image of Unity of Being, and the dry well which is "any ambition inimical to human happiness or any unattainable goal, spiritual or sexual."[14] The generation of all life is through water. The well, therefore, represents the source of life. Cuchulain is about to undertake a process of transition into heroic immortality, and his quest for self and life purpose exemplifies Mircea Eliade's assertion that the purpose of initiation ceremonies in traditional societies is to reconnect the initiate with the source of his life.[15]

The Musicians' are the tragic chorus in the play. Their faces are made up to resemble masks, unlike Cuchulain and the Old Man who actually wear masks. The difference between the two is, as Leonard Nathan suggests, that between "those who are simplified to some essential and intense quality, defined by the fate that formulates itself in the tragic moment of choice", and those who mediate between the human and the supernatural, for example, the Musicians, and those who participate now in the human and now in the supernatural, like The Guardian."[16] The Musicians first deliberate on the hero's quest, prior to his arrival: "What were his life soon done! / Would he lose by that or would he win?"[17] The answer they provide not only reinforces the symbolic thrust of the whole play, but also anticipates the Old Man:

> A mother that saw her son
> Doubled over a speckled shin,
> Cross grained with ninety years
> Would cry, 'How little worth
> Were all my hopes and fears
> And the hard pain of his birth!'[18]

Yeats himself explains in the subsequent stage direction that the words "speckled shin" are familiar to readers of Irish legendary stories in descriptions of old men bent double over fire. It denotes a life spent in loyalty to the values of the hearth, which symbolizes the unheroic, mundane or materialistic man.

The same reflection on the worth of long life informs also the poem "Among School Children," a dream poem in descriptive, meditative form which affirms the transcendence of art over time and change:

What youthful mother, a shape upon her lap.
Honey of generation had betrayed
And that must sleep, shriek, struggle to escape
As recollection or drug decide
Would think her son, did she but see that shape
With sixty or more winters on its head
A compensation for the pang of his birth,
Or the uncertainty of his setting forth?[19]

Cuchulain's quest for immortality is, in effect, a search for heroism, for that which would give meaning to his life, that which would make a mother's hopes and fears worth something, that which would justify the labor pains she endured in giving birth to him.[20]

The Musicians' answer reinforces the fact of Cuchulain's quest for immortality, and celebrates the heroic man, as opposed to the man whose loyalty is to the values of the hearth. Their bitter reflection on the worth of long life crystallizes in the figure of the Old Man, who embodies the fate the Young Man must endure, should he repeat the Old Man's folly. Yeats develops the two central figures by highlighting the differences between them. That the Old Man and the Young Man are opposites is first hinted at in the Musicians' song, "The heart would always awake / The heart would turn to its rest."[21] The aspiration towards eternal waking is clearly made manifest in Cuchulain's spirit, just as the desire for rest is in the Old Man's dogged wait.

The lines also suggest the various external forces which act on one, or the other, or both at the same time. The metaphor of the eternally wakeful heart suggests immortality as well, and it is this immortality that has drawn both Cuchulain and the Old Man to the well. The second line of the song suggests death, a force which overshadows them both and which is extended in the image of the Guardian of the Well, "sitting / Upon the old gray stone at its side / Worn out from raking its dry bed / Worn out from the gathering of the leaves."[22]

The dialogue subsequent to the antagonistic introductions between Cuchulain and the Old Man further establishes the differences between the two. The Old Man has waited fifty years for the Well to fill up, only to "find it empty / Or but to find the stupid wind of the sea / Drive round the perishable leaves."[23] Cuchulain, on the other hand, believes he will be lucky the first time around, for the "luck / Of Sualtim's son" will not desert him, and for "never / Have I had long to wait for anything."[24] The Old Man believes he is the victim of a deceit practiced by the Guardian of the Well and the people of the Sidhe. Cuchulain wonders why he should "rail / Upon those dancers that all others bless"?[25] The antinomies thus set up are significant

Cuchulain and the Old Man both seek immortality, but both initially, have misconceptions about the source of immortality. They both believe that they will achieve immortality by drinking the waters of the well. The Old Man does not realize that there is another means to attaining immortality, that is, the way of the hero, the direct confrontation with one's daemon or totem animal. In certain agrarian societies rites for the initiation of warriors involve a ritual coming to terms with a totem animal. Cuchulain, on the other hand, does not realize that the heroic destiny he will attain through confrontation with the heroic woman of the hawk will be a tragic one. The action in the play, therefore, gears towards their epiphany, the recognition scene in the manner of the great Greek tragedies, when both the Old Man and Cuchulain will be enlightened to true implications of their quest. The catalyst to this recognition is the woman of the hawk, who cries out intermittently and possesses the Guardian of the Well.

The importance of the hawk to Cuchulain's initiation is indicated in his earlier confrontation with it, when the spirit hawk was an actual hawk, during his climb up to the Well:

YOUNG MAN: – As I came hither
  A great gray hawk swept down out of the sky,

And though I have good hawks, the best in the
    world,
I had fancied, I have not seen its like. It flew
As though it would have torn me with its beak,
Or blinded me, smiting with that great wing.
I had to draw my sword to drive it off,
And after that it flew from rock to rock.
I pelted it with stones, a good half-hour,
And just before I had turned the good road there
And seen this place, it seemed to vanish away.
Could I but find a means to bring it down
I'd hood it.[26]

The image of the circling hawk evoked in Cuchulain's description of his contact with the hawk, is the same as that Yeats uses to mark the end of one historical cycle and the beginning of another in the poem, "The Second Coming."[27] A parallel ending of one phase of his life and the beginning of another befalls Cuchulain in this play, for through his confrontation with the hawk, he will commit himself to a life of anarchy, violence and war.

The hawk, according to the Old Man, is "the woman of the Sidhe herself, / The mountain witch, the unappeasable shadow / She is always flitting upon this mountainside / To allure or to destroy."[28] The hawk woman is Yeats' personification of the element of fate or the supernatural which intervenes in human existence to cause a deviation from the desired, heroic path. She is the "mountain witch," the mountain being symbolic of the mysterious realm of mystical or psychological experience. She is the "unappeasable shadow," which suggests her intangibility, her origins in darkness, the void, the visible manifestation of the invisible void. In *On Baile's Strand* these cruel spirits are represented in the witches of the air, the "Shape-Changers" whom Cuchulain blame for his failure to listen to the promptings of his heart in his confrontation with the Young Man from Aoife's country. Soyinka also dramatizes this daemonic or trickster aspect of the supernatural in the plays to be examined.

In *At the Hawk's Well,* this trickster factor is inherent in the Young Man's character. It is his daemon, his attendant or indwelling spirit. The Guardian of the Well is merely a medium through which she manifests herself. The hawk is Cuchulain's totem animal, his daemon, as the snake is for Ogun. In contrast with the polyvalent symbolism of the snake, the hawk is essentially an attribute of all sun-gods, and represents the heavens, power, royalty and nobility. The Rosicrucian Order of the Golden Dawn, the framework within which Yeats developed the traditional idea of a daemon, projected the daemon as a quasi autonomous inner spirit with a potential for both good and evil. It also exerts a profound influence on man's personal character and ultimate destiny. The rituals of the Order were basically, directed towards effecting contact between the initiate and his inner Daemon, in order to experience union with God, the source of all life. In this play, Yeats emphasizes the negative aspect of this daemon, externalizing and personifying it, in order to convey, dramatically her importance to Cuchulain's quest for immortality and her role in Cuchulain's union with his tragic destiny. We will see that Soyinka uses this technique too in *The Road,* where he emphasizes the negative, destructive aspect of Ogun's totem animal, the snake, externalizes and imbues it with feminine characteristics to dramatize her significance to Professor's quest for the Word and to his final, confrontation with death.

The hawk spirit's capacities to allure and to destroy are especially significant. They are the two means whereby she deceives Cuchulain as well as the Old Man. They are also the attributes she confers on Aoife, the Scottish warrior queen to whom Cuchulain runs at the end of the play. Aoife will bring up Cuchulain's son to challenge him and to eventually die at his hands, the core of the dramatic action in *On Baile's Strand.* The tragic, destructive qualities of the hawk-spirit are pointedly embodied in the Old Man's warning to Cuchulain:

> OLD MAN: – There falls a curse
>   On all who have gazed into her unmoistend
>   eyes;
>   So get you gone while you have that proud step
>   And confident voice, for not a man alive
>   Has so much luck that he can play with it.
>   Those that have long to live should fear her most,
>   The old are cursed already. That curse maybe
>   Never to win a woman's love and keep it;
>   Or always to mix hatred in the love;
>   Or it may be that she will kill your children
>   That you will find them, their throats torn and
>   bloody
>   Or you will be so maddened that you kill them
>   *With your own hands.*[29]

The "curses" form the basis for the drama in Cuchulain cycle of plays. The first curse manifests itself in Cuchulain's ambiguous relationship with Eithne Inuguba in *The Death of Cuchulain*, the second in his relationship with Aoife in the same play while the third obtains in his fight with his son in *On Baile's Strand*.

The Old Man typifies the intellect, the reasoning faculty in man which will always pursue the safe, and consequently "unheroic," line of action. Yeats frequently distinguishes between the reasoning faculty and the imaginative one, with the latter always emerging as the more preferable of the two. He attributes a number of negative factors in his contemporary world to the preeminence of the former, ranging from the failure of his relationship with Maud's Gonne to the prominence of materialistic mindset in contemporary Ireland. Reason has kept the Old Man waiting for the waters of immortality for fifty years; reason will keep him from the "heroic" means to immortality, which Cuchulain achieves. Cuchulain ignores the Old Man's warning, asserts his will and stares blatantly into the "unmoistened eyes" of the hawk spirit. This daring act of his marks the climax of the ritual.

The hawk spirit initiates this daring by first spinning a trance atmosphere into which all the figures fall. Trance is the prelude to the final dance to transition. Having possessed the Guardian of the Well, she begins the highly stylized dance which, by drawing his attention, will lure Cuchulain into gazing into her unmoistened eyes. This dance, as in the Japanese Noh theater, is the supreme moment in the ritual, when the initiate Cuchulain is reconciled with his destiny, with the source of his life

> YOUNG MAN: Why do you fix those eyes of a hawk
>   upon me?
>   I am not afraid of you, bird, woman or witch.
>   [*He goes to the side of the Well, which the Guardian
>   of tie Well has left*]
>   Do what you will, I shall not leave this place
>   Till I have grown immortal like yourself.
>   [He has sat down; the Guardian of the Well has
>   begun to dance, moving like a hawk. The Old
>   Man sleeps. The dance goes on for sometime].[30]

Under the spell of the hawk-spirit, Cuchulain "grows pale and staggers to his feet," rising to pursue her. The waters of the Well, in the meantime, bubble up as a reflex response to Cuchulain's possession by the hawk spirit, but because she has spun a web of trance, the hawk-spirit ensures that neither Cuchulain nor the Old Man notice this. In rising to pursue her, Cuchulain, as the Musicians communicate, has lost:

> What may not be found

> Till men heap his burial – mound
> And all history ends.
> He might have lived at his ease
> An old dog's head on his knees
> Among his children and friends.[31]

Peace will elude Cuchulain forever. The alternative would have been to live long and die peacefully amongst his children and friends. Skene rightly comments that "ordinary happiness and contentment are lost forever to devotees of the hawk-goddess".[32] Cuchulain confronts a tragic destiny as innocently and willingly as he confronts the Guardian of the Well. In so doing, he defines himself as a being of courage, ready to face whatever fate throws up at him.

The hawk spirit has projected her image unto Aoife and the tribes of female warriors who worship her, this we are told. They, as the Old Man indicates, have consequently been roused to fight Cuchulain. Ready and doom-eager, Cuchulain goes out to fight them, "no longer as if in a dream," but shouldering his spear and calling: "He comes, Cuchulain, son of Sualtim, comes!"[33] He goes into battle like a man consumed by desire. Later, we learn that he will make love like one overwhelmed with hate. He is no longer in a trance but fully accepts his hawk nature, his tragic destiny and the commitment to courage and heroism on which defines that destiny. Cuchulain embarks on the creation of his own myth.

That Cuchulain embarks on his life through combat is significant. It is intricately related to Yeats' reaction of the unfolding of contemporary world history. The play was published in 1917, one year after the bloody Easter 1916 Rising and when the First World War was in the final stages of its rage. War, to Yeats was the ultimate manifestation of the fact of man's destructive and tragic destiny. Cuchulain's final battle ready cry evokes this fact of human life. He will create his own myth, that which informs the other plays in the cycle. He is the perfect epitome of what Frank Kermode calls "romantic image," that image which lacks "simple intellectual content, bearing same relationship to thought as the dancer to the dance. As in dance there is no disunity of being, the body is the soul."[34] Cuchulain is both image maker and image.

The Road

Like Cuchulain, Professor in Soyinka's *The Road* wants to achieve immortality, that which makes, as the Musicians in the preceding play would put it, a mother's "hopes and fears / And the hard pain of his birth worthwhile." While Cuchulain hoped to attain this immortality by drinking the waters of the Well, Professor sets out to do so through a deliberate search for the an elusive "Word," both in its immediate cognitive meaning as printed matter, and in its more metaphysical connotations. He first reaches out to the supernatural world which he believes, like all mortals, controls human existence and meaning. As Cuchulain's quest in *At the Hawk's Well* takes him to a place whose physical geography is highly evocative of the supernatural, Professor's takes him to two contrasting earthly mediums of communication with the supernatural – the Christian Church and the traditional passage of transition.

Professor's quest for the Word in the Church has already taken place; it is dramatized via flashbacks to the past and from Samson's histrionic recounting of the search. We realize immediately that it was not successful, but an understanding of the context of this search is necessary to a comprehension of the subsequent search for the Word in the transitional abyss, which drives the present dramatic action. The Bible proclaims the doctrine of the Word and of the Church herself as its sole Guardian. The divinely inspired opening to St. John's Gospel proclaims:

1:   In the beginning was the Word, and the Word was with God, and the Word was God.

2:   The same was in the beginning with God.

3:   All things were made by Him; and without Him was

4:     not anything that was made.

4:     In Him was life, and the life was the light of men.

5:     And the light shineth in darkness; and the darkness comprehended it not. –

14:    And the Word was made flesh, and dwelt among us, (and we beheld his glory the glory as of the only begotten Son of the Father), full of grace and truth. –

16:    And of his fullness have all we received, and grace for grace.[35]

The Bible tells us that the Word is the Lord Jesus Christ, the true Light that enlightens, the Light that shines in the darkness of uncertainty of existence. Professor was attracted to these attributes of the Christian Word and, like a latter day pastor hoping to tap into its miraculous powers for his own self-aggrandizing ends, he was a very diligent Christian.

His reverence for the power of the Word was such that he bowed his head every time his pastor mentioned the name of Jesus Christ. He developed spiritually to a point where his powers of oratory drew new converts. The Church, however, soon began to lose her luster for him basically because he was unable to harness the awesome power of the Word to his nefarious intentions. He grew disillusioned with the Church and soon the hypocrisy of his studied Christian humility began to manifest itself. He began to question doctrinal values, by engaging in debates and battles of will with his Bishop, during which he used his apparently superior powers of oratory to humiliate the latter. Samson recounts the story:

SAMSON: B.D. Bachelor of Divinity, stupid. But B.D. or no B.D. the man just couldn't knack oratory like the Professor. In fact, everybody always said that Professor ought to preach sermons but a joke is a joke, I mean, the man is not ordained. So we had to be satisfied with him reading the

lesson and I'm telling you, three-quarters of the
congregation only came to hear his voice. And
the Bishop was jealous. When the Bishop came
on his monthly visits and preached the sermon
after Professor's lesson, it was a knockout pure
and simple. Before Bishop open in mout' half
de church don go to sleep. And the ones who
stayed awake only watched Professor taking
notes. [*Whips out his notebook and stabs it with
furious notes.*] That means, serious grammatical
error. Bishop done trow way bomb![36]

The war of wills between Professor and the Bishop came to a head in
the wall of Jericho incident, a farcical parody of the Old Testament
incident which marked Professor's formal withdrawal from the
search for the Word in the Church.

The wall, obviously an unstable wall bounding the Church,
fell down because the congregation watching the battle of wills
was "riding the wall like a victory horse. Everybody, grown-up
customers and all the riff-raff, turning somersaults in and out of
the Churchyard. Suddenly – Gbram!" It all came tumbling down.[37]
In the recollections of Professor's association with the Church
Soyinka satirizes the Church in contemporary Nigeria to capture
the prevalence of an increasingly corrupt apostolate in the formal
Churches, and the new, money-spinning evangelism, originating
from abandoned garages and warehouses all over the country.
Salubi nails it down when he concludes, "Dat one no be Church,
na high society," where corrupt leadership subvert the biblical
dictum to read "Give us this day our daily bribe.[38] Professor's own
reminiscences of the Wall of Jericho incident reveal the contempt
subsequent to his search for the Word in the Church:

PROF: Sin and wages, wages and sin. (*Stops. Turns
and faces the Church*). If you could see through

> that sealed Church window, you will see the
> lectern bearing the Word on bronze. I stood
> often behind the bronze wings of the eagle;
> on the broad span of the eagle's outstretched
> wings rested the Word. Oh what a blasphemy
> it all was but I did not know it – Oh the Word
> is a terrible fire and we burned them by the
> ear. Only that was not the Word you see, Oh
> no, it was not. And so for every dwelling that
> fell ten more rose in its place until they grew
> so bold that one grew here, setting its laughter
> against the very throats of the organ pipes,
> Every evening until I thought, until one day I
> thought, I have never really known what lies
> beyond that window. And one night, the wall
> fell down. I heard the laughter of children
> and the wall fell down in an uproar of flesh
> and dust. And I left the Word hanging in the
> colored light of sainted windows...[39]

His rejection echoes the young Soyinka's conscious decision to turn from the deep, Christian beliefs of his mother, nicknamed "Wild Christian" and his father, "Essay" to the traditional religious world of his grandfather at Isara, the world where Ogun reigns supreme.

Disillusion with the Church leads Professor's to search for the Word in the more macabre realm of the Road. The physical road, black tar clearing through what originally was an impassable forest or stretch of barren land, is the one major aspect of man's technological proficiency in transport eminently associated with Ogun in Yoruba cosmogony. It symbolizes the technological proficiency which he used to clear the transitional abyss, which he inherited from *Orisa-nla* or Original Oneness. In the metaphysical sense, the Road is the abyss of transition which links the dead, the living and the unborn, and within which there is a free flow of the essences from the past to the present to the future. Professor envisages the enigmatic Word as being "trapped" within this metaphysical road. His primary objective, therefore, is to crack its kernel, through a deliberate subversion of the functional utility of the physical road.

His brief flirtation with the Church teachings comes in handy, for the Church provides him with the necessary terminology with which to define his present nefarious purposes. He sets up his "Askident Store" in direct competition with the Bishop's church and uses Christian terminology to define his new creed of the Agemo, the religious cult of flesh dissolution. Agemo is the deity believed by the Ijebu tribe of south western Nigeria to be the supreme god. To them Agemo is the almighty god in preference to Olodumare, for whom this title is reserved among the other communities in the Yoruba nation. Agemo shares certain characteristics with Sorinka's Ogun; for example, he is possessed of an extreme vindictive temperament when he is offended, which is complemented by a more humane manifestation of his essence as soon as he is placated with rites and offerings. During his annual festivals he is virtually the god of the road, like Ogun.[40]

In professor's new search the Word is now to be found companion, not to abundant, eternal life, but to death. He concerns himself with the rites of with Agemo, the dark, mysterious, incomprehensible spirit of death whose prologue frames the play:

> My roots have come out in the other world.
> Make away. Agemo's hoops
> Are path ways of the sun.
> Rain-reeds, unbend to me. Quench.
> The burn of cartwheels at my waist!
> Pennant in the streams of time – Now,
> Gone, and Here the Future

Make way. Let the rivers woo
The thinning, thinning Here and
Vanished Leap that was the Night
And the split that snatched the heavy-lidded
She-twin into Dawn.
No sweat-beads droop beneath.
The plough-wings of the hawk.
No beetle finds a hole between Agemo's toes
When the whirlwind claps his feet
It is the sundering of the – name no ills –
Of – the Not-to-be
Of the moistening moment of a breath
Approach. Approach and feel
Did I not speak? Is there not flesh
Between the dead man's thumbs?[41]

The Agemo spirit forecasts a life of anarchy and violent death using the same image of the circling hawk as Yeats' uses in the poem, "The Second Coming". Humanity, according to the spirit's predictions, will be completely shrouded in darkness and thus fail to comprehend the plumage of this mysterious spirit of the future.

Things will fall apart completely. There will be no resistance to the violence of the elements. Professor is toying with this dangerous spirit in trying to uncover its essence. Soyinka, therefore, identifies Agemo as *Oro*, literally the word, as the dark, mysterious spirit of death. The spirit's negation of the periods – Here, Gone and the Future (Present, Past and Future times) – and its urging the merging of all periods of time into one continuous river of time projects the theme of transition. Soyinka, therefore, manipulates this most intricate aspect of the Yoruba psyche to frame the prophecies of doom and violence for the community which the spirit makes. Ben Okri in *The Famished Road*, opens his multi-dimensioned window into the world of the *abiku* thus:

In the beginning there was a river. The river became a road and the road branched out to the whole world. And because the road was once a river it was always hungry. – In that land of beginnings spirits mingled with the unborn. We could assume numerous forms. Many of us were birds. We knew no boundaries.[42]

Professor is convinced that the Word can be found in man's daily encounter with Agemo, the lord of the road and the spirit of death. This drives his intense study of the tools of the road and a conscious familiarization with the humans whose lives revolve around the road.

Soyinka presents the central symbolism of the road is presented in much the same way as Yeats does the hawk in *At the Hawk's Well*. The Road is projected as a snake which is personified and imaged as a woman who lures in order to destroy:

PROF.: But there is this other joke of the fisherman, slapping a loaded net against the sandbank. [*Looks around him.*] When the road is dry, it runs into the river. But the river? When the river is parched what choice but this? Still, it is a pleasant trickle – reddening somewhat – between barren thighs of an ever patient rock. The rock is a woman you understand, so is the road. They know how to lie and wait.

SAMSON (*anxiously*): Kotonu!

PROF. (writing): Below that bridge, a black rise of buttocks, two unyielding thighs and that red trickle like a woman washing her monthly pain in a thin river. So many lives rush in and out between her legs, and most of it is a waste.[43]

When "the road raises a victory cry" to announce new victims, the scene of the accident is like "a market of stale meat, noisy with flies and quarrelsome with old women." [44] The "Askident Store" is Professor's store house of readily collected data for his quest. To augment this data, he deliberately causes fatal accidents, chiefly by removing cautionary roads signs from their designated spots to ensure accidents then rushes to the scenes to collect more spare parts for his store, and to acquire further insights into the meaning of the Word from the death throes and configurations of the accident victims.

The road sign with the word "BEND" which he carries into the play amply explains his *modus operandi*. He found the sign "growing from the earth till I plucked it"; his arm is, therefore, armed "with the unbroken word." [45] And when the road subsequently raised "a victory cry to break my sleep" (when an accident was taking place) he hurried to "a disgruntled swarm of souls full of spite for their rejected bodies." [46]

When he removed BEND, "three souls you know, fled up that tree. You would think, to see it that the motor car had tried to clamber after them. Oh there was such an angry buzz but the matter was beyond repair. They died, all three of them crucified on rigid branches. I found this word growing where their blood had spread and sunk along plough scouring of the wheel." [47] He deliberately perverts the Christian image of Christ crucified on Mount Calvary, with the two robbers on each side, to describe the *rigor mortis* of the three victims. It is through such perversions that he arrives at a metaphysical middle ground of Christian doctrine and Yoruba metaphysics that affords him easy access to the powers inherent in the two.

His associates, the motor-park touts and drivers, all live off the road. They are nearly all steeped in the indigenous metaphysics. They all respond to him with a concatenation of emotions, ranging from terrifying awe to fear, to contempt. To Salubi,

Professor is a menace, "pulling up road-signs and talking all that mumbo-jumbo."[48] In trying to find out what all the mumbo-jumbo means, he busies himself with unraveling the mystery of Murano's importance to Professor. Samson on the other hand, is more daring. He persistently confronts Professor with clarification on the Word, knowing full well that their self-imposed *Oga* is dangerously prodding into action a god that is best left alone. That god is Ogun, the god of all professional drivers and touts who they all know needs to be appeased constantly with dog sacrifice. Kotonu has witnessed enough instances of the god's vindictiveness to be wary of driving. His partner, Say Tokyo Kid, a contemporary Americanized African avers that Professor is an "awright guy but he sure act crazy sometimes and I'm telling you, one of these days, he's gonna go too far."[49]

Professor is aware of the fear and reverence which the drivers and touts hold for the god and for the road and manipulates these to his own advantage. He mesmerizes them into serving him with his necromantic powers, and with his threats of death at the hands of the Invincible Word. To him they are "fools, vermins and insects;" the metaphors he uses to describe their action elaborate his utmost contempt for them. They are like the butterfly who "thinks the flapping of his wings fathered the whirlwind that followed," or the "burrowing beetle," who "feels he powered the arm of the [volcanic] eruption."[50] He exploits them and charges them fees on any matter which needs clarification. He forges drivers' licenses for them to keep them in the trade, ensuring further road deaths to gleans new insights into the meaning of the Word. To perpetrate his diabolical search he manipulates every situation. He transfers Kotonu's license to Salubi. He plays upon Kotonu's fear of driving in order to ensure a steady helper at the Askident Store and to tend to his daily needs, while in search of the Word. Finally, he uses his drinking parlor or bar to perpetuate his macabre kingdom of the quest for the essence of death, to expose the more sinister aspects of man and his death by sponsored accidents.

Murano, his mute personal servant, is one victim of such accidents. He was knocked down during a drivers' festival when he was wearing the *Egungun* mask to represent the drivers' god. Professor found him "neglected in the back of a hearse. And dying. Moaned like a dog whose legs have been broken by a motor car." He took him in and "looked after him till he was well again." As a result of the accident which happened when he was possessed by a spirit, Murano is now in a transitional state between life and death. To Professor, Murano is trapped within the metaphysical road to which he aspires to arrive via the physical road. Apart from his surface function as Professor's palm-wine tapper, he, in Professor's view, holds the secret to the elusive Word:

PROFESSOR: Deep. Silent, but deep, Oh my friend, beware the pity of those that have no tongue for they have been proclaimed the sole Guardians of the Word. They have slept beyond the portals of secrets. They have pierced the guard of eternity and unearthed the Word, a golden nugget on the tongue. And so their tongue hangs heavy and they are forever silenced. Do you mean you do not see that Murano has one leg shorter than the other? — When a man has one leg in each world, his legs are never the same. The big toe of Murano's foot — the left one of course — rests on the slumbering chrysalis of the Word. — When that crust cracks my friend — you and I, that is the moment we await. That is the moment of our rehabilitation.[51]

Professor hides the full facts about Murano form the other drivers and touts he caters to, awaiting a propitious moment when he will use him to serve his own purposes.

Professor also searches for the Word as printed matter, as the Yoruba *oro*. This aspect of his quest is not given the same prominence as the first two contexts but it is significant nevertheless. He carries about with him bundles of old newspapers supplementary to the cautionary road signs he collects from the scenes of accidents. The *guguru*, a delicacy made from corn starch, he orders from the Tapa woman, for example, is not so important as the paper she uses in wrapping it. Salubi gratefully accepts the *guguru*, while Professor carefully peruses the paper – one of football pools – where he attempts to glean cabalistic signs within which he hopes the key that leads to the Word may lie. Samson's efforts to confront his boss with the reality of the situation prove futile. "You cannot read, and I presume you cannot write, but you can unriddle signs of the enigmatic Word."[52] Contemptuous, he remains convinced that his final hope for unraveling the mystery of the Word rests with Murano, the spirit god he has held captive, and with whom he intends to "cheat, to anticipate the final confrontation" with the word, "learning its nature, baring its skulking face."[53]

Murano's renewed interest in the mask he was wearing when he was knocked down catalyzes Professor's dramatic confrontation with Ogun. He notices and immediately encourages the interest; he orders the dance of possession and restores the mute back to his *egungun* phase, hoping on a face to face meeting with the god: "I feel powered tonight, but that is usual. But I also feel, at last, a true excitement of mind and spirit. As if that day has been lowered at last which I have long awaited."[54] Professor subverts the dance of the spirit to his purposes he merges the traditional belief that a god becomes manifest during the transitional dance of possession with the Christian belief in the power of the Word made flesh. To the drivers and touts this is going too far. To their thinking no one can see a god made flesh and survive. His ultimate act of sacrilege, despite the fears and warnings of his associates on the physical road, is akin to Cuchulain's decision to stare into unmoistened eyes of the hawk woman in *At the Hawk's Well*. It is the assertion of will on the part of the protagonist, which inevitably leads to a denouement fraught with tragic consequences for himself and for his community.

In the silent drama which follows the complete possession of the *egungun,* Professor pays for the tragic penalty for his pride, his daring. Out of fear of Ogun's retribution and at his wit's end with Professor's constant sacrilege, Say Tokyo Kid engages the *egungun* in combat. With Salubi's collusion, he stabs Professor and mortally wounds him. He becomes the agent whereby Professor comes face-to-face with what the Word means, especially to all those who dare to usurp its essence. Man's constant efforts to overreach himself, to become immortal, are inevitably functions of his *hubris.* It is significant that each attempt only reinforces his punyness, the fact of his mortality. Death still remains the only certainty: "Spread a broad sheet for death with the length and the time of the sun between you, until the one face multiplies and the one shadow is cast by all the doomed."[55]

On Baile's Strand

Yeats second play in this chapter dramatizes one consequence of Cuchulain's tragic choice in *At the Hawk's Well.* Here we meet an older Cuchulain who was challenged to a war by Aoife, following the hawk-spirit's projection of her alluring and destructive capacities unto Aoife. Cuchulain falls in love with her and, in spite of her aggression, overcomes her in war and in love. He leaves her pregnant, though unwittingly. Aoife gives birth to a son whom she brings up to hate his father, just as much as she hates him for his desertion. The arrival of Aoife's now grown up son on the shores of Dundealgan, the seat of High King Conchubar, to whom Cuchulian is *supposed* to be subject is the legendary context of *On Baile's Strand.* His arrival is the catalyst that spurs Conchubar's demands of the oath of allegiance from Cuchulain. Conchubar and Cuchulain represent the dark and light sides of the moon respectively.

Conchubar is the mythical definition of what the Old Man represents in *At the Hawk's Well.* He embodies the values of the hearth, the mundane concern with reason and right government, and with rearing up children to ensure one's posterity. His symbol is water. Cuchulain, on the other hand, represents the fiery, heroic, individualist spirit, one who is not to be bound by conventions. He is the willful, instinctual man, as opposed to the reasoning man. His symbol is fire. The action of the play dramatizes the quenching of Cuchulain's fiery spirit by Conchubar, the water spirit. By this means Yeats warns of the increasing preeminence of materialist values in contemporary Irish society, at the expense of the heroic, individualistic spirit. Yeats also hints at the eternal consequences of this preeminence, namely, petty greed, materialism and, ultimately, war.

Conchubar has, on trust, a verbal oath of submission from Cuchulain, but "from Conchubar's point of view the problem with service offered as a free gift is that it may be withheld any time the giver loses respect for the receiver of the service. The gift of Cuchulain's loyalty is personal and does not relate to the office of the High King."[56] In his demand for this oath, Conchubar is motivated by both public and personal considerations. He cites the landing of the Young Man from Aoife's country on a shore which Cuchulain has left ill-guarded, the fact that "everyday / Our enemies grow greater and beat the walls / More bitterly," and the need to "make this land safe for them and theirs," as public reasons why Cuchulain must be bound.[57] However, there are hidden, more personal motives informing his request, the real reasons why he wants the oath of allegiance from Cuchulain. His attitude towards Cuchulain's reveals his spiritual affinity with the Blind Man. The Blind Man tells the Fool that Conchubar is to impose an oath on Cuchulain because "he ran too wild."[58] Conchubar characterizes Cuchulain as possessing "wildness of blood" and sees in the oath an instrument for curbing his "wild will."[59]

Cuchulain refers to a previous kinship between himself and

Conchubar but one which Conchubar has negated through marriage, public service and a hypocritical concern with public good.
Both he and Conchubar trace their origins to some time when
fire and earth were in greater contact; but while Cuchulain's fiery
nature still burns passionately, that of Conchubar has been diluted
beyond recognition: "Are you so changed / Or have I grown more
dangerous of late? / But that's not it. I understand it all. / It's you that
have changed. You've wives and children now, / And for that reason
cannot follow one / That lives like a bird's flight from tree to tree."[60]
The image of the bird flitting from tree to tree is particularly apt
in the context of the conflict between the two. Cuchulain's initial
repudiations of attempts to bind him are based on his conviction
of his birthright to limitless freedom, freedom to soar and land
when and where he wills, like the hawk, his daemon and totem
animal, whom "as men say, begot this body of mine / Upon a
mortal woman." He insists that he'll "not be bound / I'll dance or
hunt, or quarrel or make love, / Where and whenever I've a mind
to / If time had not put water in your blood. / You never would
have thought it."[61]

Against Conchubar's argument of the need for order and "right
government," for a politically stable state, Cuchulain champions
the individual will to do as he wishes. He is hardly perturbed by
the landing of the Young Man from Aoife's country since mention
of his name in the past has kept enemies at bay. He does not care
about having children to entrust his name to posterity because
his heroic exploits have been translated into songs which will
outlive him. Moreover, Conchubar's "pithless" and "marrowless"
children are enough to turn his thoughts against having any. In
sexual relationships, he finds that men of heroic temper like him
prefer women of spirit, like Aoife, the Queen of the North, to
Conchubar's women, who are weak, meek and submissive.

The difference between the two types of women is the difference between the woman who sits at the spinning wheel all day,
and defines her life in terms of her husband and her children, and

one who leads armies to war and lives solely on her own terms, like Aoife:

> CUCHULAIN: You call her (Aoife) a 'fierce woman of
>   the camp',
>   For having lived among the spinning wheels.
>   You'd have no woman near that would not say,
>   'Ah! how wise! What will you have for supper?'
>   What shall I wear that I may please you, Sir??'
>   And keep that humming through the day and
>   night
>   For ever. A fierce woman of the camp!
>   But I am getting angry about nothing.
>   You have never seen her. Ah! Conchubar, had you
>   seen her
>   With that high, laughing, turbulent head of hers
>   Thrown backward, and the bowstring at her ear,
>   Or sitting at the fire with those grave eyes
>   Full of good counsel as it were with wine,
>   Or when love ran through all the lineaments
>   Of her wild body – although she had no child,
>   None other had all beauty, queen or lover,
>   Or was so fitted to give birth to kings.[62]

Any relationship between men of heroic temper and like Aoife will always be a form of conflict, for the love is always as "a kiss / In the mid-battle, and a difficult truce / Of oil and water, candles and dark night, / Hillside and hollow, the hot footed sun / And the cold sliding, slippery-footed moon- / A brief forgiveness between opposites / That have been hatreds for three times the age / Of this long-'stabilized ground."[63]

This conflict in sexual relationship recalls Nietzsche's view of sexual relations in *The Birth of Tragedy*: "Procreation depends on the duality of the sexes, involving perpetual strife with only periodically intervening reconciliation."[64] In *Per Amica Silenia Lunae* Yeats relates this to the conflict a man must engage in with his daemon in the working out of his destiny:

> Then my imagination runs from Daemon to sweetheart, and I divine an analogy that evades the intellect. I remember that Greek antiquity has bid us look for the principal stars that govern enemy and sweetheart alike among those that are about to set in the Seventh House as the astrologers say; and it may be 'sexual love', which is 'founded upon spiritual hate,' is an image of the warfare of man and Daemon; and I even wonder if there may not be some secret communion, some whispering in the dark between Daemon and sweetheart.[65]

To Cuchulain, and to Yeats, this conflict in sexual relations is infinitely more preferable to the docility of Conchubar's type of woman.

A similar incompatibility of "hot-footed sun" and the "slippery footed moon" characterizes Cuchulain's relationship with Conchubar.[66] It is the conflict between subjectivity and objectivity. Yet, Cuchulain decides to submit to taking the oath he mere pretext that he should fall in line with his retainers who have all married and generally imbibed Conchubar's values:

> A YOUNG KING: Cuchulain, take the oath.
>   There is none here that would not have you take it.
>
> CUCHULAIN: You 'd have me take it? Are you of one mind?
>
> THE KINGS: All, all, all, all, all, all!
>
> THE YOUNG KING: Do what the high King bids you.
>
> CONCHUBAR: There is not one but dreads this turbulence

Now that they're settled men.

CUCHULAIN: – It's time the years put water in my
    blood
And drowned the wildness of it, for all's changed,
But that's unchanged. – I'll take what oath you will.
The moon, the sun, the water, light, or air,
I do not care how binding.[67]

His decision to take the oath is the preliminary submission to worldly values that facilitates the intervention of the trickster quality in the life of man, the Shape-changers. Here they are represented by the three Women, Yeats' version of the Witches of Endor, the keepers of the sacred fire who chant the intervention of the Shape Changers:

THE WOMEN: May this fire have driven out
    The Shape-changers that can put
    Ruin on a great King's house
    Until all be ruinous.
    Names whereby a man has known
    The threshold and the hearthstone,
    Gather on the wind and drive
    The women none can kiss and thrive,
    For they are but whirling wind,
    Out of memory and mind. [68]

The shape changers, presented as spirits borne on the wind are the harbingers of anarchy and destruction. Although the ritual of oath-taking is performed on his own element, fire, it is a fire lighted from the hearth, and, therefore, "fire brought into the service of domestic values, not the fire of the fiery cloud, the sun, or the old fiery fountains which are the source of all life."[69] Cuchulain vows to abide by the oath, for "I never gave a gift and took it again." His sense of duty towards his retainers and desire to lead by example will force him to adhere to it.

However, the entrance of the Young Man from Aoife's country triggers into being the consequences of Cuchulain's submission to Conchubar's values, the values of Dundealgan. Cuchulain is immediately drawn to the Young Man. He recognizes the Young Man's nobility and his uncanny resemblance to Aoife and throws aside the challenge the Young Man throws to him and proffers friendship in instead. The Young Man accepts his offer and the friendship is sealed with a ritual exchange of gifts. The exchange of gifts symbolically establishes the relationship between father and son for the benefit of the audience. To reinforce this, Yeats reinterprets the traditional account of Cuchulain's meeting with his father, Lugh:

> CUCHULAIN: — My father gave me this.
>   He came to try me, rising up at dawn
>   Out of the cold dark of the rich sea.
>   He challenged me to battle, but before
>   My sword had touched his sword, told me his name,
>   Gave me this cloak, and vanished.[70]

By accepting the Young Man's gift, Cuchulain is tacitly accepting him as his son, although he is ignorant of the relationship

Conchubar, the voice of reason and right government, intervenes in the developing friendship between Cuchulain and the Young Man. He forbids the friendship on the grounds of Cuchlain's just-pledged oath of allegiance to him. He bristles at his sudden loss of control over this flighty, brave knight of his kingdom and accuses Cuchulain of being under the influence of some witch of the air. Cuchulain is affected by the accusations. He is torn between his feelings of friendship towards the Young Man and his allegiance to

Conchubar. In the end, he submits easily to Conchubar's treacherous reasoning, aided and abetted by his courtiers:

FIRST OLD KING: Some witch has worked upon
    your mind, Cuchulain.
  The head of that Young Man seemed like a
    woman's
  You had a fancy for. Then of a sudden
  You laid your hands on the High King himself!

CUCHULAIN: And laid my hands on the High King
    himself?

CONCHUBAR: Some witch is floating in the air above
    us.

CUCHULAIN: Yes, witchcraft! Witchcraft! Witches
    of the air! [*To Young Man*]. Why did you? Who
    was it set you to this work?

Out, out! I say now It's sword on sword!

YOUNG MAN: But … but I did not.

CUCHULAIN: Out, I say, out, out![71]

In the ensuing battle Cuchulain easily triumphs over the Young Man, killing him instantly. Cuchulain has chosen the pragmatic and the reasonable, over the heroic and the imaginative, and thus ensured the continuous victory of the Conchubars over the Cuchulains of the world.

The full horror of his choice emerges with the awareness that he has also betrayed the Young Man, in the process of betraying himself. Cuchulain recognizes his folly through the agency of the Fool and the Blind Man, the chorus – protagonists in the play. The Young Man has been robbed of the honor which would have come from the clean acceptance of a direct challenge; given the sequence of events following his arrival at Dundealgan, we can only presume that he was not prepared psychologically for the fight.

The "quenching of greatness" which the Second Woman invites us to witness is all more tragic because of this fact. The terse, direct, question and answer dialogue between the trio of Cuchulain, the Fool and the Blind Man orchestrate and precipitate the revelation. In the stylized dialogue cited below Cuchulain's subconscious subtly but swiftly pieces together the scraps of information offered by the Fool and Blind Man, and connects these with his own recollected memories of his exploits with Aoife:

> BLIND MAN: None knew whose son he was.
>
> CUCHULAIN: None knew! Did you know, old listener at doors?
>
> BLIND MAN: No, no; I knew nothing
>
> FOOL: He said a while ago that he heard Aoife boast that she'd never but the one lover, and he the only man who overcame her in battle. [*pause*]
>
> BLIND MAN: Somebody is trembling, Fool! The bench is shaking. Why are you trembling? Is Cuchulain going to hurt us? It was not I who told you, Cuchulain.
>
> FOOL: It is Cuchulain who is trembling. It is Cuchulain who is shaking the bench.
>
> BLIND MAN: It is his own son he has slain.[72]

With this epiphany, Cuchulain inevitably moves into a madness that originates from the mind's inability to grasp and retain a pure truth. He sees Conchubar as the source of his tragedy, a "maggot" which has eaten up his earth, and like the thieving "magpie" that he is, has flown away:

> CUCHULAIN: 'Twas they that did it, the pale windy people

Where? where? where? My sword against the
　　thunder!
But no, for they have always been my friends;
And though they love to blow a smoking coal till
　　it's flame,
The wars they blow aflame
Are full of glory, and heart-uplifting pride,
And not like this. The wars they love awaken
Old fingers and the sleepy strings of harp.
Who did it then? Are you afraid? Speak out!
For I have put under my protection
And will reward you well. Dubtbach the Chafer?
He's an old grudge. No, for he is with Maeve.
Legaire did it! Why do you not speak? What is this
　　house? [pause]
Now I remember all.
[Comes before Conchubar's chair; and strikes out with
　　his sword, as if Conchubar was sitting upon it]
'Twas you who did it – you who sat up there.
With your old rod of Kingship, like a magpie
Nursing a stolen spoon. No, not a magpie,
A maggot that is eating up the earth!
Yes, but a magpie, for he's flown away.[73]

The resuscitating hawk in him goes after the magpie. Insane at this
juncture he goes out to the sea to fight the waves.

His fight with the waves is a re-interpretation of the original
saga material to conform to the total dramatic picture. In the
traditional saga, Conchubar is said to have arranged that his druids
bewitch Cuchulain into mistaking the sea for the assembly of the
Red Branch Kings. Yeats makes Cuchulain's fight with the sea
a function of his madness, a symbolic act representing his final
struggle against the water spirits, the objective, earthly values, that
have caused him immense suffering:

CUCHULAIN: Conchubar! Conchubar! The sword
    into your heart!
    [*He rushes out. Pause. Fool creeps up to the big door
    and looks after him.*]

FOOL: He is going up to King Conchubar.
    They are all about the young man. No, no, he is
    standing still.
    There is a great wave going to break, and he is
    looking at it.
    Ah! now he is running down to the sea, but he is
    holding up his sword as if he were going into a
    fight. [*Pause.*]
    Well struck! well struck!
    — There, he is down!
    He is up again. He is going out in the deep water.
    There is a big wave. It has gone over his head.
    I cannot see him now.
    He has killed Kings and giants, but the waves have
    mastered him![74]

The world of greed and materialism thrives upon the suppression
leading to the elimination of the individual spirit, the spirit that
presents it with the unvarnished truths about itself. It is through
this process of elimination that this world of greed perpetuates itself,
a fact extended in the Blind Man thinking of scavenging untended
ovens for food, while Cuchulain drowns

Death and the King's Horseman.

This play is inspired by historical events which took place in Oyo,
ancient Yoruba city of Nigeria in 1946. That year, the lives of Elesin,
his son, and the colonial District Officer intertwined, with the
fatal results set out in the play.[75] Soyinka is however, more than
concerned with the mere dramatization of the conflict of cultures,

such as found in his earlier play, *Camwood on the Leaves*. In *Death and the King's Horseman*, he returns once more to the theme of leadership and its impact on the well-being of the community, which forms the focus of the action in such plays as *Kongi's Harvest* and *The Bacchae of Euripides*. Soyinka modifies historical events and sets the action in the play back two or three years to embrace the period of the Second World War to capture his real intentions. This also bears out the artistic kinship with Yeats.

The Second World War was, among other things, another example of the archetypal tendency on the part of world leadership to exploit their poor for self-serving expansionism, just as Yeats saw the First World War as symptomatic of the continuing triumph of the Conchubars of this world over Cuchulains. The confrontation in the play is, as Soyinka directs in the notes to the play, largely "metaphysical, contained in the human vehicle which is Elesin, and the universe of the Yoruba mind." This suggests his primary objective of evoking consciousness to the eternally recurring archetype of leadership betraying the led for its own selfish goals.[76]

The play was written in 1974, fourteen years after Nigerian Independence in 1960, during which the nation had been plunged into a civil war that was basically another instance of the assertion of selfish wills on the part of leadership of the conflicting sides. In reviewing the state of the nation following the war and Independence in 1960, Soyinka harps back to an incident that had occurred fourteen years before Independence, evoking awareness of the fact that the negative forces which were at work in colonial 1946, are still at work in post-colonial 1974.[77]

Elesin Oba is the ritual vehicle through which this consciousness is evoked. As the play opens, the Alafin Oyo (the king of Oyo) has died, and Elesin Oba, in keeping with tradition as the Alafin's Chief Horseman, is to prepare to join his king in the realm of the ancestors. When we meet Elesin Oba, he is already on the metaphysical road to transition. He is at the precise point where he embodies the transitional passage, and in this sense, the Yoruba world itself. He is, therefore, the archetypal Yoruba or African man. The ritual of transition which he is about to perform is on behalf of his community, of which the market is a microcosm. It is a re-enactment of Ogun's daring to plunge into the fearful abyss of transition in order to forge a path for the other gods on their way to earth, the ritual which in Soyinka's view, encapsulates the Yoruba cosmogony's coming into being. The ritual is, thus, to be undertaken to ensure existential continuity in the community, in the contiguity of the relationship between the dead, the living and the unborn, integral to the community's system of beliefs.

As the Praise-Singer indicates, "Our world was never wrenched from its true course," and "there is only one world to the spirit of our race. If that world leaves its course and smashes on the boulders of the great void, whose world will give us shelter?"[78] Elesin Oba is initially insistent that he will not fail the community, for the communal world was not smashed on the boulders of the great void in the "time of my forebears, and it shall not in mine." To reinforce his promise he uses the riddle of the "Not I bird." Through this riddle, he images the traditional act by warding off evil, specifically death, by snapping the fingers round the head, as performed consecutively by the farmer, the hunter, the courtesan, the Mallam, his good kinsman, Ifawomi, and the palm-wine tapper in his story. He assures the Praise-Singer and his community that his own reaction to the "Not-I bird" was completely different:

ELESIN: Not-I
   Has long abandoned home. This same dawn
   I heard him twitter in the gods' abode.
   Ah, companions of this living world
   What a thing this is, that even those
   We call immortal
   Should fear to die

IYALOJA: But you, husband of multitudes?

ELESIN: I, when that Not-I bird perched
Upon my roof, bade him seek his nest again,
Safe, without care or fear. I unrolled
My welcome mat for him to see. Not-I
Flew happily away, you'll hear his voice
No more in this lifetime You all know
What I am.[79]

He assures the community that he is "master" of his Fate, and that "when the hour comes / Watch me dance along the narrowing path / Glazed by the soles of my great precursors. / My soul is eager. I shall not turn aside."[80]

His arrogant confidence recalls the *hubris* characteristic of the Nietzschean *Ubermensch*. The problem with such overweening pride is, as shown in Cuchulain's case, that it precludes awareness of the operation of negative force in life, which is the complement of the positive. In Elesin Oba's case, the operation of this negative energy is compounded by the colonial factor. Simon Pilkings is the colonial counterpart to Elesin, and just as Elesin feels duty-bound to serve the Alafin and the community, Pilkings feels equally so as regards King and Empire. The confrontation between the two is the inevitable conflict of cultures; the only difference is that Pilkings stands firm in his loyalty to the tenets of his own culture.

Motivated by a colonial sense of mission to civilize, Pilkings epitomizes colonial strategy of superimposing colonial laws upon a culture completely at variance with it. He had been instrumental to Olunde's, Elesin Oba's eldest son's, departure to a medical school in England, in the misplaced conviction that he was helping the son's escape from the clutches of an "obnoxious tradition." He has an appreciable awareness of the traditions of his subjects, enough to know which aspects of it to try to subvert to eliminate all potential threats to his government. He is further strengthened in his mission by his belief that the "Blackman's juju cannot touch him because he is a good Christian." He holds his imbecilic houseboy,

Joseph, in eternal thrall with this claim of infallibility from juju. He had once confiscated *egungun* masks and costumes, sacred to the spiritual life of the community, during a festival and imprisoned the masquerade and his acolytes in the belief that they posed significant threats to the peace of the community. This and subsequent actions signal a pathetic disregard for the elements of indigenous culture which contributes in its own way to the tragic outcome of the play.

To exacerbate the conflict of cultures, Pilking and his wife become the stars of the masque (a parody of the mask) held in honor of the visiting Prince Regent, by virtue of the *egungun* outfit they wear to the costume ball, and their derisive simulation of *egungun* festival antics, all in the name of entertainment. The following stage direction explains:

> *The prince is quite fascinated by their costume and they demonstrate the adaptations they have made on it, pulling down the mask to demonstrate how the egungun normally appears, then showing the various press-button controls they have innovated for the face-flaps, the sleeves, etc. They demonstrate the dance steps and guttural sounds made by the egungun, harass other dancers in the hall, Mrs. Pilkings' playing the 'Restrainer' to Pilkings manic darts. Everyone is highly entertained, the Royal Party especially who lead the applause.*[81]

One is therefore not surprised by his intervention in Elesin's ritual suicide since he typifies colonial's derision of non-western or alien traditional values. News of the impending suicide reaches him and he decides to put a stop to the ritual suicide, just because he cannot allow such to happen on his watch. What he and his ilk fail to realize is that the concept of self-sacrifice on behalf of community is not endemic to nonwestern cultures: it is fundamental to a number of cultures and religions, its most famous form being found in the life, sacrificial death and resurrection of Jesus Christ so that we might be saved.

However, the consequences of Pilking's intervention pale into oblivion when they are juxtaposed with those of Elesin Oba, the maker of his own destiny. Assuring the community of his readiness to complete the ritual of transition, he is honored in both verbal and concrete terms, in imitation of the promise of kingship and other rewards made by the gods to Ogun prior to his plunge into the primordial marsh in the mythical parallel. The Praise-Singer calls him a man who "Chanced upon the calabash of honor / You thought it was palm wine and / Drained its contents to the final drop."[82] Iyaloja and the market women clothe him in the richest and most colorful materials in the market – damask, alari, *sanyan* and indigo cloth – the material manifestations of honor.

The material rewards for daring to bridge the gulf of transition engender, however, Elesin's excessive appetite for the pleasures of mortal life, and an unacknowledged reluctance to let go of such pleasures. His lusts after a beautiful young girl, one of the spectators urging on his journey; he yields to an appetite for the world that draws him from his pre-ordained, honor-laden destiny. Knowledge of the girl's betrothal to Iyaloja's son does not even deter him. He insists on sexual intercourse, and almost upbraids the market women for expressing their doubts about the union.

He sees sexual union with the girl as a right and a duty, which he justifies in the context of his impending transition:

> ELESIN: – Do me credit. And do me honor.
> I am girded for the route beyond
> Burdens of waste and longing.
> Then let me travel light. Let
> Seed that will not serve the stomach
> On the way remain behind. Let it take root
> In the earth of my choice, in this earth
> I leave behind.[83]

He arrogates to himself the task of leaving behind the fruit of the union of the transitional passage and of the world. Thus, after sexual intercourse with the girl, the stain is "no mere virgin stain, but the union of life and the seeds of passage. My vital *flow*, the last from this flesh, is intermingled with the promise of future life."[84]

Worldly pleasures preoccupy his mind, even in the final moment prior to transition. It is precisely this triviality of thought, in face of such a momentous occasion, with its implications for the community, that causes his failure to attain the perfect state of trance necessary for successfully completing the transition. He asks his new bride to stay by him until his final passage. He has chosen to do his leave-taking in the market, "this hive which contains the swarm of the world in its small compass", where he has "known love and laughter away from palace", and where "nothing ever cloys."[85] Although he falls into a trance and experiences the ritual anguish consequent upon reaching out into the spiritual void, and of uttering visions symbolic of the gulf, the sense of failure, of having been too contaminated with worldly thoughts is pervasive:

PRAISE-SINGER: – Is the darkness gathering in your
        head, Elesin?
    Is there now a streak of light at the end of the
        passage, a light
    I dare not look upon?
    Does it reveal those whose touches we often-felt,
        whose wisdom come suddenly into the mind
        when the wisest have shaken their
    Heads and murmured, 'It cannot be done?'
    Elesin Alafin, don't think I do not know your lips
        are heavy,
    Why your limbs are drowsy as palm oil in the cold
        of harmattan.
    I would call you back but when the elephant heads
        for the jungle,

The tail is too small a handhold for the
hunter that would pull him back.[86]

The elephant is, however, pulled back in spite of its miniature tail
relative to its size, for we do meet Elesin Oba again, this time in
prison in the Residency.

In an article on mediation in the play, Dan Izevbaye refers
to the significance of *Esu-Elegba* in the context of Eleshin's failure.
Esu-Elegba is "the principle of uncertainty, fertility and change, and
the one god who makes possible the reconciliation of opposites
which we associate with mediation."[87] Izevbaye also refers also to
Joan Wescott's definition of *Esu*, the Yoruba trickster-god, which
is used to explain the trickster trait in the personality of the non-
conformist. [88] Yoruba creation myth details the role played by Esu
in Ogun's massacre of friends and foes alike during his sojourn at
Ire, bringing to bear forcefully the god's destructive complement to
his creative attributes. Soyinka had earlier personified this trickster
trait in *A Dance of the Forests,* in the character of Eshuoro, whose
conflict with Ogun over preeminence at the Gathering of the Tribes
formed the focus of consciousness in the play. There he emphasizes
Esu's mischievous traits at the expense of his more important role
as the messenger or public relations officer between man and the
supreme deity.

In *Death and the King's Horseman,* Soyinka recreates the
essences of both gods rather than actual personification. Elesin
Oba has manifested an Ogun-like courage in his willingness to
bridge the gulf of transition on behalf of the community. But he
also harbors an Ogunnian weakness, in this case lust for young
virgins. It is this weakness that opens the door for the intervention
of the trickster god, Esu, as part of an on-going archetypal struggle
between himself and Ogun. Esu's intervention in Elesin Oba's
destiny and that of the community is akin to the influence Shape-
Changers had on Cuchulain in *On Baile's Strand.* The implications

of the intervention for Elesin Oba are, as in the case of Cuchulain, ultimately tragic.

In prison and at the nadir of his spiritual fortunes, Elesin Oba first blames external forces for his failure. He accuses Pilkings of having "shattered the peace of the world forever," of having destroyed "not merely my life but the lives of many," and of having to "push our world from its course and sever the cord that links us to the great origin." Iyaloja, however, confronts him with the truth in a passage replete with images of heroism familiar to him:

> IYALOJA: You have betrayed us.
> We fed you sweetmeats such as we hoped
> awaited you on the other side. But you said
> No, I must eat the world's leftovers. We said
> you were the hunter who brought the quarry
> down; to you belonged the vital portions of the
> game. No, you said, I am the hunter's dog and I
> shall eat the entrails of the game and the faeces
> of the hunter. We said you were the hunter
> returning home in triumph, a slain buffalo
> pressing down on his neck; you said wait, I first
> must turn up this cricket hole with my toes. We
> said yours was the doorway at which we first
> spy the tapper when he comes down from the
> tree, yours was the blessing of the twilight wine,
> the purl that brings night spirits out of doors to
> steal their portion before the light of day. We
> said yours was the body of wine whose burden
> shakes the tapper like a sudden gust on his
> perch. You said, No, I am content to lick the
> dregs from each calabash when the drinkers are
> done. We said, the dew on earth's surface was
> for you to wash your feet along the slopes of

honour. You said No, I shall step in the vomit
of cats and droppings of mice; I shall fight them
for the left-overs of the world.

ELESIN: Enough, Iyaloja, enough.[89]

Elesin Oba fails because of his addiction to "left-overs," his pro-
clivity for the pleasures of mortal life in preference to the honor
and glory accruing from service to the community. In the wider
context, modern leadership fails the masses precisely because of
its self-serving proclivities, to use Iyaloja's metaphors, to be the
hunter's dog that eats the entrails of the game and the hunter's
faeces, rather than the hunter.

The tendency is innate and cannot be attributed to any
external colonial force or energy. Elesin himself recognizes this
fact when he admits:

ELESIN: It is when the alien hand pollutes the
source of the will, when a stranger force of
violence shatters the mind's calm resolution,
this is when a man is made to commit in his
thought, the unspeakable blasphemy of seeing
the hands of the gods in this alien rupture of
the world. I know it was this thought that killed
me, sapped my powers and turned me into an
infant in the hands of unnamable strangers. I
made to utter my spells anew but my tongue
merely rattled in my mouth. I fingered hidden
charms and the contact was damp; there was
no spark left to sever the life-strings that should
stretch from every finger-tip of an alien race,
and all because I had committed this blasphemy
of thought – that there might be the hands of
the gods in the stranger's intervention.[90]

The consequences of his "blasphemy of thought," of his attempt to rationalize and justify his weakness for "left-overs" is that the world he leads is now "set adrift and its inhabitants are lost." In the same manner, Cuchulain's staring into the "unmoistened eyes of the hawk-woman" inaugurates a life that drifts between a Fool and Blind Man to the end, and nobody can know his end.

Soyinka however, goes beyond Yeats tragic ending to develop the idea of regeneration seen in his earlier plays, the hope for a kink in the tragic cycle of life. That hope is, once again, embodied in the artistic sensibility. Demoke in *A Dance of the Forests* is the first dramatic intimation of the hope for change which the artist represents in the community. Emman in *The Strong Breed* also embodies this hope in his willingness to undertake the burden of the carrier in place of Ifada, on behalf of the community. In *Death and the King's Horseman*, it is Elesin Oba's son, Olunde who personifies Soyinka's perfection of his vision of the artist, and of the artist's significance to the community. Precisely because of his dramatic evocation of the abyss of transition, he transforms the concept of the artist's self-sacrifice on behalf of his community into myth, the ritual of which, he suggests, needs to be constantly re-enacted by contemporary leadership.

The ritual of Olunde's apotheosis begins in the third scene, where the reference to him misleads one into presuming that he has abandoned his culture and absconded from ordained responsibilities to the community. He is away at medical school in England. His return in the fourth scene, however, changes that impression. He had heard news of the Alafin's death and, instinctively, knew it was time for him to return home. From his conversation with Jane Pilkings, it is obvious that his sojourn in England, far from representing an abscondment from tradition and duties the Pilkings' had hoped it would be, has rather enlightened him to the necessity of the continuity in the traditions of his community.

His experiences in England have taught him that the colonial culture has "no respect for what you do not understand," and that its leadership, rather than sacrificing itself for the generality of its people, sends masses of young men to their deaths in the misplaced sense of survival.[91] Olunde's reaction to Jane Pilkings' story of the ship-captain who blew himself up rather than risk the life of others is significant, especially in the context of his own function in the play. He finds it "rather inspiring," an "affirmative commentary on life." In this sense also he sees his father's impending ritual suicide as one that will earn him the "honour and veneration of his own people." Hence his disappointment when his father fails to complete the transitional rites. Olunde's disappointment in Elesin Oba informs his scathing renunciation:

ELESIN: Olunde! (He moves his head, inspecting
   him from side to side)

OLUNDE! (He collapses slowly at Olunde's feet)
   Oh son, don't let the sight of your father turn
   you blind!

OLUNDE: (He moves for the first time since he heard
   his voice, brings his head slowly down to look
   on him): I have no father, eater of left overs.
   [He walks slowly down the way his father had
   run. Light fade out on Elesin, sobbing into the
   ground][92]

Olunde feels duty bound to act where his father has failed. He rushes to complete the ritual suicide because in Iyaloja's words, "he could not bear to let honour fly out of doors, he stopped it with his life."[93]

  But his ritual suicide hardly guarantees the spiritual safety of the community for, as the Praise-Singer tells Elesin, "this young shoot has poured its sap into the parent stalk, and we know this is not the way of life. / Our world is tumbling in the void of strangers, Elesin." [94] This final consciousness of the magnitude of his betrayal forcefully brought to bear by Olunde's suicide, the vituperations of Iyaloja and the Praise-Singer, induce Elesin Oba to strangle himself in one swift, decisive movement. It is all too late. Although he completes the passage, Olunde "will feast on the meat and throw him the bones. The passage is clogged with droppings from the King's stallion". Elesin will arrive "all stained in dung."[95] The fate of the community still hangs precariously in the balance.

Chapter five
Consciousness of War:
Cyclical History and the
Apocalyptic Vision

War is the most violent expression of man's destructive proclivities. Soyinka and Yeats witnessed first hand the destruction of human lives and property that are byproducts of war, and were profoundly and permanently affected by their experiences. The experience of war in each case was made all the more painful because each had foreseen and sounded the warnings of war years before the actuality. Yeats had predicted a bloody Anglo-Irish confrontation that manifested itself as the Rising of Easter 1916, and the Anglo-Irish War of 1919–1921, as can be seen in his early play, *Cathleen ni Houlihan*. In *On Baile's Strand*, as well as in other works, he had predicted the bloody clash of wills which harbinger would be the triumph of materialistic and aspiritual values in the Irish and world communities. His fears were concretized in both the Irish Civil War of 1921 to 23, and the two World Wars that occurred in his life time. Soyinka also foresaw the bloody conflict of sectional interests which actualized as the Nigerian Civil War, in addition to the various internecine wars that have since played themselves out throughout the African continent. The Three Triplets in *A Dance of the Forests,* for example, prophesied doom and fratricidal fighting as the *sine qua non* of the new nations.

Both dramatists reacted in much the same fashion to the reality of war. They overlooked the self-righteous reasons often advanced by the conflicting forces to condemn vehemently, the unnecessary bloodshed and carnage visited upon innocents. Both saw wars as major testimony of man's innate predilection towards the actualization of his tragic destiny, and corroboration of the repetitive, cyclical nature of human history. Their articulations of this repetitive, cyclical concept of human destiny reflects the significant influence of Nietzsche's *ewige Wiederkehr* in *Thus Spake Zarathustra,* where all life is perceived in terms of a pattern of birth and decay, ebb and flow, integration and disintegration, drought and rain, exhaustion and rejuvenation.[1]

In that philosophical treatise, Nietzsche asserts that the conflicting tension of opposites is predicated on man's hubristic infractions on nature which, in response, engender nature's countering contingency measures for the reassertion of her wholeness. Through *ewige Wiederkehr,* we comes face to face with the gravity of our insignificance in the grand scheme of things, with the reality that this present life is just an infinitesimal pause in the endless return of the forces that constitute and define us. We can only overcome perpetual nihilism by the strength of our willing ourselves to a higher sphere, redeeming and conditioning all existence, past, present, and future. The eternal conflict of opposing forces, therefore, derives chiefly from the utilities to which we put our energy, our will to power, either for positive or negative uses.

Human history is littered with examples of both positive and negative uses of this energy, seen, respectively, in the construction of great civilizations and monuments, and in the destruction of these same civilizations and its progenitors. The Apollonian-Dionysian polarity of the Greek Age, alternates throughout history, with all higher cultures beginning in barbarism, then ascending, descending, and being revitalized again by the energy of barbaric forces. This concept of human history and of life as cyclical, for both Yeats and Soyinka, are inexorably linked with myth. Both were less concerned with the actual achievements of past and present life than with their eternal and repetitive symbolisms. The past provides insight into the characters and events of the present, and offers a vision of the future. Their particular experiences of war in this century, for both, are testimonies to the eternally repetitive pattern of life. Two plays, *The Dreaming of the Bones* by Yeats, and *Madmen and Specialists* by Soyinka, particularly capture both artists' vision of human life and history as repetitive. But before we proceed with the exegesis of the plays we will examine in some detail the socio-political contexts informing their concept of cyclical history.

With war, Yeats' concern with the erosion of the heroic man, the increasing hegemony of the Conchubars over the Cuchulains of this world, as he would put it, climaxed. The First World War, the so-called war to end all wars, convinced him that "many ingenious, lovely things are gone" from this world, although the issues involved were far removed from the Irish problem.[2] The Rising of Easter 1916 took him, like many others, by surprise, in the sense that it posed the most definitive threat to English rule ever. He eulogized the heroes of the Rising in such poems as "Easter 1916" and "Sixteen Dead Men," but still wondered:

> Was it needless death after all?
> For England may keep faith
> For all that is done and said.
> We know their dream, enough
> To know they dreamed and are dead;
> And what if excess of love
> Bewildered them till they died?
> I write it out in a verse –
> MacDonough and MacBride
> And Connolly and Pearse

Now and in time to be,
Wherever green is worn,
Are changed, changed utterly:
A terrible beauty is born.[3]

The "beauty" that is born as a result of the martyrdom of these freedom fighters has a "terrible" aspect, and as such, poses greater problems for the life of the nation than ever. The Irish Civil War of 1922 to 23 left him with the conviction that out of all "the murder and rapine" will come "not a demagogic but an authoritarian government – I always knew that it would come, but not that it would come in this tragic way."[4] In "Meditations in Time of Civil War," he sets up images of permanence with which he contrasts the destruction and violence he sees all around him; such images include his tower, his sword, the unicorn, and his descendants. But he admits he could not avoid the realities of, "A barricade of stone or of wood; / Some fourteen days of civil war; / Last night they trundled down the road / That dead young in his blood."[5] The incidence of war is partially responsible for his attempts at propounding a mythical basis for the cyclical pattern of the life of man in *A Vision* – a scheme emerging from the *Spiritus Mundi*, his term for defining the vast unconscious of the human race through which he achieves a reconciliation with the opposing forces in the universe.

The principal symbol in both the 1925 and 1937 versions of the schema is that of a Great Wheel, which is constantly turning. Its revolutions signify not only all the antinomies (those opposites which contain each other) but also all the various cyclical patterns of death and rebirth. These cycles and antinomies can be identified in and used to explicate every facet of life in the universe: the psychological life of mankind, the whole course of human history, the movements of the four seasons and the heavenly bodies, and life after death. Four main essays elaborate Yeats' vision of the life of man: "What the Caliph Partly Learned," "What the Caliph Refused to Learn," "Dove and Swan," and "The Gates of Pluto."

The first and second essays are particularly relevant to our intentions in this chapter.[6] In "What the Caliph Partly Learned," Yeats classifies human beings into twenty-eight archetypes, each type symbolically associated with one of the twenty-eight spokes of the Great Wheel. The classification is made according to the individual's subjectivity or objectivity, words for which Yeats often substitutes the symbolical abstractions, *antithetical tincture* and *primary tincture*.[7] As the moon revolves around the Great Wheel, it waxes and wanes. At the fifteenth phase, which is a full moon, subjectivity is at its height; and at phase one, the dark of the moon, life is entirely objective.

Yeats divides human personality into four faculties, paired on the Great Wheel as conflicting opposites: Will and Mask, Creative Mind and Body of Fate. He considers them in relation to other divisions in the human personality: the conscious and unconscious aspects of the mind, the bi-sexual desires in every individual, the psychological as opposed to the supernatural Daemon, and the four principles, which are all in perpetual conflict. Such conflict is necessary for the existence of life itself, for, out of psychological discord, there emerges, for every human being, a consciousness of self-hood and a masterful individuality. In each human being's sublimation of conflict – the search for Daemon or Mask – the creation and enjoyment of art is made possible, as are all the noteworthy achievements of men. In "What the Caliph Refused to Learn," Yeats elaborates on his doctrine of cycles, antinomies and eternal recurrence.

The geometrical symbol on which he concentrates is that of a *gyre*, or whirling cone which at different times he describes as a triangle, a perne or a spindle, a wheel or a circle. He speaks of his symbolic cones as being two interpenetrating pernes or gyres, one subjective, the other objective, self-generating, whirling around inside of each other, revolving in opposite directions, and alternately expanding and contracting, a movement which can be diagrammatically represented as follows:

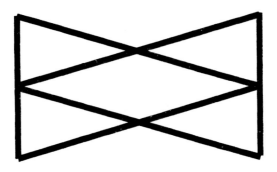

The Interpenetrating Gyres

Wedded in antagonism, the gyres symbolize the opposing elements that make up existence: male and female, sun and moon, life and death, love and hate, permanence and change, the natural and the supernatural. The centrifugal movement their interpenetration generates posits a situation where man or movement of life is conceived of as moving from left to right, then right to left. Once the fullest expansion of the objective cone is reached the counter movement towards the fullest expansion of the objective cone begins. The events of his time suggest to Yeats that history is swinging back again towards objectivity; mass movements, such as democracy, socialism and even communism are evidences of this shift towards objectivity when every man tries to look like "his neighbor and repress individuality and personality."[8]

The movement of the interpenetrating cones or gyres afforded him a vision into the future. This is a nightmarish vision captured in the figure of the Sphinx – the most potent symbol of man's predilection for violence and self-destruction foreshadowed in "The Second Coming."[9] The "widening gyre" in the poem is the gyre of objectivity which presages the beginning of a new age, as does the traditional myth of a second coming. The falcon is one bird which in Yeats' system is symbolic of this new age of objectivity; it is also the totem animal associated with the Cuchulain. The disintegration of order and the breaking of the "blood-dimmed tide" intimate the violence and destruction attendant upon the emergence of the Sphinx.

As with Yeats, the fact of war confirmed Soyinka's belief in the cyclical movement of all life, and in an apocalyptic vision of the history of man, of his irrevocably tragic destiny. The Nigerian Civil War was the long expected justification of the predictions of doom and cataclysm in the earlier plays; the war provided an immediate frame of reference for the disturbed apprehension of the African situation, to which he had given expression in his previous writings, especially in the progression along the line of vision which connects *A Dance of the Forests* with *Kongi's Harvest*.[10] The first rumblings of the Civil War, the massacres of Igbos in Northern and Western Nigeria, saw him trying to force awareness of the cataclysmic consequences of war on all sides concerned. These attempts, already catalogued in chapter two, led to his detention and subsequent imprisonment from 1967 to 1969. He paid the same price for confronting "leadership" with the reality of its intentions as the Warrior in *A Dance of the Forests*, and as does the Old Man in *Madmen and Specialists*.

Soyinka, however, does not relate his conception of the movement of the history of man as cyclical to a separate grand scheme of things as Yeats does in A *Vision*. Rather, his theory can be culled from the various references to it scattered throughout his works, especially in the collection of poems, *Idanre and Other Poems* (1967). The poem, "Massacre, October '66", with its superscription "Written in Tegel," places the massacres of Igbos in Northern Nigeria within a historical context. As Tanure Ojaide argues, "the Nigerian killings are portrayed as indirectly comparable to the Nazi holocaust as the poet uses the environment to which he has briefly fled to express the inhumanity taking place in his home country."[11] The Tegel referred to in the superscription is the district in Berlin where, during World War Two Hitler had supervised the flourishing of the Aryan myth, revolting for its decimation of millions of Jews and other non-Aryans, which the massacres in Northern Nigeria replicated. It is in the poem, "Idanre," however, that Soyinka refers more pointedly to the cyclical movement of the history of man.

Man is a mere speck in the cycle of birth and death, integration and disintegration which is infinite or never ending. This is the basic symbolism of Mobius Strip, a mathe-magical ring infinite in self-recreation into independent but linked rings. It is especially evoked by the image of a snake eternally devouring its own tail, which he identifies with the god Ogun:

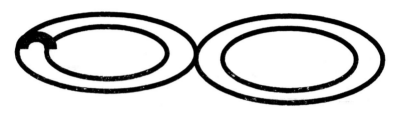

The Mobius Strip

The snake is an important totemic element in Ogunnian worship, just as the hawk is in Cuchulain rites. The Mobius Strip embodies the connotations of birth and death, of flux and cyclical repetition conjured up by the "whorl" and "whirl" in the poem; just as the falcon, a bird similar in nature to the hawk, embodies the turning, "whirling" of the interpenetrating gyres in Yeats' poem, "The Second Coming". This is probably the basis for Soyinka's claim that "in the human context of my society, Idanre has made abundant sense," for the bloody events narrated therein anticipated the bloodbath in Nigeria during the Civil War.[12] Identification of the cyclical movement of history, of all life with Ogun implies that the god's creative/destructive duality is, therefore, cyclical.

The year in which *The Dreaming of the Bones* is set, 1916, latently suggests the war theme. The First World War had yet to run its course and the bloody Uprising of Easter 1916 had just taken place. Although there is no specific reference to it in the play, the Nigerian Civil War forms the point of departure for the dramatic action in *Madmen and Specialists*. Along with the collection of poems, *A Shuttle in the Crypt*, Soyinka drafted the play on scraps of paper made available to him by sympathetic wardens while in prison on the orders of then Nigerian Head of State, General Gowon. It was the one means by which he maintained his sanity under the mentally debilitating conditions of solitary confinement.

The Young Man in *The Dreaming of the Bones* had participated in the Rising of Easter 1916, specifically, in the famous siege of the General Post office. He is consequently, on the run from the British forces, in order not to suffer the same fate as the sixteen men executed for their part in the Rising. The metaphysical super-structure of the play is hinted at in the description of the figures in the play. The three main figures, the Young Man, the Stranger and the Young Girl, wear masks; their movement is deliberately dance-like, suggestive of the presence of archetypes rather than individuated characters. The Young Man is the archetypal Irish peasant; he seems "an Aran fisher," that is, a fisherman from the Aran Isles, the westerly islands which both Yeats and Synge associated with the quintessential Irish peasant. That he is wearing "the flannel *bawneen* and the cowhide shoes" reinforces the peasant archetype. *Bawneen* is the traditional jacket of the West of Ireland made of homespun flannel and without lapels or pockets.[13] He is about to climb to the mountain top over the village of the Abbey of Corcomroe, from where he is to look out for a ship which would take him to safety on the continent.

Dr. Bero is the "Specialist" in Soyinka's play. Like the Young Man in Yeats' play, he had participated actively in a war, but now returns home severely wounded, psychologically. The tag, "Specialist", defines both his pre-war and post-war activities. Before the war, the due diligence he exercised as he performed his medical duties had, as the priest infers, marked him out as a specialist in his own field. War however, affected him profoundly to the point where it led to a turning point in his attitude towards his profession. His responsibilities as head of Intelligence Service in the Army had confronted him with humans' ingrained tendency towards accommodating, and even rationalizing, brutality to fellow humans. Service in Army Intelligence confronts him with absolute power, which the aphrodisiac that corrupts absolutely; it leads to his resolve to achieve absolute power and control over human destiny: "Control, sister, control. Power comes from bending nature to your will. – The specialist they called me, and a specialist is, – well a specialist. You analyze, you diagnose, you – [*He aims an imaginary gun*] – prescribe." [14]

The Dreaming of the Bones

The Young Man in Yeats' play meets a Stranger and a Young Girl, the dead couple who "dream back" their crime of passion. The "dream back" process is integral to Yeats' conception of the movement of man's spirit. Its basic postulate is that the dead dream back, or "re-live" for a certain length of time, the more personal thoughts and deeds of their lives:

> Spiritism, whether of folklore or of the seance-room, the visions of Swedenborg, and the speculations of the Platonists, and Japanese plays will have it that we may see at certain roads and in certain houses old murders acted over and over again, and in certain fields dead hunts men riding with horse and hound or ancient armies fighting above bones or ashes. We carry to *Anima Mundi* our memory, and that memory is for a time our external world; and all passionate moments recur again and again, *for passion desires its own recurrence more than any event*, and whatever there is of corresponding complacency or remorse is our beginning of judgment. [15]

Yeats creates a romantic-cum-political scenario to dramatize this re-living process. The crime of passion which the Stranger and the Young Girl "dream-back" constantly is their illicit love affair, which facilitated English colonialism in Ireland, the operation of which is responsible for the Young Man's current situation as a war fugitive. In a modification of a Japanese Noh technique, Yeats identifies the young couple who wear heroic masks as the historical characters, Diarmuid and Dervorgilla. Their story is the Irish version of the Hellenic triangle of Helen, Menelaus and Paris. Briefly, the legend goes that in 1152, Diarmuid MacMurrough, King of Leinster, eloped with Dervorgilla, daughter of the King of Meath and wife of Tegernan O'Rourke. For his daring, Diarmuid was ostracized and banished from Leinster. To regain his kingdom, he appealed to Henry the Second of England, the Norman King, for help. The latter, in 1169, subsequently gave him an army under Strongbow, the nick-name for Richard Fitzherbert de Clare, Earl of Pembroke (1130–1176). Diarmuid's request thus initiated the series of conquests of the Irish and derogation of Irish culture by English forces, and Irish counteractive measures at reclaiming their land and culture which culminated in the Rising of Easter 1916.

In the play, the Stranger and the Young Girl are presented as beings from an earlier subjective era. Their subjectivity is symbolically represented through the darkness, the calls of the night birds, the hovering nebulous clouds, the wind blowing out the lantern, the dim path to the ruined Abbey of Corcomroe and on up the ridge where the grave of the lovers is located. These are the symbols of the dizzy dreams that spring from the dry bones of the dead, the consciousness of tragic guilt in the past.[16] In contrast, the Young Man starts out as an objective man who deals effectively with reality, whose notion of duty is simple and intense. He has pursued the hard service of Cathleen ni Houlihan and is determined that only through it shall he be remembered forever. He is not concerned with the purgatorial life of the dead, but with the objective details relevant to his escape. His objectivity is encapsulated in the references to the dawn and sunlight, the crowing of the cocks and the panorama of the landscape ruined by Civil War

For their passionate crime, the Stranger and the Young Girl

remain spiritually distant from each other, and suffer the immense anguish resulting from the separation of once united souls. They wander the lonely hills and valleys of the scene of their crime of passion, an endless purgatory; they seek forgiveness in order that they may not only enjoy eternal rest but also consummate their love:

> YOUNG GIRL: Although they have no blood, or
> living nerves,
> Who once lay warm and live the live-long night
> In one another's arms and know their part
> In life, being now but of the people of dreams.
> Is a dream's part; although they are but shadows;
> Hovering between a thorn-tree and a stone
> Who have heaped up a night on winged night;
> although
> No shape however harried and consumed
> Would change his own calamity for theirs,
> Their manner of life were blessed could lips
> A moment meet; but when he has bent his head
> Closer to her head, or hand would slip in hand,
> The memory of their crime flows up between
> And drives them apart.[17]

Although they are dead, these shades live a fully human torment and have no power to overcome the guilt that flows up between them. Only a member of the living can liberate them from their suffering, the constant re-living of their passionate crime

The Stranger is their only hope for liberation from this eternal penance. The path to the mountain top is dark and uncertain, and they offer to help him to the look-out point in the hope of a *quid pro quo*:

> STRANGER: We know the pathways that the sheep
> tread out

> And all the hiding places of the hills
> And that they had better hiding-places once.
>
> YOUNG MAN: You'd say they had better before
>   English robbers
> Cut down the trees or set them upon fire.
> For fear their owners might find shelter there.
> What is that sound?
>
> STRANGER: An old horse gone astray.
> He has been wandering on the road all night.
>
> YOUNG MAN: I took him for a man and horse. Police
> Are out upon the roads. In the late Rising
> I think there was no man of us but hated
> To fire at soldiers who but did their duty
> And were not of our race, but when a man
> Is born in Ireland and of Irish stock,
> When he takes part against us –
>
> STRANGER: I will put you safe,
> No living man shall set his eyes upon you.
> I will not answer for the dead. [18]

In anticipating the *quid pro quo* between the Young Man and the dead couple, Yeats projects the idea of a marriage of aristocratic and peasant values, which he expounded in preference to the materialist mentality that defined the Ireland of his times. This merging of values he saw as a necessity, since both the peasant and the aristocrat shared Unity of Image and Unity of Culture; and as a result of these shared values, were much closer to the attainment of the Unity of Being.

The images and symbols in description of the journey to the mountain top, however, prophesy the failure of such a union of values. The journey itself is transformed into a concrete fact by the accompanying circuits of the figures on the stage, creating the impression of a spiral path in a Dantesque mountain valley that is filled with darkness. They go from "the shallow well and flat stone," past "grassy fields" and "ragged thorn trees," to a place "among the stones above the ash."[19] The images in the description suggest the actual ascent to the mountain summit as a ritual movement from a temporal state through death to a state of pure spirit, revealed in the distancing from the "cat-headed bird." Wilson associates the "cat-headed birds" with the man-headed birds of the earlier Yeats play, *The Shadowy Waters,* where they are the spirits of the dead. The function of the image, he argues, is purely atmospheric, to paint the atmosphere of dark expectancy against which the action is played out.[20]

The songs with which the Musicians intersperse their description of the journey are filled with symbols which develop the mood and suggest the apocalyptic vision in the play. The symbolism of the Red bird of March which features prominently is particularly significant. March is an important month in Yeats' system. It is associated with the moment in which one cycle of life dies or ends, and another begins or is created, as engendered by the centrifugal tendency of the widening cones or gyres. The red color of the bird, the animal image which defines Yeats' movement of the gyres, suggests the red bird of Mars, the god of war after which the month is named, and of the blood letting and destruction consequent upon the dawning of a new cycle.

Yeats expected the new objective age to begin with world-wide wars – involving, *inter alia*, the liberation of Ireland – at a full moon in March, the month of Mars – and the Easter Rising of 1916 came almost exactly at this time."[21] The First and Second World Wars, as well as the war of Independence in 1921 were preamble to the anarchy which Yeats foresaw would mark the Second Coming. The Red bird of March in the play, therefore, suggests Yeats' vision of this anarchy, the "things" that "fall apart" in the present objective age, which the 1916 Dublin Rebellion seemed to symbolize.

The Young Man's attitude towards the Stranger and the Young Girl, the representatives of an earlier era, has been particularly conditioned by this rebellion. He is totally against quislings in any form, the situation which obtains as he says, "when a man / Is born in Ireland and of Irish stock, / When he takes part against us." This makes him equally suspicious of historical personages like Donough O'Brien, who rebelled against the King of Thomond and brought the Scots into Ireland, and, therefore, "made Ireland weak."[22] As expected, the Young Man has no sympathy for the, plight of the dream-back couple:

> YOUNG MAN: What crime can stay so in the
>   memory?
> What crime can keep apart the lips of lovers
> Wandering and alone?
>
> YOUNG GIRL: Her king and lover
> Was overthrown in battle by her husband
> And for her sake and for his own, being blind
> And bitter and bitterly in love, he brought
> A foreign army from across the sea.
>
> YOUNG MAN: You speak of Diarmuid and Devorgilla
> Who brought the Norman in?
>
> YOUNG GIRL: Yes, yes, I spoke
> Of that most miserable, most accursed pair.
> Who sold their country into slavery and yet;
> They were not wholly miserable and accursed.
> If somebody of their race at last would say
> 'I have forgiven them'.
>
> YOUNG MAN: O, never, never,
> Shall Diarmuid and Dervorgilla be forgiven.[23]

The Young Man realizes that he faces greater danger from the dead bones before him than from the living English colonialists from whom he is fleeing. He could lose his head in a cloud, or fall victim to the passionate mood of the lovers, be overcome and forget what the lovers had done to Ireland, forgive them and end their endless torture in purgatory. The Stranger and the Young Girl act out their love and torment in a ritual dance which the Young Man watches intently. For a brief moment, we are caught up in a brief hope we that the much longed for Unity of Being of the peasant class, represented by the Young Man, and the aristocratic Stranger and Young Girl will play itself out before our eyes.

The Young Man however, resists the temptation to become subjective and imaginative, to imagine so vividly the private passion and suffering of Diarmuid and Dervorgilla that he forgives them, and accept what history has done to Ireland. He neither yields nor forgives, in spite of his being entranced by the ritual dance. His refusal to forgive and forget signals the end of heroism in Ireland; and the continuity of the constant hatreds, guilt and bickering which Yeats believed, and variously propounded, had done more damage to Ireland than the English colonialists themselves. For him, the Young Man's lack of vision and magnanimity is a refusal to give modern objective Ireland its heroic mask, its fullness of being:

> YOUNG MAN: – So here we are on the summit I can
>   see
> The Aran Islands, Connemara Hills
> And Galway in the breaking light; there too
> The enemy has toppled roof and gable
> And torn the panelling from ancient rooms
> What generations of old men had known
> Like their own hands, and children wondered at,
> Has boiled a trooper's porridge. That town had lain
> But for the pair you would have me pardon
> Amid its gables and battlements
> Like any old admired Italian town;
> For though we have neither coal, nor iron ore
> To make us wealthy and corrupt the air,

> Our country, if that crime were uncommitted,
> Had been most beautiful.[24]

Although the Young Man had fought gallantly to defend Ireland, it is the ghostly couple who wear the heroic masks. The "music of a lost Kingdom" with which the Musicians end the play and the crow of the "red," "strong March birds" intimate the end of heroism and proclaim the anarchy resulting from upon the dawning of a new age of objectivity and war.

Madmen and Specialists

Dr. Bero, like the Young Man in *The Dreaming of the Bones,* has also been so hardened by war that it warps his relationship with his fellow men. He is "uniformed, carrying a hold all."[25] He is a doctor, a medical specialist but in a pointed betrayal of the Hippocratic oath of his pre-war medical studies, he is now a specialist of a different kind, the kind so intoxicated by power and bloodlust of war, now fully manifest in his control of the System, an abstraction for the totalitarian state. Dissent is inimical. The Mendicants, Aafaa, Goyi, Blindman and the Cripple, their disabilities notwithstanding, are mere pawns in his power game. He has commanded them to keep an eye on the his father, the Old Man, whom he has imprisoned in a cellar for daring to challenge him, and on his sister, Si Bero, to keep her from going down to the cellar. Whenever Dr. Bero feels the Mendicants are falling out of line, he is quick to remind them of his authority. When they remind him of his promise to them that he will reward them for their services, he

> [(*c*)*uts the Aafaa's face with his swagger stick.*
> *Aafaa staggers back, clutching the wound. Bero*
> *stands still, watching him. At the sound of pain*
> *Iya Agba looks our of the hut and impassively*
> *observes the scene.*]

BERO: That should remind you I do know how to

slap people around. And you'd better remember
some other things I know. You weren't
discharged because of your – sickness. Just
remember that and other things. [26]

The Mendicants' constant contact with the Old Man has, however, enlightened them to the reality of a being known as AS, and to their present circumstances as pawns in the System. They spend their waking lives trying to decipher AS, and what he / she / it stands for:

A...   As is Acceptance, Adjustment. Adjustment of Ego to
       the
       Acceptance in As. –
B...   Blindness...Blindness in AS. – All shall see As who
       render themselves blind to all else.
C...   Contentment. A full belly
D...   Divinity. That's us. For Destiny too Destiny is the
       Duty of Divinity. D-D-D.
E...   Epilepsy. For your Divinity to have control the flock
       must be without control
F...   As Fulfils. As Farts.
G...   As is Godhead.
H...   Humanity, the Ultimate Sacrifice to As, the eternal
       oblation on the altar of... I am, I, thus sayeth As[27]

Dr. Bero is irked by their constant attempts to unravel AS, because it is an existential philosophy originated by the Old Man his father to situate his son's predilection towards cannibalism and the general violence in society in its proper ontological context. "AS" is predicated on an apocalyptic vision of human leadership. The Old merges traditional Yoruba and Christian concepts of eternal recurrence, defining AS is the supreme manifestation of the destructive essence of Ogun, the natural complement of his creative aspect. As a god, AS' nature is cyclical and eternal. Its eternality is particularly suggested by a deliberate subversion of the second part of the Christian prayer, the Gloria Patri – As it Was in the Beginning, Is now, and Ever Shall Be World Without End, Amen:

> OLD MAN: As Is, and the System is its mainstay
> though it wear a hundred masks and a
> thousand outward forms. And because you
> are within the System, the cyst in the System
> that irritates, the foul gurgle of the cistern, the
> expiring function of a faulty cistern and are part
> of the material for re-formulating the mind of a
> man into the necessity of the moment's political
> As, metaphysic As, sociologic As, you-cannot-
> escape! There is but one constant in the life of
> the system and that constant is As. What can
> you pit against the priesthood of that constant
> deity, its gospelers, its enforcement agency? And
> even if you say unto them, do I not know you,
> did I not know you in Rompers, with leaky
> nose and smutty face? Did I not know you
> thereafter, know you in the haunt of cat-houses,
> did I not know you rifling the poor boxes in
> the local church, did I not know you dissolving
> the night in fumes of human self-indulgence
> simply simply, simply did I not know you, do
> you not defecate, fornicate, prevaricate when
> heaven and earth implore you to abdicate
> and are you not prey to disc displacement, in-
> growing toe nail, dysentery, malaria, flat-foot,
> corns and childblains? Simply, simply, do I not
> know you man like me? Then shall they say
> unto you, I am chosen, restored, redesignated,
> and redestined and further, further shall they

say unto you, you heresiarchs of the System,
arguing questioning querying weighing
puzzling insisting rejecting upon you all shall
we practice, without passion – [28]

AS is here presented as the negative life force in the universe, the System that informs the constant, systematic annihilation of the rest of humanity by the megalomaniac few. Humans are mere cysts in the System, the "foul gurgle of the cistern": that is, an insignificant speck in a vast, eternal system of death and destruction that he questions or confronts on pain of death.

The Old Man has taught the Mendicants this philosophy, leading them to realize that they their disabilities only exacerbates their uselessness to the System. He teaches them the AS song, which they chant regularly to try to garner some meaning from their miserable lives. This of course, incenses Dr. Bero the more; in his view thinking is the ultimate sacrilege, because thinking leads to asking questions; questionings threaten the very fabric of authoritarianism here represented as the System. The potential threat the Mendicants pose to him fuels Dr. Bero's determination to keep them in thrall to him and his persisting warfare with the whole of humanity: "Can you picture a more treacherous deed than to place a working mind in a mangled body?"[29]

African leadership has invariably been characterized by a preponderance of Dr. Beros, each drunk with a sense of importance, to the point of co-opting their nation-states as their own personal properties, divinely given, instituting their own systems of governance and brutally quashing any form of dissent. The Old Man is one such dissenter, who has "questioned and queried" the System, and upon whom Bero now "practises." Bero is so de-humanized that he has lost all filial compassion. The Old Man's "crime" is that he had made Dr. Bero and his cohorts face the reality of their dehumanization, of their tendencies to feed off other humans both literally and figuratively during and after the war. They, unwittingly, had become disciples of AS:

> BERO: — it was no brain-child of mine. We thought it was a joke. I'll bless the meat, he said. And then — As was the Beginning, As is Now, As Ever Shall be…World without We said Amen with a straight face and sat down to eat.[30]

Constant arguments with his father in the basement surgery are, consequently, attempts, not only to put a stop to his father's brainwashing the Mendicants, but also, to some extent, attempts to better understand the philosophy. Bero however, only sees and hears what reinforces his sense of power; he cannot see beyond the borders defined by his new god, and remains deaf to the Old man's delineations. He toughens the Old Man's prison conditions, and proceeds with plans to eliminate him.

Dr. Bero's thirst for absolute power and control does not stop with humanity. In his warped sense of self-importance, he hankers after the control of the supernatural as well. The two old women, Iya Agba and Iya Mate, earth mothers, represent the supernatural forces which Bero attempts to bring under his domain. They are witches in traditiona Yoruba cosmogony "who are acknowledged to be close the ultimate source of human life and can influence individual lives for good or ill."[31] They are the custodians of the basic natural laws of continuity of the human race. Bero had relied on their powers for survival on the warfront for they had provided the supernatural leeway necessary for his survival of such a brutal war. Si Bero, his sister, had been the medium through which their protective powers were transported to him:

She collects dried twigs and barks for them, the ingredients they demand to enable them achieve their supernatural protection of her brother. The twigs and barks are metaphors for human beings, the good and the evil:

IYA AGBA: You can cure with poison if you use it
right. Or kill.

SI BERO: I'll throw it in the fire.

IYA MATE: Do nothing of the sort. You don't learn
good things unless you learn evil.

SI BERO: But it's poison.

IYA MATE: It grows.

IYA AGBA: Rain falls on it.

IYA MATE: It sucks the dew.

IYA AGBA: It lives.

LYA MATE: It dies.

IYA AGBA: Same as any other. An-hn, same as any
other.[32]

Now back from war, Dr. Bero's objective is to control them and the
power they exert. He is totally contemptuous of the earth mothers,
although Iya Agba tells him, "We move as the Earth moves, nothing
more. We age as the Earth ages."[33]

He dismisses them as old hags with nothing better to do than
maintain a petty thieving cult. He threatens to proscribe them
and eject them from their hut, supernatural or not. In retaliation
the Earth Mothers withdraw their supernatural support from him,
suggesting a repudiation of evil by both Earth and Nature. Their
retaliation is total: they set fire to the collection of twigs and barks
used hitherto to protect Dr. Bero.

Their decision is to do so simultaneous with the movement
towards the elimination of the Old man. The Old Man had foreseen
that with AS, death at the hands of its disciple, is the only possibility and sets about rehearsing his elimination with the Mendicants.
Bero the specialist sees the process of eliminating his father as a
surgical operation to "excise the cyst in the body politic of AS,"
and aims to actualize the elimination.

He enters the cellar just as the Old Man and the Mendicants are rehearsing his death. In the rehearsal before the fact, Cripple plays the Old Man, while the Old Man himself role plays his son Dr. Bero:

OLD MAN: Practice… on the cyst in the System –
  you cyst, you cyst, you splint in the arrow of
  arrogance, the dog in dogma, tick of a heretic,
  the tick in politics, the mock of democracy the
  mar of Marxism, a tic of the fanatic, the boo in
  buddhism, the ham in Mohammed, the dash
  in the crisscross of Christ, a dot on the i of ego
  an ass in the mass, the ash in ashram, the boot
  in kibbutz, the pee of priesthood, the pee pee
  of perfect priesthood, oh how dare you raise
  your hindquarters you dog of dogma and cast
  the scent of your existence on the lamp-post
  of Destiny you HOLE IN THE ZERO OF
  NOTHING!

CRIPPLE: I have a question

OLD MAN: [*turns slowly towards the* interruption): It's
  the dreamer.

CRIPPLE: I have a question.

OLD MAN: Black that zero! [Aafaa, Goyi and
  Blindman begin to converge on the Cripple] [34]

Cripple (as The Old Man) is about the pay the supreme price for questioning the System. He is the hole in the zero of nothing which must be blacked out, the cyst in the System, the minutiae in all the earthly systems and beliefs known to man. The parodying of various principles of governance or religious dogmas of AS, from Marxism, to Buddhism, to Islam to Christianity, conveys the message that despite man's attempts to rationalize his existence and control his life in terms of defined systems and beliefs, he remains essentially insignificant, puny in the larger scheme of things that are beyond his imagination.

The final elimination scene is reinforces of the theme of transition, a final brutal statement on a soulless society.[35] As the Old Man is about to exercise the cyst, Bero shoots him and we assume he dies instantly. The Earth Mothers who must have determined that they were not going to tolerate Bero's patricide, now appear and thrash all the weed and herbs of their trade into the cellar, setting all inside it including Dr. Bero on fire. Si Bero and the Mendicants survive the resulting conflagration, but no indication is given that Dr. Bero himself survived it:

> OLD MAN: Let us taste just what makes a heretic tick.
> [*He raises his scalpel in a motion for incision. Bero
> fires. The Old Man spins, falls face upwards on
> the table as the Cripple slides to the ground from
> under him. A momentary freeze on the stage.
> Then Si Bero rushes from the Old Women towards
> the surgery. Instantly Iya Agba hurls the embers
> into the store and thick smoke belches out from
> the doorway, gradually filling the stage---Both
> women walk calmly away as Si Bero reappears in
> the doorway of the surgery. The Mendicants run
> to look at her, break gleefully into their favorite
> song.*][36]

The symbolic fire which engulfs the weeds store, and from which the Earth Mothers calmly walk away marks the dissociation of the Earth forces from man and his evil propensities. The play ends with a nightmarish vision of the human condition, a world where AS continues to triumph, celebrated in the Mendicants' closing song:

Bi o ti wa
Ni yio se wa
Bi o ti wa
Ni yio se wa
Bi o ti wa l'atete ko se.[37]

Translation:

As it was in the beginning
As is now
As ever shall be
World without end.

Chapter six
The Dramaturgy of Dance

The study of dramatic technique or method is a means to the discovery of meaning in a work of art. Soyinka has variously been termed the dramaturge *par excellence,* because of his abiding concern with the mechanics of the message, as well as with the message itself. This preoccupation with technique is probably partly responsible for the charges of elitism and obfuscation frequently leveled at his works. Soyinka shares an oblique consciousness of dramatic with his Irish counterpart. Yeats, in his critical writings, frequently refers to the primacy of art over propaganda. He was disdainful of those contemporaries of his whose predilection towards the simple subordination of art to the message in the name of ideology or realism. To him this often resulted in a cold immediacy, topicality and banality of art. This chapter examines Yeats' and Soyinka's dramaturgy in terms of structure, space and time, characterization and language, to determine how they facilitated the communication of the dance of the ritual heroes.

Structure as Drama

Structure fundamentally refers to the architectural framework of a work of art. Conventional Western dramatic criticism, deriving primarily from classical rules of rhetoric, projects five aspects of this architecture, the organic interaction of which advances the action in the play. They are the *exposition,* or the introduction, whereby the necessary information about the action and the characters needed to set the plot in motion are introduced; the *complicatio,* the substance of drama, whereby the conflicting interests of the characters clash with each other; the *climax,* from which the action derives its final configuration; the *peripeteia* or the reversal at which point the protagonist suffers a reversal of fortunes; the *catastrophe* which fleshes out the consequences of the climax and reversal in order to evoke in the audience a catharsis of emotions.

Working within a milieu conditioned by the forced knowledge of these tenets of literary criticism, Soyinka, like Yeats before him, modified the five-part structure of conventional criticism in terms of his consciousness of traditional theater. He emerges with a composite that not only reflects his traditional bias but also individuates him artistically. Yeats and Soyinka conceive of their plays as rituals. The ritual framework in each case is the composite of the Dionysian ritual dithyrambic origins of conventional western drama specifically, tragedy, as well as of the ritual structure of traditional society and art, be it Celtic, Nigerian, or even Japanese, as exemplified by Yeats' interest in the Noh, the rituals of the Japanese warrior caste. The ritual framework is predicated upon their belief that audience participation in the tragic rites of passage of a recognizable mythical hero, leads to transference of the implications of the ritual to the contemporary scene. It leads a cerebral almost subconscious understanding of that scene, and of the metaphysical and universal truths incorporated in the ritual.

The three plays in this book which were inspired by the colonial experience in Ireland and Nigeria – *The Countess Cathleen, Cathleen ni Houlihan* and *A Dance of the Forest* – pronounce the traditional, ritual bias of both artists, despite a marked amateurism in the choreography of ritual evidenced in them. *The Countess Cathleen*, in particular, with its re enactment of the rite of sacrifice, is a striking example of Yeats' attempts to evoke a sense of Ireland's "other worldliness", its irrevocable difference from, and superiority to, the banality and materialism of English colonialism, achieved through a recourse to the traditional beliefs and practices of the Irish peasantry and aristocracy. *A Dance of the Forests* inaugurates Soyinka's concern with the dramatization of the rites of passage of the Yoruba hero gods. The Welcoming of the Dead can be interpreted in terms of the Yoruba gods' arrival at the edge of the transitional abyss, while the Dance of the Unwilling Sacrifice undertaken by Demoke in the final movement is a modification of Ogun's plunge into and disintegration within the transitional abyss.

The four plays discussed in chapter four – *At the Hawk's Well, On Baile's Strand, The Road, Death and the King's Horseman* – reflect a perfection of the ritual format by both dramatists, signaled in the choreography of the tragic rites of passage of Cuchulain and Ogun, the two most prominent hero gods of their respective pantheons. In *At the Hawk's Well*, Yeats modifies the structure of the Noh ritual to suit the Celtic mythological material with which he hoped to both perfect his concept of theater, and to impact upon consciousness. In *The Road* and *Death and the King's Horseman*, Soyinka evokes the essence of the numinous fourth level of existence in Yoruba cosmogony, the abyss of transition that is integral to the Yoruba psyche and is specifically associated with Ogun. The two plays discussed in the fifth chapter – *The Dreaming of the* Bones and Mad*men and Specialists* – reveal further modifications of the rituals of the two hero gods to the expression of their consciousness of war.

The fundamentally ritual conceptual framework appears to impel both dramatists towards the evocation of a physical or external framework that would reinforce the ritual action. All of the Yeats plays studied, with the possible exception of *The Countess*

Cathleen, are deliberately structured within the one act play convention. The compression of action, concentration of emotions and the preclusion of scene shifts and changes consequent upon the one act structure most appropriately impress the sense of ritual, of communion with the supernatural, and the ageless, universal truths associated with the form. The one act structure of *Cathleen ni Houlihan,* with its uninterrupted action from the sound of cheering beyond the peasant cottage to Patrick's vision of Cathleen ni Houlihan as a young girl who had "the walk of a queen", subtly impresses the mood of the traditional *aisling* form which inspired the play, in addition to a sense of the enormity of the evil that is Ireland's bondage to England.

As Yeats evolved artistically from a concern with mere cultural nationalism, the one act structure also facilitated his attempts to impact upon the whole psyche of man, which he felt was the preliminary to effecting changes on particular contemporary facts, events and issues. The one act structure of *At the Hawk's Well,* for example, ensures the communication of a very intense experience, what Yeats himself describes as "the joy (action) of a thousand years – crushed into a moment."[1] It ensures that nothing stands between the audience and the "deeps of the mind," the collective subconscious to which the whole play appeals. As with Yeats, the physical structure in the Soyinka's plays reflects the attempt to impress the concept of drama as ritual. With the exception of *Death and the King's Horseman,* each of his four plays studied is divided into two parts, each of which ends in a ritual or psychological climax.

The climax in the first part of each of the plays is often marked by a stampede towards the scene or subject of ritual consciousness by one or more of the characters. Fear is often the factor that motivates this stampede, a fear often engendered by the chief protagonist who also attempts to re-enact the Ogunnian plunge into the transitional abyss. The first part of *A Dance of the Forests,* for example, ends with the Chimney of Ereko incident. Adenebi, one of the three protagonists whom Forests Head / Aroni wants to confront with the mirror of original nakedness, emerges from the uproar and the smoke in mortal terror of being lost in the dark forest. He rushes to Obaneji, who with Rola and Demoke proceed to the Welcoming of the Dead. The first part of the action in *The Road* ends with the failure of Salubi's attempt to identify Murano, the living embodiment of the Word towards which Professor gropes. The attempt is motivated by Professor's manipulation of their natural fear of his sorcery and their curiosity over Murano. In *Madmen and Specialists* there is a precipitation of movement towards the surgery, the scene for the dissection and examination of AS and its physiology. The movement is motivated by Si Bero's unease over her brother Bero's growing dehumanization and her fears for her father the Old Man's safety.

Part Two in each of the Soyinka plays encapsulates the actual moment of ritual consciousness. The action too, takes the form of a stampede towards ritual epiphany; in each case, this stampede is incited by the catalyst of the epiphany. In *The Road*, for example, Professor's restoration of Murano to his *egungun* phase is the catalyst that prompts the drivers and touts' recognition of Murano as the god come alive, and awareness of Professor's mission, culminating in Professor's final confrontation with the Word, one which he elaborates in his dying injunction. In *Madmen and Specialists*, the Old Man's attempt to "Black a Zero," and to "hear the expiring suction of an imperfect system" is the catalyst that forces the ultimate consciousness of AS, extended in Dr. Bero's shooting the Old Man, and by Mendicants song on the eternality of AS.

The division of action into two parts, each culminating in a precipitation of movement that leads to the final consciousness, can also be identified in *Death and the King's Horseman*, despite its five-part structuring in terms of western classical tragedy.[2] The structure of the play consists of two converging movements. The first begins with Elesin Oba's preparations for the transitional plunge in Part One, and follows him through Part Three, where the audience is led to believe that he has actually danced and joined the ancestors, to Part Five, where he is in prison. The second movement begins in Part Two with the Pilkings' tango on the verandah of their bungalow, through Act Four to the masque in honor of the Prince Regent in the Residency. It merges with the first movement in Part Five, where Pilkings stands colonial witness to first Olunde's, then Elesin Oba's dance to transition. The formal structuring into the five parts of classic western tragedy does not preclude the essence of continuity and contiguity of ritual in the traditional sense.

A structural feature adopted by both dramatists is the framing of the dramatic action with choric elements, consisting of one or more figures who evoke the ritual essence, and who place the dramatic action in its proper perspective. This choric feature in the plays is, in each case, the composite that results from the manipulation of the traditional and classic western concepts of ritual drama. Yeats modifies the allusive half-sung and half-spoken declamation of the ancient bards, the structural conventions of the Japanese Noh ritual drama, and the stylized, but direct, choric chants of classic Greek tragedy to effect a composite of the Musicians in both At the Hawk's Well and The Dreaming of the Bones. The faces of three Musicians in both plays are made up to resemble masks, as distinct from the figures in the play who wear actual masks, a device which impresses their roles as mediators between the subconscious and the conscious, between the figures in the play and the minds of the audience. In each of the two plays, the Musicians introduce the protagonists, set the action into perspective, narrate the progress and evoke the general metaphysical tenor of the play in their final song. The Musicians' folding and unfolding of a cloth, in each case, also reinforces the ritual context. In At the Hawk's Well, the cloth is black and upon it is a gold pattern suggesting a hawk; the hawk figure immediately suggests Cuchulain whom they then introduce via evocation of other archetypal images long associated with the Celtic hero-god.

They also intimate the central conflict in the play, between the heart that would always be awake, and the heart that will forever turn to its rest, as well as set the action, such as it is, in motion:

> FIRST MUSICIAN: [*speaking*]:
> Night falls;
> The mountain side grows dark;
> The withered leaves of the hazel
> Half-choke the dry bed of the well;
> The Guardian of the Well is sitting
> Upon the old gray stone at its side,
> Worn out from raking its dry bed,
> Worn out from gathering up the leaves.
> Her heavy eyes
> Knowing nothing, or but look upon stone.
> The wind that blows out of the sea
> Turns over the heaped-up leaves at her side,
> They rustle and diminish.[3]

The Musicians' final song is an affirmation of the individual heroism that defines Cuchulain's tragic choice, captured in the metaphors, the choice of folly and a "pleasant life / Among indolent meadows," in preference to the wisdom and the calling of "the milch cows / To the comfortable door of his house," epitomized by the Old Man.

In *The Dreaming of the Bones*, the three Musicians introduce the "dream-back" process as well as place the action of the play into perspective. They ask:

> Have not the old writers said
> That dizzy dreams can spring
> From the dry bones of the dead?
> And many a night it seems
> That all the valley fills
> With those fantastic dreams.
> So passionate is a shade,

Like wine that fills to the top
A gray-green cup of jade,
Or maybe an agate cup.[4]

The "passionate shade" song anticipates the Stranger and the Young Girl, the Dead Couple who are condemned to eternal penance because of their crime of passion. The contrasts between the Dead couple and the Young Man on the run from English forces is also evoked in the Musicians' song. Since the Young Man is an objective being, a part of reality, they "hear" his footfalls, in contrast to their trembling and uncertainty generated by the flitting past of the shadows of the dead. They describe the progress of the characters to the mountain summit and reiterate the central symbol of the Red Bird of March, as a means of impressing its significance in the context of the play. Their final song, the "Music of a Lost Kingdom" affirms the resolution; their call to the strong red birds of March to crow, to "stretch neck and clap the wing, / Red cocks, and crow!" proclaims the triumph of war, the repetitive and inevitable consequence of the failure of vision to transcend hatred, patriotism and fanaticism.

The choric feature in Soyinka's plays does not consist of Musicians but usually of supernatural beings who initiate and direct the dramatic action. or who epitomize the spirit of the abyss evoked in the play. In *A Dance of the Forests,* Aroni is the god whose prologue sets the action in perspective, and who, indeed, directs the action throughout the play. He is an agent of Forest Head, *Olodumare,* the supreme deity, and, like him, he is the Spirit of Wisdom who is omniscient, ubiquitous and timeless. In response to the human community's request for illustrious ancestors to mark the feast of the Gathering of the Tribes, he sends "two spirits of the restless dead," who were "linked in violence and blood with four of the living generation" in their previous lives. He elaborates on the four and their respective crimes in the past and the present; the Dead Couple are to be the means to their awareness of their crimes. Aroni also elaborates on the conflict of the gods, Ogun and Eshuoro, and their manipulation of Demoke and Oremole, two humans as pawns in the conflict.

Halfway through the action in the play Aroni takes both Forest Head and us his audience to the scene in the Court of Mata Kharibu. The flashback is to take us as far back as "about eight centuries, possibly more. / One of their great empires." Following the flashback, he, together with Forest Head, stares continuously "into the spectacle," reflecting upon man's eternal propensity towards the destruction of his fellow man, an example of which they have just shown us. Prior to the Welcoming of Dead, Aroni momentarily stops Eshuroro from the execution of his plan of revenge against Demoke, and the new community:

OGUN: Will you foresee the many confusions
　　　Eshuoro hatches in his mind? Aroni, let my
　　　servant go. He has suffered enough.

ARONI: I need him most of all.

OGUN: He has no guilt. I, Ogun, swear that his
　　　hands were in every action of his life.

FOREST HEAD: Will you all never rid yourselves of
　　　these conceits![5]

Demoke is significant to the consciousness of man's own regenerative potential in the subsequent Welcoming of the Dead. Aroni impresses this fact upon Demoke, following the Dance of the Forest Spirits, culminating in the tussle for the Half-Child. Demoke intercepts it and returns it to the Dead Woman who is immediately led off by Aroni, indicating that the cycle of evil will continue to define the new nation.

Three structural devices characteristic of Soyinka's plays but totally absent in Yeats' are the flashback, the dovetailing, and the play-within-the-play techniques. Yeats' compression of action and concentration of emotion into the one act structure precludes the effectiveness these structural devices. In Soyinka, these devices are a means to suggesting the continuity of the past in the present and the future, an integral aspect of African world view and of the abyss of transition central to Yoruba creation myth. The flashback to the court of Mata Kharibu in *A Dance of the Forests* is an excellent example of this sense of continuity. In *The Road,* Soyinka treats the flashback scenes as part of a continuous forward action rather than breaks in time. They are re-called and consciously relived by the characters as a means of passing away their time with Professor. A perfect example is Samson and Kotonu's re-enactment of an accident at a dilapidated bridge, which ends with Samson's plea to Kotonu to "Kill us a dog before the hungry god (Ogun) lies in wait and makes a substitute of me."

The dovetailing technique features most prominently in *Madmen and Specialists,* where it serves to convey the sense of the simultaneity of action between the three levels of setting suggested by structural intervals. There are twelve such intervals and the triple-layered action merge into the thirteenth interval. In the penultimate interval, the Old Man deliberately makes a conspicuous gesture when he "freezes with his arms raised towards the next scene as if in benediction." The gesture forces the audience to forge a nexus between this interval and the next one which witnesses the triumph of AS. The very short sketches which the Mendicants perform at strategic points exemplify the play-within-the-play technique. These sketches highlight the various attributes of the god AS, as the Mendicants have come to understand him and his acolytes. An example is Aafaa's gimmick of practicing upon Goyi with the Specialist's needle in the opening scenes of the play:

> AAFAA: [*Voice change. He points a 'needle' held low, at Goyi*] Say anything, say anything that comes into your head but SPEAK, MAN! [*Twisting the needle upwards. Goy: hand over crotch, yells*]

BLIND MAN: [*solemnly*] Rem Acu Tetigisti.

AAFAA: Believe me, this hurts you more than it hurts
me. Or – vice versa. Truths hurts. I am a lover
of truth. Do you find you also love truths? Then
let's have the truth. THE TRUTH!
[*He gives another push. Goyi screams*]

BLIND MAN: Rem Acu Tetigisti.

AAFAA: Think not that I hurt you but that Truth
hurts. We are all seekers after truth. I am a
Specialist in truth. Now shall we push it up all
the way, the truth, all the truth. [*Another push.
Goyi screams, then his head slumps.*]
Hm, the poor man has fainted.[6]

Aafaa in this sketch mimics a common ruse used by African leadership to excuse their hypocrisies, and thereby continue to eliminate
any form of dissent. The use of the needle links this ruse with the
Mendicants' favorite Latin expression, *Rem Acu Tetigisti* – or "You
have touched the matter with a needle," – the "matter" in this
sense being AS.

Space and Time

The plays all incorporate the unities of time, space and action,
prescribed by classic western rhetoric. As expected, however,
recourse to their traditional heritage also induces a merging of
the conventional western sense of time and space, which is linear,
precise and demarcates a time past from a time present and a time
future, with the traditional sense, which is cyclical and which denies
periodicity to the past, present and future. Space and time in the
plays are, therefore, mainly symbolic and suggest the metaphysical
or ritual framework of the dramatic action.

An examination of setting in Yeats' plays reveals an initial
emphasis on the house and the hearth in the early plays – in conformity with his cultivation of a cult of the peasant to celebrate the

Irishman and to indict the Englishman – to an enduring emphasis on the symbolic and the supernatural. This corresponds to the shift as he matures artistically from a mere cultural nationalism to a concern with metaphysical, universal truths, the apprehension of which is made more imperative by the immediate sociopolitical experiences of the Ireland of his time. *The Countess Cathleen* and *Cathleen ni Houlihan* are set within the house and hearth context. This setting is characteristic of the early Abbey's avowed intention to create a Celtic world view through highlighting and promoting aspects of peasant lifestyle. The action in *The Countess Cathleen* vacillates between the peasant cottage of the Rua family, with its lighted hearth, and the interior of the Countess' castle. Mediating between these two locations is the forest or the woods, which, as in Soyinka's *A Dance of the Forests*, is a repository of the unknown, of the ominous. The two demon merchants who represent English colonialism are first sighted as "horned owls", in "the bush beyond." The woods serve also as the back-ground for Cathleen's indecision as she vacillates between service to self by retreating to the beautiful world of dreams and art epitomized by Aleel, and service to the community by entering into the Faustian pact with the demon merchants.

Time in the play is that of pre-colonial Celtic Ireland, when feudalism was the only form of government in operation; this is seen in the dynamics of the relationship between an aristocratic Countess and her peasants. It was also a time when traditional religious practice of a mixture of pagan druidism and Catholic Christianity was the norm. Yeats' attempts to evoke a sense of mystical, other worldliness of Ireland is also reflected in the setting. The opening scene in the Rua cottage is, per the stage directions, *"that of a room with a lighted fire, and a door into the open air, through which one sees, perhaps, the trees of a wood, and these trees should be painted in flat color upon a gold or diapered sky. The walls are of one color. The scene should have the effect of a missal painting."*[7] Into this innocent mystical world step the two-demon merchants, and they cataclysmic change that trails their entrance is reflected in the change in the Rua cottage in the final scene.

The room is now dominated by a large table upon which the merchants arrange and count the money stolen from the peasants and the castle coffers. The dim light in the house symbolizes death, of Mary Rua whose body lies on the bed with candles round it, and of innocence. Light no longer reinforces the sense of life it did prior to the arrival of the merchants. Total darkness descends upon the room and the whole land, following Cathleen's signature of the Faustian pact, suggesting the triumph of the demons. As an Old Man puts it, "The Almighty's wrath at our great weakness and sin / Has blotted out the world and we must die."[8] The darkness, is however, broken by a visionary light, signifying the benevolence of the Almighty who has forgiven both Cathleen and the errant peasants, since He "Looks always on the motive, not the deed."

Cathleen ni Houlihan is set in a cottage similar to that of the Rua family, with the exception that it is close to Killala Bay. The time is 1798, the place and year when a French expeditionary landed in Ireland and, with the help of the peasants, defeated a large body of British yeomanry. Thus, time and setting correspond with the action of a play intended to incite the revolutionary spirit in the colonized Irishman.

The definitive framework provided by the rituals of the two mythical heroes – Cuchulain and Ogun – results in overt attempts by Yeats and Soyinka to evoke the supernatural, specifically, the actual location of passage of transition. Time and space are, therefore, identified with the hero-gods and essentially, reflect the movement away from the world of the conscious to the world of the unconscious, the twilight world between being and nonbeing where eternal truths about man are made manifest. Setting in these later plays invites psychic, rather than physical comprehension. *At the Hawk's Well*, for example, has none of the stage properties of the realistic theater of Yeats' Abbey Theater contemporaries such as Lennox Robinson. Rather, the stage is "any bare space before a wall against which stands a patterned screen."9 The only props on the stage are a drum, a gong and a zither, musical instruments whose sounds particularly evoke the ritual atmosphere.

The action takes the form of a quest that takes Cuchulain to a well on a windswept, barren mountain, a far cry from the hearth which is the common setting of the earlier plays. The setting here is one where sky, land and water meet or become one another, a place of mystical union and transformation. The time is sunset, a time of transformation from light to darkness, from life to death; time is, therefore, suggestive of the resolution of the quest. As the sun-god in Yeats' system, Cuchulain embarks on a quest that will inaugurate his setting, his demise. The three hazel trees by the well are leafless and dry. The well itself is in a hidden rocky place; the physical geography of Cuchulain's quest is therefore, suggestive of death, of the preternatural, the appropriate location for Cuchulain's transition into a tragic, heroic mortality.

The action in *On Baile's Strand* takes place in the great hall of an assembly house in Dundealgan, near Baile's strand, the gaelic term for a peninsula. The big door at the back, through which "misty light, as of sea mist" can be seen is the first of Yeats' constellation of symbols which represent the psyche, the "deeps of the mind" opening into the *Anima Mundi*, the racial subconscious. The symbolism of the door invites the audience member to suspend material reality, manifest either in an apprehensible present, a documentable past or a hypothetical future, and to seek instead the transcendant truth found through psychic participation; by which "many crooked things are made straight."10 It is through this door that the Fool and the Blind Man, and subsequently, Cuchulain and Conchubar, enter.

The time and setting for Professor's inordinate grope towards the essence of death in *The* Road are symbolically significant. They communicate the movement of transition from the past to the present and future and the spirit of death which permeates all. It begins with "dawn breaking on a road-side shack." Dawn, is the hour traditionally associated with Ogun. That Murano goes out in this dawn with his palm-wine tapper's implements suggests his portrayal as the epitome of transitional abyss, and his significance to the unfolding of the drama. The play ends with the onset of dusk, which is suggestive of the descent of darkness, the spirit of death towards which Professor gropes. The Church with its cross-sur-mounted steeple and its closed stained glass windows represents one area of the search for the Word. The decrepit "bolekaja" or cargo truck whose rear Professor now uses as the "Askident Store," and the make-shift beer parlor just beyond this represent current fields of his research on the essence of death. The sprawling, motionless figures lying close by the Askident Store further communicate the theme of death. Samson, Salubi and the other motor-park touts are sprawled out prior to awakening to a day whose very movement is towards death.

Setting in *Death and the King's Horseman* alternates between the marketplace of the Yoruba community, and the government reservation areas of the colonialists, until the fifth part where both worlds converge in Elesin Oba's prison quarters. The market is microcosmic of the Yoruba spiritual world, a fact Dan Izevbaye elucidates through reference to two concepts:

> First while the major Oba are addressed as Alayeluwa (Owner of the world and life), the minor Oba who are founders of their towns have the title, Qioja (Owner of the market). Second, there is the common Yoruba say-ing, *Oja L'aiya, Orun n'ile* (the world is market, heaven is home.)[11]

The market in the play is the location for Elesin Oba's dance. He enters along a "passage" in the market on his way to the "great market," meaning the world of ancestors. The market is "my roost, where I become a monarch whose palace is built with tenderness and beauty", and where "I have known love and laughter away from the palace." Iyaloja is the mother of market, "mother of multitudes in the teaming market of the world." The market is the abyss of transition itself, whose passage by Ogun encapsulates the Yoruba cosmogony's corning-into-being. The colonial world of the Pilkings, on the other hand, is a sterile, existential wasteland where the drumming preparatory to transition is "bush," and where the holy water of Christianity is absolute "nonsense". That the two worlds meet in Elesin Oba's prison reinforce the fact of his failure to successfully complete the passage, as well as the "deadlock" which obtains from contact between the two forces.

The Dreaming of the Bones is set in Clare, County Galway in 1916, the year which already evokes the war theme in the play. The stage is basically any bare place in a room close to the wall but with a screen patterned with mountain and sky, the mountain being suggestive of the subconscious, circuitous path to the truths engendered by the Young Man's encounter with the bones of the dead. The sky suggests the universe to which that truth relates. Time in the play is the hour before dawn, the darkest hour and the phase of complete objectivity in Yeats' system. It is the hour which defines the "dreaming back" process, when the dead couple are said to enter into the Shade, and are consequently able to communicate with the living. It also defines the dawning of the new objective age, epitomized by the Young Man on the run from the Easter 1916 Rising.

To the Musicians it is the hour that frightens the heart, and "sets it beating so." They, therefore, call upon the Red bird of March to wake up and begin to crow. Dawn will also announce the inauguration of a new cycle of hatred and fanaticisms which are often the substance of wars. The onset of dawn awakens the Young Man once again, to his near yielding to the temptation of the Stranger and the Young Girl and to the destructive effects of English colonialism. From the mountain summit he perceives far and wide into the Aran Islands, Connemara Hills and Galway, where, "The enemy has toppled roof and gable, / And torn the panelling from ancient rooms."[12] This perception reinforces his decision never to forgive Diarmuid and Dervorgilla, the implications of which are re-echoed in the Musicians final song, "now the night which is gone. / I have heard from far below / the strong March birds a-crow."[13]

In *Madmen and Specialists*, the action is spread over three levels of setting – the surgery down in a cellar, the level ground in the fore where Si Bero dries her barks and twigs, and where the Mendicants spend most of their time, and the higher structure to one side in the form of a semi-open hut where the Old Women sit. Qyin Ogunba's symbolic interpretations of the three levels are appropriate here:

> Level One is the level below normal human dignity and, correspondingly, the nature of the action there is sub-human, for each of the four scenes on it – is a reflection on man's depravity. – The matter in the scenes [in Level Two] is treated superficially – we see the people and their actions essentially from outside. It is as if the characters are unwilling to disclose themselves fully until they are back in the safety of Level One or Level Three. – All the four scenes on Level Three are extremely short ones – As this is the level of the supernatural, it is understandable that very little is said. Witches, after all, have a gift for brevity.[14]

The distribution of the dramatic action between the three levels of setting captures the frenzy, the total breakdown of basic human laws, reason and sanity consequent upon the rule of AS. The Mendicants on the second level gamble away sections of the already mangled bodies in a macabre game of dice. The Dr. Bero who returns from the war front on the same level appears to have lost all sense of familial ties and duties in the all-consuming bid to achieve control over human destiny. The immediate temporal context is the Nigerian Civil War but, despite this context, a sense of the timelessness of the action pervades the whole play. The war in which Bero participated and from which he returns could be any war, just as Bero himself is the archetypal representation of the destructive instinct in humanity.

Figures in a Dance

Characterization of the figures in the plays is defined by complementarities. The gods are characterized in terms of the humans, and vice versa. These gods are often drawn from the mythical repository of both artists' respective cultures and are compartmentalized into those that are benevolent and wise, who use their omniscient wisdom to work for the benefit of humans, and those that are decidedly malevolent, whose sole objective is the destruction of humans. Mediating between the two extremes are supernatural beings who exhibit both beneficent and malevolent attributes, the manifestation of either being dependent upon the assertion of the individual will. Beyond these groups are figures suspended between the natural and the supernatural, due to some quirk of fate.

The Christian God in *The Countess Cathleen*, Aroni and Forest head in *A Dance of the Forests* and the Old Women in *Madmen and Specialists* all fall within the first group of supernatural beings, the benevolent, the wise and who love humans. In Yeats' play, God Himself intervenes to save the peasants from the machinations of the demon merchants, and to redeem the Countess from the pact of blood she signed with them. Aleel seizes one of the armed angels standing in the "half light... half shadow" to ferret out the fate of the Countess from him. He learns that the "gates of pearl are wide" open for the Countess, and that "she is passing to the floor of peace" to her Creator.[15] In *A Dance of the Forests,* Forest Head or Olodumare, intervenes to play the same omniscient role.

Contrasting the benevolent supernatural beings are the malevolent ones who work solely for the destruction of mankind. The demon-merchants who represent English colonialism in Yeats'

The Countess Cathleen have deliberately created a situation of severe famine and abject poverty to force the peasants into desperation, into selling their own souls in return for money to buy food. Their ultimate goal is the soul of the Countess but they are thwarted by the "Light of Lights" declaration of the Faustian pact null and void. In *A Dance of the Forests,* Eshuoro is presented in terms of a malevolent being whose sole aim is the destruction of Demoke, with the new community he represents. Most prominent in the plays are the gods who exhibit the dualities of good and evil. Cuchulain and Ogun clearly fall within this category. *A Dance of the Forests* is the only play in which Ogun is personified. His characterization as a churlish god in perpetual conflict with Eshuoro tends to negate the awe, grandeur and nobility normally ascribed to him in the later plays. In *The Road,* the road is the chief protagonist in the play; it is an aspect of the god. In *Death and the King's Horseman* the passage through the market place where Elesin Oba dances on his way to transition corresponds to the internal abyss of transition, associated with Ogun.

The fourth group of supernatural beings consists of those characters who are suspended midway between life and death, in limbo or purgatory which affords them contact with humans and are at their mercy The Dead Couple in *A Dance of the Forests* are representatives of this kind. As the Warrior and his pregnant wife in the flashback to the Court of Mata Kharibu, they confronted a society predicated on war and its spoils. For their pains, they were forced to wander aimlessly in the streams of the world for centuries, until Forest Heads orders them to the Gathering of the Tribes in order to prick the conscience of the new community. Demoke's decision to hand the Half-Child back to its mother, the Dead Woman, at the end of the play (in recognition of the irreversibility of the cycle of evil and destruction) plunges them once more into the purgatory.

Murano in *The Road,* is the visual embodiment of the transitional abyss. He was knocked down in his "agemo" phase by Kotonu's lorry during a driver's festival, an incident re-enacted in a flashback in the second part of the play. To Professor, he is the one person "in this world in whom the Word reposes." Consequently, he attempts to confront the transitional realm by restoring Murano to his mask state, his former state of possession. In Yeats's The *Dreaming of the Bones*, the Stranger and the Young Girl are supernatural beings who have transformed into Shades, in order to effect contact with a member of the living who can release them from purgatory, from their state of eternal penance. But the Young Man's resolve never to forgive them ensures the continuity of their penance.

In close interaction with these supernatural beings is the generality of humanity. These can be compartmentalized on the basis of similarities into three broad groupings – the protagonists, the characters who motivate the protagonists or act as counterf6il to them, and the community at large upon whom the actions of the protagonists reverberate. These protagonists are often juxtaposed with characters who either motivate them or act as counterfoils to them, with the resulting conflict of opposites highlighting the central issues in the plays. In *The Countess Cothleen*, Aleel represents the world of dreams and art to which Cathleen would like to escape, but which she subordinates to the call for self-sacrifice on behalf of her peasant subjects. In *On Baile's Strand*, the war of wills between Conchubar and Cuchulain reflects the larger conflict of greed and materialism with the heroic individual. The war of nerves between Elesin Oba and Pilkings in *Death and the King's Horseman* intimates the conflict of cultures in the play, extended in the alternation of the scenes between the passage in the marketplace and the verandah of the Pilkings' bungalow, as well as in the dance of the market and the waltz and masque on the Pilkings' verandah and the residency, respectively.

Iyaloja functions simultaneously as Elesin Oba's motivator and antagonist. Along with the Praise-Singer and the market women, she motivates him in his dance to transition, showering praises on him and meeting even his most banal needs. Following his failure to successfully complete the dance, she execrates him for having betrayed the community, and confronts him with the dangers inherent in his failure which are heightened, rather than lessened, by his son's Olunde's completing his task for him. The conflict between Dr. Bero and his father in *Madmen and Specialists* is symptomatic of the wider conflict between the oppressive system and the sensitive individual. The Old Man, whose Socratic wisdom is encapsulated in his namelessness and his age, confronts his recalcitrant son with the fact of the evil that reigns supreme within him, and in the System he serves.

The community at large, so to speak, find themselves at the mercy of the conflicting protagonists. The peasant families in the two early Yeats plays represent the larger community of Ireland. Their simplicity, innocence, belief in the mixture of pagan druidism and Christianity are projected as being the very same attributes that define the Irish. These characteristics contrast with the a-spirituality, greed and materialism of the English. In *On Baile's Strand*, however, this innocence disappears and the community becomes the precipitator of the tragic denouement. The junior kings in the play manifest the same materialistic mentality as Conchubar, and, threatened with Cuchulain's fame, heroism and fiery spirit, they urge him to take the oath of allegiance, to "do what the High Kings bids you since "(t)here is none here that would not have you take it."

The community in the Soyinka's *A Dance of the Forests* is much more complex, reflecting the wide spectrum of life in Nigeria. The group of characters comprising the Old Man, Demoke's father, two councilors and Agboreke, the diviner, represent the larger, post-independent Nigerian community whose preoccupation with the celebration of Independence blinds them to the truths whose apprehension is mandated by Forest head and Aroni. Ignorant of the significance of the Dead Couple, the Old Man complains that they "are slaves and lackeys. They have only come to undermine our strength. To preach to us how ignoble we are. They are disgruntled creatures who have come to accuse their tormentors as if this were a court of law."[16] In his view, they have come to foul the feast of the Gathering of Tribes, dominated by his son's totem and, therefore, must be eliminated. His attempts to do so provide most of the comic relief in the play.

He brings in a group of beaters to make a lot of noise and drive the obscenities away, in the belief that the dead cannot bear high noise decibels. Failing, he orders the Chimney of Ereko, a death trap in iron, back on the road in the hope that the poisonous fumes it emits will fumigate the forest of the couple. The vehicle, however, emits enough fumes to choke not only the Old Man and his associates but also a host of other forest spirits who "all hold leaves to their noses, and grumble all the way. Some sniff in disgust, others spit, all stop their noses, disapproving strongly of petrol fumes."[17] Agboreko is brought in next to use his powers of divination to rid the Gathering of the couple. But he ensures the failure of his plan by first consulting Murete, a tree demon who admits to a laxity of concentration at times. Thus, Agboreko's invocation of the demon as the "Bar (drinks) that never shuts" or "the Eye that never closes" is ironical, especially in the light of this admission. The ritual of divination he mounts is faulted by the nature of the metaphysical postulates in the incantations, they are merely re-statements of the most mundane facts of life, and bear no relationship to the seriousness of the issue at hand: "If the wind can get lost in the rainstorm it is useless to send him an umbrella"; "The eye that looks downwards will certainly see the nose", "The hand that dips to the bottom of the pot will eat the biggest snail."[18] The farcical nature of the whole ritual is confirmed when the Chimney of Ereko descends upon it in all its thunder and fumes.

The community of drivers and motor-park touts in *The Road* contribute, in one way or the other, to Professor's quest. For example, Samson, "the Champion Tout of the Motor Park," is the primary means whereby Professor's multifaceted conceptions of the

Word are made public. For him, the Word is Ogun, a potentially dangerous god that is best left alone. This is the root cause of his frustration with Professor's manipulation of Kotonu's fear of driving, and his desperate plea to Kotonu in the flashback enacting their hair-breadth escape from death to "serve Ogun his tit-bit so the road won't look at us one day and say Ho, ho! you two boys look juicy to me."[19] Soyinka, however, introduces an ironic twist to Samson's toying with death. At certain strategic points in the play, he pokes at a spider's web with a stick and alternatively feeds it with a fly:

> SAMSON: Your brother is having a dinner –
>
> HM: Just the wings left of that fly.
>
> KOTONU: The road and the spider lie gloating, then
> the fly buzzes along like a happy fool
>
> SAMSON: [*very hurriedly*] All right, all right.[20]

In Yoruba creation myth, Ogun is said to have surveyed the awesome gulf of transition dangling from a spider's web.[21] Like his mentor, Samson subverts the positive attributes of the god's own daring, albeit unwittingly. His feeding the spider with the fly suggests his complicity in the macabre game of death on the road engineered by Professor. As the champion tout, he herds unwitting passengers to their deaths – a fact he innocently confirms in one of the mimes in the play:

> *Samson finds himself doing a running battle with a fly. He loses eventually, and the fly succeeds in loading in his wine. Samson leaps up angrily scoops up the froth with the fly in it, and carefully rakes the fly between two fingers. After a moments thought he takes the fly to the spider's web, throws it in, and stays to watch the spider seize it, a satisfied grin spreading over his face.*[22]

Alongside the drivers and touts are a number of stereotypes who are not directly associated with the road, but who are also predators, since they typify a number of social ills in Nigeria. They congregate in Professor's drinking bar, a secret haven where they can give full rein to planning their nefarious activities without fear of detection. Particulars Joe, as his name suggests, exemplifies the corrupt policeman who facilitates the high incidence of deaths on the road, by feigning ignorance of forged drivers' licenses in return for a bribe. Chief-in-Town is the typical corrupt, loud politician endemic to Nigerian politics, who relies upon thugs for effective political campaigns, maintaining their loyalty by bribing them with an ample supply of hard drugs.

In *Death and the King's Horseman* the conflict between Amusa and the daughters of the market women provides the comic relief in the play. Amusa is the archetypal alienated African who has thoroughly imbibed the culture of the colonials. The market daughters on the other hand, like their mothers, are the custodians of the culture whose continuity is threatened by the likes of Amusa. Their play-acting effectively impresses upon Amusa his actual insignificance to the colonial masters he serves, and their common perception of the native as an object for anthropological study, rather than a human being:

- But you do manage to cope?
- Yes, indeed I do.
- I have a rather faithful ox called Amusa
- He's loyal?
- Absolutely.
- Lay down his life for you what?
- Without a moment's thought.
- Had one like that once.
- Trust him with my life.
- Mostly of course, they are liars.
- Never known a native to tell the truth.[23]

Another approach to characterization common to the two artists is the presentation of physically handicapped characters, often actually identified by their physical disability, to serve as ironic counterpoints to the central conflict of opposites. In this context they also reinforce the metaphysical, existentialist milieu of the plays in the manner reminiscent of handicapped figures in Samuel Beckett's *Waiting for Godot.* The Fool and the Blind Man in *On Baile's Strand*, for example, are the ironic counterpoints to the central conflict between Cuchulain and Conchubar. Barton Friedman argues, Yeats created the Fool and the Blind Man to do for his play what the Greek chorus and the Shakespearean sub-plot do for their plays, that is, as "the main plot working itself out in more ordinary men and women, and so doubly calling up before us the image of multitude."[24] The Fool and the Blind Man are vehicles for audience effect, for inviting the audience-member, as the Musicians do in *At the Hawk's Well,* to participate, psychically, in the action. They frame the action of the play, forcing the audience member to recognize in the mythic giants they shadow, the same conflicting forces within themselves.

The Blind Man is Yeats' personification of moral and imaginative bankruptcy, of the materialism which besets contemporary consciousness. The Fool is overawed by the Blind Man's cleverness, particularly his pragmatism: "What a clever man you are though you are blind! There's nobody with two eyes in his head that is as clever as you are."[25] This cleverness, however, is the direct result of spiritual blindness, of his inability to apprehend other than sensuously, to comprehend other than empirically. It is a cleverness that realizes maximum utility in stealing chickens when the hen wife is asleep, and in deceiving the Fool, in plotting to get all the lean parts of the chicken, leaving the Fool with the feathers and bones. The fact that he puts into perspective the action of a play which will climax with the triumph of materialism and reason over imagination and heroism, is an index of his role as the embodiment of those triumphant forces. The Blind Man also knows who the father of the Young Man from Aoife's country is, but refuses to disclose it, for Cuchulain must play out his tragic demise.

In contrast to Blind Man's practical intelligence and prudential values, the Fool represents the imagination, the things of the spirit. He is unable to cope with the problems of subsisting in the present world – hence his dependence on the Blind Man. He prefers the companionship of supernatural beings. While the chicken is "being done to the turn," he could "go out and run races with the witches at the edge of the waves and get an appetite," and he is on intimate terms with "Boann herself out of the river", and "Fand out of the deep sea."[26] Although he calls these supernatural beings "witches," the word holds none of the terror for him that it does for the Celtic Warriors we meet in the next scene. His naiveté and honesty make him an easy target for the Blind man's treachery. When he learns of Cuchulain's impending oath of allegiance to Conchubar, he becomes confused; he like many others in Dundealgan believed that Cuchulain has limitless freedom to do any thing he likes. But the political strategy by which Conchubar accomplishes his aims is alien to the Fool. The Blind Man tells him, "You have no wits to understand such things."[27] He watches helplessly as his hero falls prey to the world of the Blind Man and Conchubar.

Following the fatal battle with the young Man, the Fool attempts to intimate Cuchulain with the Blind Man's treachery through a song he sings which plays on the legendary longevity of the eagle by comparing it with the oak:

> When you were an acorn on the tree-top,
> Then was I an eagle-cook
> Now that you are withered old block,
> Still am I an eagle cook.[28]

The eagle refers to the spiritual aspect of man, and the oak, its material counterpart. By rejecting his eagle or hawk-like nature, Cuchulain has irrevocably identified with the material world. The feathers which the Blind Man leaves the Fool after the chicken feast, and with which Cuchulain wipes the blood of his son from his sword, are symbolic reminders of Cuchulain's rejected bird-like nature; the contact of the feathers with the Young Man's blood signals a connection which Cuchulain makes unconsciously. The trance induced by the tragedy of Cuchulain's mastery by the waves is broken by the Blind Man's persistent demands for attention to plot his next foray into untended ovens, encapsulating the theme of the continuity of the world of treachery, greed and materialism.

The Mendicants in *Madmen and the Specialists*, like the Fool and the Blind Man, act both as participants and poets in the tragedy of As. They are presented as the casualties of war in various stages of physical disintegration, which they exploit to their own advantage; Aafaa's St. Vitus spasms for example, are "designed to rid the wayfarer of his last pennies in a desperate bid to be rid of the sight."[29] Their every activity is conditioned by AS. Their mock trial and execution of Goyi, for example, is an enactment of a principle of AS: Execution before trial. In the "line of duty," Goyi is shot with an imaginary gun; the others realize he was not tried and Goyi resurrects, is accused for an unspecified crime and is promptly executed – all in the name of a 'fair trial'. Another important sketch is Blind Man's parody of former British Prime Minister Harold Macmillan's "Wind of Change" pronouncement in the 1950s, on approaching independence for the colonies in Africa.

Blind Man makes topical allusions to the old colonial powers, to the new regimes of Africa, to class and race prejudices, and, in the reference to Katangese, to the armed struggle in the former Belgian Congo which parallels the Nigerian-Biafran war. The significance of the speech is pointedly suggested in Soyinka's stage direction that it be constantly revised in keeping with the topicality of the times:

> It was our duty and a historical necessity. It is our duty and a historical beauty. It shall always be. – What we have we hold. – What though the wind of change

is blowing over the entire continent, our principles and traditions – yes, must be maintained. For we are threatened, yes, we are indeed threatened. Look at the hordes, I implore you. They stink. They eat garlic. What on earth have we in common with them? – If we don't stop them now, who knows but it may be our turn next moment. I ask you do you want to wake up murdered in your beds? – Rape is more natural to them, if it must be, lie back and enjoy it. That coming from their greatest – er-er-atomic scientist is not a statement to be taken lightly The black menace is no figment of my father's imagination – Yes, we are indeed threatened. Excuse me, but we are entitled to match you history for history to the nearest half-million souls.[30]

The speech also alludes to the covetousness which reveals itself in the tenacious clinging to power by individuals, in the proliferation of economic and political exploitation by conglomerates and political parties, and in the perpetuation of spheres of influence by the superpowers. That the speech is made by Blindman, the man "without vision," suggests the blind passions and policies of powerful men who resort to bloodshed and the carnage of war to achieve their aims.

Language

Language in the plays reflects the traditional bias of the two dramatists, and their fundamental conceptions of theater as sacred ritual. The centuries old close association with the earth found in all agrarian societies results in a form of communication that is vibrant and vigorous, rather than pallid and smooth; it ends also, and in the use of images and symbols that have firm roots in the terrestrial cosmos. It is the language which most requires a simultaneous stylized, physical expression, a dance, for greater communication and comprehension.

The language of the old Woman in *Cathleen ni Houlihan* reflects Yeats' indebtness to the linguistic conventions of the *aisling* or vision poem, in its profusion of archetypal images which are understood by only the native Irish. Language in *At the Hawk's Well* evokes the cosmic entirety, the supernatural framework of the play. The Old Man and the Young Man communicate in a terse, poetic language that is appropriate to their portrayal as figures in the unfolding of a universal and eternal truth. The Old Man's language is bitter and resigned; it is the result of having waited for fifty years for the water of the well to rise, of his being at the mercy of the dancers who have cheated him continuously:

> OLD MAN: I came like you when
>   Young in body and mind, and blown
>   By what had seemed to me a lucky sail
>   The well was dry, I sat upon its edge,
>   I waited while the years passed and withered me
>   away
>   I have snared the birds for food and eaten grass
>   And drunk the rain, and neither dark nor shine
>   Wandered too far away to have heard the plash,
>   And yet the dancers have deceived me. Thrice I
>   have awakened from a sudden sleep
>   To find the stones were wet.[31]

It contrasts with the vibrancy and challenge inherent in the Young Man's language, who believes his "luck is strong", that he will "take" the waters of the well in his hands. He is not afraid of the Guardian of the Well, "Do what you will; I shall not leave this place / Till I have grown immortal like yourself."

A similar allusiveness and symbolism marks the language of the Stranger and the Young Girl in *The Dreaming of the Bones*. That they are from an earlier, subjective era is reflected in their allusive and mysterious speeches, which contrast with the direct, matter-of-fact language of the Young Man who represents the objective world:

> STRANGER: We're almost at the summit and can rest.
>   The road is a faint shadow there, and there
>   The Abbey lies amid its broken tombs.
>   In the old days we should have heard a bell
>   Calling the monks before day broke to pray;
>   And when the day had broken on the ridge
>   The crowing of its cocks.
>
> YOUNG MAN: Is there no house
>   Famous for sanctity and architectural beauty
>   In Clare or Kerry, or in all wide Connacht,
>   The enemy has not unroofed?[32]

While The Stranger describes the Abbey in terms of its present structure and past functions, the Young Man sees only its destruction, its illustration of the destruction of ancient Irish buildings by the colonizing forces.

Language in the Soyinka plays is also highly allusive or symbolic. The language of the Alagemo preface poem in *The Road* identifies the spirit and his attributes; his embodiment of the timelessness: "Pennant in the stream of time – Now, / Gone and Here the Feature Make way", and of destruction as in, "When the whirlwind claps his feet / It is the sundering of the – name no ills – Of- the Not-to-be / Of the moistening moment of a breath – Approach."[33] The language used by Forest Head and Aroni and *A Dance of the Forests,* and by the Old Women in *Madmen and Specialists* reflects their comprehension of the human condition and their transcendence of earthly values that drives them. Forest Head's terse language in his direction of the course of the action in the Dance recalls the equally commanding language of the Christian God in the creation of man in Genesis, as seen in these excerpts:

FOREST HEAD: Eshuoro, you came here to bathe in
blood,
Ogun, you to defend the foibles of your ward.
Let this night alone, when I layout the rites of
the dead or my anger will surpass our spleen.
Aroni, you know my will. Proceed – Do not
deny that all goes as you planned it – But only
because it is my wish. And so we all must be
content. Call the questioner and let no one
foully intervene for the furthering of his cause.[34]
Aroni, relieve this woman of her burden and let the
tongue of the unborn, stilled for generations, be
loosened.[35]
Demoke, you hold a doomed thing in your hand.
It is no light matter to reverse the deed that was
begun many lives ago. The Forest will not let
you pass. [36]

The same authority and arbitrariness is inherent in the language of
the Old Women in *Madmen and Specialists.*

Dance is the most stylized form of communication and is
integral to the traditional theater of both Ireland and Nigeria. Along
with music and song, dance forms an intricate part of festivals
and celebrations which mark the spiritually significant points in
the life of the agrarian based societies. The use of Dance in the
plays manifests both artists modification of the communicative
form in terms of their consciousness of national imperatives,
and in terms of their exposure to literary influences, such as the
Japanese Noh convention in Yeats' case. *They resort to dance at the
point where spoken language becomes inadequate, usually the ritual
climax in the play.* Dance in Yeats' plays embodies an idealized
image of the experience felt or aroused on the stage, and in the
audience. It occurs at the moment when it will be impossible
to "know the dancer from the dance", when both the actor and

the audience become one, enraptured in the lofty emotion being evoked.

The dance of the Guardian of the Well in *At the Hawk's Well* is like the movement of a hawk. It occurs when Cuchulain goes into the ritual trance prior to his final transition. The dance is a symbolic definition of the hero-god, of Cuchulain himself. He, in mortal life, is to be like the hawk, in its limitless freedom in the sky, in its ability to challenge the sun, as well as its ability for destruction. The dance of the Stranger and the Young Girl in *The Dreaming of the Bones* fails to entrance the Young Man; it is a symbolic communication of the latter's failure of vision, and corresponds to man's repetitive failure to transcend the narrow confines of fanaticism and hatred.

Dance in the Soyinka plays, as in those by Yeats, is the language of communion in the supernatural. It is the motif used by Forest Head and Aroni to confront the three protagonists, with the mirror of original nakedness in *A Dance of the Forests*. The dance motif plays a particularly significant role in the Welcoming of the Dead section; the dance of the forest spirits with their apoclayptic vision of man, that of Eshuoro and the Interpreter on one side, and Ogun and Demoke on the other for the possession of the Half-Child, and Demoke's own dance of the Unwilling Sacrifice are media with which Forest Head communicates the need for regeneration in Nigeria.

The dance motif also defines the action in *The Road*. Murano is the visual suspension of the transitional dance, towards which Professor gropes. Restoring Murano to his former state of possession at the end of the play is his promethean attempt to subvert the cosmogonic functions of the dance. In *Death and the King's Horseman*, Elesin Oba dances towards the transitional abyss in conformity with the traditions of the Yoruba community. He is goaded towards the abyss by the music of the market women, the drumming and praises of the Praise-Singer and the pander of Iyaloja. Music, as Soyinka avers, is "the intensive language of transition and its communicant means, the catalyst and solvent of its regenerative hoard."[37] Elesin Oba dances into the state of trance within which he utters the visions symbolic of the abyss: "I have freed myself of earth and now, / It's getting dark. Strange voices guide my feet."[38] Failure to dissociate himself completely from worldly pleasures, however, constitutes the dangerous pause in the momentum and rhythm of music and dance that alter the preordained course to transition.

The language of the protagonists in the plays is alternately highly allusive and direct. The Countess Cathleen's language in the Yeats play effectively suggests the internal conflict between the world of dreams and art and that of the peasants. The Gaelic syntax and speech inflections of the language of the peasants merges with the highly poetic, allusive language of dreams and art, as spoken by Aleel:

> CATHLEEN: Bend down your faces, Oona and Aleel;
> I gaze upon them as the swallow gazes
> Upon them as nest under the eve, before
> She wanders the loud waters. Do not weep
> Too great a while, for there is many a candle
> On the High Altar though one fall. Aleel,
> Who sang upon the dancers of the woods
> That know not the hard burden of the world,
> Having but breath in their bodies, farewell!
> And farewell, Oona, you who played with me,
> And bore me in your arms about the house
> When I was but a child and therefore happy,
> Therefore happy even like those that dance.
> The storm is in my hair and I must go. [39]

Cuchlain's speeches in *On Baile's Strand* are filled with images of the conflict of opposites which he embodies, of earth and air, fire and water, the cold moon and the hot sun, of heroism and weakness. His language identifies him as the embracer of the curses consequent upon his daring to stare into the "unmoistened eyes" of the hawk-woman.

> CUCHULAIN: No wonder in that, no wonder at all in
> that,
> I have never known love but as a kiss
> In the mid-battle, and a difficult truce
> Of oil and water, candle and dark night
> Hillside and hollow, the hot-footed sun
> And the cold, sliding, slippery footed moon
> A brief forgiveness between opposites
> That have been hatreds for three times the age
> Of this long 'stablished group. [40]

The language of the protagonists in the Sovinka plays betrays the artist's love for words and word play. Professor's language in *The Road* defines his quest for the Word as word, for the definition of meaning. Hence it is obscure and mystifying, qualities which set the user apart from the linguistic environment of the community of touts and drivers. In his quest for the meaning of the word, Professor proffers constantly changing definitions and contexts for the Word. There are three main contexts in which he uses the Word: the Word as printed matter, the Word as divine power manifesting itself in potent utterances, and the Word in terms of images associated with Mother Earth.[41] In this third context, he sees himself as "a gleaner" of the Word, in the air and the earth; his favorite "paths are those trickles among green fastnesses, on which whole forests are broken up, between the falling dew and the evening mists the nature of those paths changes right beneath my feet."[42] The Word may be found where, "ascent is broken and a winged secret plummets back to earth." Izevbaye attests this last context to the influence of *Ogboni*, an occultic cult in Yoruba land thought on Professor: "the ascent is the spirit's aspiration towards its maker, Olorun the father, while the plummeting back to earth is the return to *Ogboni*, the earth, the mother of all life."[43]

The association of the Word with Mother Earth dovetails neatly into its identification with the natural seasonal cycle of sowing and harvest, with birth and death. It also reinforces the identification of the Word with Ogun, who embodies the seasonal tensions. Professor sees himself as a "faithful gleaner" of the Word from the road. The bundles of paper he carts around with him assume another more potent symbolism, as the "granary" where he stores his harvest; the Word, being the "elusive kernel" in that granary.[44] He found the word "BEND" where it "sprouted for heaven knows how long" to prevent accidents and uprooted it, to cause the accidents it was designed to prevent. When language fails to adequately define the Word, Professor resorts to the mask idiom, with tragic consequences. He restores Murano the mute to his former state of possession as the Agemo masquerade in anticipation of a final confrontation with the Word. In the final consciousness, Professor uses the symbolic language of myth, with its capacity to encapsulate "in a single image the tenor of a complex and coherent experience."[45] He images the road as a snake and captures not only the sense of its treachery, its winding nature but also of its manifestation of Ogun, the god of the road.

Elesin Oba's language is filled with metaphors and symbols which crescendo as he actually arrives at the edge of the transitional abyss. The market is "his roost," and among the market-women, he is like "a chicken with a hundred mothers."[46] He executes brief, half-taunting dances, in tune with Olohun-Iyo's drumming and praises. As he nears the edge of the abyss, his language assumes a mystifying, lyrical quality:

ELESIN: My sash is of the deep purple *alari*;
It is no tethering-rope. The elephant
Trails no tethering-rope, that king
is not yet crowned who will peg an elephant.

Not even you my friend and king.

PRAISE SINGER: And yet this fear will not depart
from me.
The darkness of this new abode is deep.
Will your human eyes suffice?

ELESIN: In a night which falls before our eyes
However deep, we do not miss our way.[47]

As he falls deeper into the trance necessary for transition, his images of the transitional abyss become more stylized, and his dance gestures become weightier.

More direct language in the plays is used with the minor characters. These speak a type of English which has been dramatically conditioned by the cultural or sociological changes effected by the colonial contact. The peasants in Yeats' plays speak an Anglo-Irish dialect, an English language that has been deeply modified by Gaelic. It is consequently characterized by inflections of speech and turns of phrase that are more expressive and more poetic than the standardized and materially oriented speech of their colonials. It is the type of language Synge compares to clothing in the Preface to *The Playboy of the Western World,* and which defines a distinct peasant or Irish identity, despite its English superstructure.[48] Neologism is a characteristic feature of this Anglo-Irish dialect and it derives from the constant quest for appropriate English words to evoke the intense Gaelic emotion.

Yeats' use of a peasant dialect was part of the nationwide cultural nationalism which witnessed the revival and projection of Gaelic as a national language, with Douglas Hyde's Gaelic League spearheading the move. The dialect of the peasantry in the West of Ireland was projected as the most ideal. It is that which characterizes peasant speech in Yeast's plays, as well as in John Millington Synge's. In the Preface to *The Playboy of the Western World,* Synge asserts, "In a good play every speech should be as fully flavored as a nut or an apple, and such speech cannot be written by anyone who works among people who have shut their lips on poetry."[49] An example is the peculiar turns of phrase and speech inflections in Bridget's reflection on Patrick's future in *Cathleen ni Houlihan*:

> I do be thinking sometimes, now things are going so well sometimes, and the Cahels such a good back to us in the district, and Delia's own uncle a priest, we might be put in the way of making Patrick a priest some day, and he so good at his books.[50]

The equivalent of the speech inflections in the Anglo-Irish dialect of the peasants in the Yeats plays is the pidgin-English spoken by the community of motor park touts in *The Road*, for example. This native English developed as a utility language without any conscious formalization through education, and this explains the peculiarities of its grammar, syntax and vocabulary.[51] Like the peasant speech of Yeats plays, it is primarily the language of the transitional masses who have partially escaped the socializing influence of traditional society without having undergone full modernization."[52]

Unlike the peasant dialect, however, it is primarily the language of the urban centers or cities, those concentrations of peoples and lifestyles inaugurated by colonial administration. It functions primarily as a means of communication between the varieties of peoples drawn from different linguistic areas to the melting pot, incorporating the many syntactical peculiarities of the vernacular languages of West Africa. It is an onomatopoeic language which can easily be turned to vulgar and abusive purposes. The community of motor park touts in *The Road* are typical of the urban drifters and *lumpenproletariat*, with inadequate educational training and skills who communicate in pidgin. Samson and Salubi try to communicate in standard English before Professor; but they revert to the most expressive form of pidgin to ridicule either each other, Professor, or any of the social vices Soyinka satirizes in the play. In the opening scene, they ridicule each other as follows:

SAMSON: Me a jobless tout? May I ask what you are?

SALUBI: A uniformed private driver – temporary
unemploy. [*Straightens his outfit*]

SAMSON: God almighty! You dey like monkey wey
stoway in side sailor suit.

SALUBI: Na common jealousy de do you. I know I
no get job, but I get uniform.[53]

Samson's description of the driving lessons he received from an
expressive instructor particularly evokes the onomatopoeic nature
of pidgin English:

Then it was Fai! Fai! You think say I get petrol for waste?
Take your foot comot for accelerator! Small, small! I say
small small – you tink say dis one na football game. Fai
fai fai! You dey press brake – Gi-am! – as if na stud you
wan' give centre back. I say do am soft soft! Fai fai fai!
All a waste of time. Everytime I started the lorry it went
like a railway – gbaga gbaga. – like clinic for hiccup.[54]

Say Tokyo Kid's quasi-American slangs: "No borer in re ol bole", "A
guy is gorra have his principles – You wanre Limousine, a Ponriac
or something like that," "Shurrup, wharre hell you mean," mark
him out as one who has thoroughly imbibed the composite culture
of the metropolis and turned it to his own advantage.

One means of communication found in the Soyinka's plays, but
which is totally absent in Yeats' plays, is mime. Like dance, mime
symbolically captures the tenor of the play. A good example is the
afore mentioned "battle" between Samson, a fly and a spider which
intersperses the action in *The Road*. It recalls Kotonu's earlier statement: "the road and the spider lie gloating, then the fly buzzes along
like a happy fool. "The mime communicates the treachery of the road
and the complicity of the drivers and touts in the destruction.

Both Soyinka and Yeats use songs as structurally strategic devices to capture the meaning of a play. The action of *Cathleen ni Houlihan* is interspersed with the Old Woman's songs, which evoke the memories of past lives lost fighting on her behalf. The lament for the "yellow-haired Donough" is based on a traditional folk song, "Donnchadh Ban" and evokes images of a young peasant farmer who readily gave up farming to die "for love of" the Old Woman:

> OLD WOMAN: – I will go cry with the woman,
>   For yellow-haired Donough is dead,
>   With a hempen rope for a neck-cloth
>   And a white cloth on his door; –
>
> MICHEAL: [*Coming from the door*]: What is that you
>   are singing, ma'am?
>
> OLD WOMAN: Singing I am about a man I know one
>   time,
>   Yellow haired Donough that was hanged in
>   Galway.[55]

The song spurs Michael into ferreting out information that will culminate in his leaving a secure future to fight on behalf of the Old Woman. The songs sung by the community of drivers and motor park touts in *The Road* evoke a sense of life on the road and of Professor's looming figure in this life. The first Drivers' dirge ridicules the fear of death engendered in passage as a result of the drivers' speed and carelessness:

Ona orun jin o eeeee	It is a long road to heaven
Ona orun jin dereba rora	It is a long road to heaven,
	Driver, slowly
E e dereba rora	Go easy- a-ah, go easy
	driver

E e dereba rora

Ona orun jin o eeeee   It is a long road to heaven

Eled a mi ma ma buru   My Creator, be not harsh
                               on me

Esin baba Bandele je l'odan   Bandele's horse galloped
                               home a winner

Won o gbefun o   But the race eluded him

Eleda mi ma ma buru   (2)

So also, the song of AS the Mendicants sing at structurally strategic points in *Madmen and Specialists* to impress the pervasiveness of AS.

Chapter seven
Figures in a Dance

The artistic sensibility connotes an acute of consciousness, a third eye which pierces deep into the matrix of society; and channels that consciousness to creative purposes. The art, the by product of such a channeling is often an accurate index of the artist's environment, its *zeitgeist*. It functions to either to affirm his or her environment's positive values, or to condemn those others that are decidedly deleterious to its well-being. Wole Soyinka is an artist whose impact on his environment is unquestionable. His abiding concern with fashioning, in poetic overtones, the drama of human existence, is fundamentally similar to that of another great artist of the twentieth century, William Butler Yeats.

The similarities between them, just like the obvious differences, transcend the borders of time and race, because both dramatists were confronted with near identical circumstances and responded to in like manner. They are both products, for example, of communities characterized by a viable traditional base, whose original structure and symbolism had been altered by contact with the forces of colonialism. The upsurge of that contact and conflict, slavery, colonialism and neo-colonialism, inevitably bred a corpus of literature concerned with the scarification and sanctification of community, as opposed to literature just for its own sake. They scoured their community's repository of tradition to awaken consciousness to the negative as well as the positive values operating in their worlds. An aspect of tradition that particularly lent itself to their intent is myth.

Myth is broadly defined as a narrative structure involving human limitations and superhuman strivings and accomplishments from which a community derives its sense of identity. Myth symbolizes human attempts to express those features of his physiological and psychological makeup, as well as those aspects of external environment that we cannot comprehend, accept or master. The periodic enactment of myth, ritual, is captured in this study as a dance, a highly stylized form of self-expression. This enactment enables communal stocktaking and re-consideration of values and directions. Yeats and Soyinka were particularly drawn to these cohesive and metaphysical facets of myths. Since ritual performance facilitated the communication of these myths, they both generated and practiced ritual theories of drama.

Both saw the theater as the most revolutionary form of communication, in its facilitation of audience cohesion and affect through the intimate interaction of the performers, the dramatist and the audience. Exposure to and study of western theatrical conventions that date from ancient Greece however, led them to modify traditional understanding of ritual to classical theatrical conventions. The resulting composite is a unique mix of traditional ritual and a reconsideration of Aristotle and Nietzsche's theories of tragedy. Fundamentally, both project a dramatic situation where the performance of the tragic rites of passage of a hero-god, drawn from the community's mythological corpora, initiates the active participation of the audience-member, whereby he or she will submerge himself or herself into the action, to re-emerge with a new consciousness of self and of community.

Early efforts at the practice of this theory were inspired by the colonial experience. Yeats' two short plays, *The Countess Cathleen* and *Cathleen ni Houlihan*, were written in the spirit of a cultural and political nationalism, as part of a nation wide drive to put an end to English colonial rule in Ireland. Soyinka's *A Dance of the Forests* is an attempt to confront the new nation of Nigeria with certain truths about itself and about the African in general, the consciousness of which would guide it on its new post-independent path.

In *The Countess Cathleen* and *Cathleen ni Houlihan*, Yeats draws upon archetypes popular in Irish peasant imagination to project a vision of English colonialists as satanic forces, conspiring, in a repetition of the temptation of man in the Garden of Eden, to deny Ireland of her innocence and spirituality. Self-sacrifice, in the manner of Jesus Christ who came to save man from Satan, and as enacted by the Countess Cathleen, is, for Yeats, the only means whereby Ireland's identity and heritage can be saved. In *A Dance of the Forests*, the enemy is not some external colonizing force as in the Yeats plays, but resides within the Black community itself. The conflict between Ogun and Eshuoro, Demoke and Oremole, respectively, is the archetypal internecine fight that obliterates the individual spirit, and as Soyinka projects, has done more damage to the socioeconomic development of the Black man than western imperialism. The hope for regeneration lies with the artist, who must always be willing to sacrifice himself for the regeneration of his community.

As both artists matured they came to focus on the tragic rites of passage of hero-gods to express their reaction to the unfolding socio-political events in their environment. Soyinka developed his interest in Ogun, the Yoruba god of iron and war, just as Yeats had been led to modifying the rituals of Cuchulain, the Celtic hero-god. Ogun and Cuchulain are, perhaps, the most prominent gods in the traditional pantheons of the respective communities, and are significant to Soyinka's and Yeats' perfection of their theories and practice of ritual drama. The two gods are characterized by a Dionysian urge to unity, to service, on behalf of the community, and by an Apollonian self-affirmation. Soyinka extends Ogun's attributes to inculcate a Promethean will to challenge, to dare, which channels anguish into a creative purpose.

In *At the Hawk's Well,* Yeats dramatizes the ritual of Cuchulain's transition into a heroic, mortal destiny to impress upon his audience a vision of man that is essentially tragic, his heroism and nobility notwithstanding. In *On Baile's Strand,* he reinterprets an incident from Cuchulain's tragic life, as the defender of the land and subject to Conchubar, to reveal his abiding concern with the continuing triumph of materialism, of greed and of the thwarting of the individual, heroic, spirit which characterized contemporary Ireland. These negatives, he believed, ultimately nurture environment enabling wars and the destruction of man.

Soyinka draws attention to the prevailing incidence of death on Nigerian roads through the drama of the malevolent aspect of Ogun in *The Road.* In its winding nature and its treachery, the road is the physical manifestation of Ogun, which Professor deliberately abuses or subverts in a bid to confront the metaphysical road of transition, within which the Word is trapped. *Death and the King's Horseman,* once again, evokes a sense of this passage of transition to highlight the problem of leadership in Africa, which constantly fails the masses. Due to his weakness for the "Leftovers" of the world, Elesin Oba fails to enact the Ogunnian plunging and disintegration in the abyss of transition, designed to facilitate the spiritual regeneration of the community.

Confronted with the realities of war, specifically the Easter Rising of 1916 and the Nigerian Civil War of 1967 to 70 respectively, in which both were directly involved, Yeats and Soyinka focused on the wars as the ultimate corroboration of man's tragic destiny, and his innate predilection towards violence and self destruction.

Turning once more to the rituals of Ogun and Cuchulain, they project the creative and destructive dichotomy of the gods as being repetitive, eternal and symbolic of a cyclical movement of all life in terms of opposites. Yeats uses the traditional symbolism of the sunbird, the hawk, the animal image often associated with Cuchulain, to define the movement of the interpenetrating gyres, the central symbol of his great scheme of life as elaborated in *A Vision*. Soyinka uses the traditional symbolism of a snake devouring its own tail, imaged as the Mobius Strip, which has a special relevance to Ogun.

The Dreaming of the Bones, the first of the two war plays, is based on a Japanese Noh ritual in which the souls of the dead are said to be bound to earth by some particularly intense human passion. The dead in Yeats' play are Diarmuid and Dervorgilla, the historical lovers whose passion was responsible for the colonization of Ireland. In Soyinka's *Madmen and Specialists*, the Old Man formulates a religion of "AS" to not only situate the demonic actions of his son but also to explain the sense of the cyclical and eternal nature of evil, of wars and human wastage. Yeats and Soyinka predicate these vicious cycles in the life on the actions of two protagonists, who have been profoundly affected by war. The Young Man in Yeats' play, on the run from the forces of English colonialism following the failure of the Rising of Easter 1916, fails to release the "dream-back" couple from their torment and purgatory. This failure to perceive beyond fanaticism and hatred is dramatized in the context of the dawning of a new objective age in the Great Wheel of life, characterized by wars, and which the Red bird of March, the animal and month associated with Cuchulain, heralds. Similarly, Dr. Bero's firm conviction that fellow humans exist only to whet his appetite for power and absolute control, and in the need to maintain the System and its machinery from such threats posed to it as that of the Old Man, his father, captures the continuing failure of African leadership to tolerate a "righteousness" other than itself.

Setting in the plays is often symbolic rather than representative. The forest in *A Dance* is a repository of the unknown, the realm of the supernatural beings with whom human beings commune to arrive at anew knowledge of self and of their environment. It also represents the transitional gulf, the chthonic realm into which Soyinka plunges man, in a reenactment of Ogun's plunge and reemergence. Similarly, the barren, windswept mountain summit and the well of immortality in *At the Hawk's Well* suggest the supernatural, the location for Cuchulain transition into his mortal destiny. *Dramatis personae* in the plays reflect the traditional belief in the inter-relationship of the supernatural with the natural. The Countess Cathleen in Yeats' play of the same name, for example, is presented in Christ-like, terms, in her nobility, purity and self-sacrifice to evil on behalf of peasant subject. Demoke in *A Dance of the Forests* is defined in terms of Ogun, the god he serves. He is both creative and destructive as an artist, but the hope for regeneration in the new community lies with him. Language in the plays is highly allusive and symbolic, serving to evoke and impress the ritual, poetic framework.

The upsurge of this subtle interaction of mythical themes and ritual techniques in the plays is a tragic vision of life and of history, with the hope for regeneration persisting in the individual, artistic and heroic sacrifice on behalf of others. The ritual framework reveals a message communicated subliminally, and grasped intuitively. Arguments that these plays constitute both artists' most obscure can then only be understood within this ritual context, where the past interweaves with the present to forecast the future.

In face of criticism and unpopularity of his dramatic form, Yeats in his life time, remained adamant in his self appointed role as the custodian of tradition, and of those ancient values from which an increasing materialistic Ireland was turning away;

> Being a creator the artist is of necessity a destroyer. His creation of a national literature will inevitably challenge

and offend the leaders of the crowd as they attempt to build the nation itself – Nevertheless, the artist builds more truly and permanently than these servants of abstract ideas, because he is more sensitive to the inexplicable purposes of life".[1]

Soyinka is equally adamant. He defends the lack of an ideological superstructure to his plays in terms of a natural concern with the negative forces in society that does not need to be structured within a specific ideology. Insisting on the autonomy of the creative imagination whose operations on social and natural phenomena cannot be legislated, he averts that myth and ritual are relevant to the spiritual needs of modern man.

In more recent plays however, the exigencies of communicating with national audiences still defined by a minimal English literacy and cultural homogeneity has seen Soyinka complementing the mythical, metaphysical framework with a more realistic and immediate one. *Opera Wonyosi* (1979) inaugurates the trend away from myth with its dramatizations of the vices of post-war oil-boom Nigeria and the excesses of the former Central African Republic dictator, Jean-Bedel Bokassa. It is continued in *A Play of Giants* (1985), a satire on African dictator-ships that differs in terms of approach from the similar diatribes in *Kongi's Harvest* and *The Bacchae of Euripides*, and extended in his guerrilla or proletarian theater shows, staged chiefly in market-places and assembly halls. Communication is through such agitation and propaganda techniques as chants, mimes and iterative images and props. His recourse to the visually affective medium of the camera and film, exemplified by *Blues for a Prodigal Son* (1983), also suggests this trend away from myth. However, even in the deliberate attempt at a wider accessibility, myth remains the substratum from which he expresses his consciousness of his environment.

The broader appreciation of Yeats and Soyinka's colossal contributions to world literature can only persist with the recognition of a mythic consciousness. This is the mindset that enables an intuitive and cosmogonist perception of the human condition as the necessary foundation for efficient and sustainable efforts at impacting this tragic condition for the better.

Endnotes

Chapter one:
The Artist and Zeitgeist

1. Erich Auerbach, *Mimesis: The Representation of Reality in Western Literature*, trans. Willard R. Trask (Princeton: Princeton Universty Press, 1953).
2. Aristotle, "Poetics.' trans. S.H. Butcher in *Criticism: The Major Texts*, ed. Walter Jackson Bate, (New York: Harcourt Brace Jovanovich, 1972.) pp. 13–19.
3. Sir Philip Sidney, An Apology for Poetry," in *Criticism: The Major Texts* (New York: Harcourt, Brace Jovanovich, 1972.) pp. 77–82.
4. Alexander Pope, "An Essay on Criticism," in *Criticism: The Major Texts,* pp. 174–181.
5. Pope, "An Essay on Criticism," p. 181.
6. Longinus, "On the Sublime," *Criticism: The Major Texts,* p. 71.
7. Immanuel Kant, *Critique of Judgment* (1790), trans. J.H. Bernard. (London Macmillan, 1931.) pp. 102–03.

8. James Joyce, *A Portrait of the Artist As a Young Man,* in *The Essential James Joyce,* ed. Harry Levin (Middlesex, England: Penguin Books, 1972.) pp. 219–220.

9. Giambattista Vico, *Scienzia Nuova* (1744) trans. T.G. Bergin and M. H. Fisch. (New York: Cornell University Press, 1948.) p. 201.

10. Hippolyte Taine, *History of English Literature,* in Diana Laurenson and Alan Swingewood, *The Sociology of Literature,* (London: Paladin, 1971.) p. 32.

11. George Lukacs, *The Meaning of Contemporary Realism* (London: Merlin Press, 1963.) pp. 66–69.

12. George Plekhanov, *Art and Social Life* (London: Lawrence and Wishart, 1953.), p. 37.

13. Lukacs, *The Meaning of Contemporary Realism,* p. 69.

14. Gobineau, "Essai sur l'inegalite des races humaines", and Lucien Levy-Bruhl, "Les functiones mentales dans les societies inferieures," cited in Claude Wauthier *The Literature and Thought of Modern Africa* (London: Heinemann, 1978.), p. 259.

15. Disreali's comment is cited in L.P. Curtis, *Anglo-Saxons and Celts* (Connecticut: University of Connecticut Press, 1963.) p. 84.

16. Patrick O'Farrell, *England and Ireland Since 1800.* (London: Oxford University Press, 1975.) p. 2.

17. Frantz Fanon, *Black Skins, White Masks* (New York: Grove Press, 1967.) p. 60.

18. Warren L. d'Azevedo, ed., *The Traditional Artist in African Societies* (Bloomington, Indiana: Indiana University Press, 1973) p. 6.

19. Jean-Paul Sartre, "Orphee Noir," in *Anthologie de la Nouvelle Poesie Negre et Malagache,* ed. Leopold Sedar Senghor (Paris, PUF, 1948.) p. 16.

20. John Millington Synge, Preface to *The Playboy of the Western*

World, in *J.M. Synge; Collected Works IV*, ed. Ann Saddlemyer. (London: Oxford University Press, 1962.) p. 54.

21. Obiechina, "Cultural Nationalism in Modern African Creative Literature." *African Creative Literature Today; A Journal of Explanatory Criticism, Omnibus Edition*, Nos. 1, 2, 3, 4. London: Heinemann, 1978.) p. 20.

22. Richard M. Kain, "Yeats and Irish Nationalism," *W.B. Yeats, 1865–1965: Centenary Essays*, D.E.S. Maxwell and S.B. Bushrui, eds. Ibadan: Ibadan University Press, 1960.) p. 64.

23. Cited in Malcolm Brown. *The Politics of Irish Literature: From Thomas Davies to W.B. Yeats* (Seattle: University of Washington Press, 1972.) p. 22.

24. Charles Stewart Parnell, often called the "uncrowned king of Ireland," was the Anglo Irish Protestant politician who, perhaps more than any of the other agitators for Irish independence, brought Irish Home Rule closer to reality. The momentum towards Home Rule was however, halted mid-stream by the scandal which erupted in the wake of his affair with Mrs. Katherine O'Shea. The Irish Catholic middle class, with their presumptuous sense of righteousness decided to make Parnell's private morality the issue of Irish national politics, oblivious to the protests of the majority who argued that Home Rule was more important than Parnell's private affairs. The Catholic priests and their allies won; Parnell died, a broken man, in 1891, and Ireland was only able to achieve semblance of Home Rule or Independence in 1921.

25. Ann Saddlemyer "The Cult of the Celt: Pan-Celticism in the Nineties" in *The World of W.B. Yeats* Robin Skelton and Ann Saddlemyer, eds. (Seattle: University of Washington Press, 1965.) p. 3.

26. Phillip L. Marcus, *Yeats and the Beginnings of the Irish Renaissance* (Ithaca: Cornell University Press, 1970.) p. 235.

27. William Butler Yeats, *Uncollected Prose I*, John P Frayne ed. (New York: Columbia University Press, 1970.) p. 350.

28. Yeats, "Nationality and Literature", *W.B. Yeats*, ed. William H. Pritchard. *Penguin Critical Anthologies* (England: Penguin Books, 1972.) p. 37.

29. Obiechina, "Perceptions of Colonialism in West African Literature", *Ufahamu*, 5, 1 (1974), p. 49.

30. Lilyan Kesteloot, *The Intellectual Origins of the African Revolution,* trans. Alexander Mboukou. (Washington: Black Orpheus Press, 1972.) p. 29.

31. Lilyan Kesteloot, The Intellectual Origins of the African Revolution, p. 30

32. Abiola Irele, *The African Experience in Literature and Ideology* (London: Heinemann, 1981.)

33. Irele, *The African Experience in Literature and Ideology,* p.69.

34. Irele, pp. 76–78.

35. Leopold Sedar Senghor, "The Spirit of Civilization or the Laws of African Negro Culture", *First World Congress of Negro Writers and Artists* (Paris: Presence Africaine, 1956) p. 52.

36. Senghor, pp. 54–56.

37. Obiechina, "Perceptions of Colonialism in West African Literature", p. 62.

38. Obiechina, pp. 63–64

39. Georges Gurvitch, "The Sociology of the Theater," in *Sociology of Life and Drama.* Elizabeth and Tom Burns, eds. Middlesex, England Penguin Books, 1973.) p. 73.

40. *Larousse Encyclopedia of Mythology* (London: Paul Hamlyn, 1959.) p. 244.

41. Isabella Augusta Gregory, *Our Irish Theater* (New York: Capricorn Books, 1965.) p. 108.

42. Yemi Ogunbiyi, "Nigerian Theater and Drama: A Critical Profile", *Drama and Theater in Nigeria: A Critical Source Book* (Lagos: Nigeria Magazine Publications, 1981.) p. 20.

43. M.J.C. Bcheruo, *Victorian Lagos* (London: Macmillan, 1977) p. 60.

44. Editorial, "Let us Build Theaters", *The West African Pilot*, July 8, 1947.

45. Yemi Ogunbiyi, Drama and Theater in Nigeria: A Critical Source Book, p.25

46. Ebun Clark, *Hubert Ogunde: The Making of Nigerian Theater* (London: Oxford University Press, 1979.) pp. 80–83.

47. Yemi Ogunbiyi, p. 25.

48. James Booth, *Writers and Politics in Nigeria* (London: Hodder and Stoughton, 1981.) p. 39.

49. Frantz Fanon, *The Wretched of the Earth* (1965, p. 175) London: McGibbon and Kee.

50. John Bernard MacCarthy, Preface, *The Long Road to Garranbraher* (Dublin: Gill, 1928.)

51. Stanley Macebuh, "Poetics and the Mythic Immigration", *Critical Perspectives on Wole Soyinka*, James Gibbs, ed. (Washington, D.C.: Three Continents Press, 1980.) p. 64.

52. Olu Obafemi, "Revolutionary Aesthetics in Recent Nigerian Theater", *African Literature Today: 12: New Writings, New Approaches* (London: Heinemann, 1982.) pp. 118–120.

53. A technique similar in nature to Bertolt Brecht's unorthodox appropriation of classical material and of Shakespearean plays.

54. Interview with Femi Osofisan, in Obafemi, "Revolutionary Aesthetics in Recent Nigerian Theater", p. 126.

55. Soyinka, "Who's Afraid of Elesin Oba," *Art, Dialogue and Outrage: Essays on Literature and Culture* (Ibadan: New Horn Press, 1988.) p. 123.

Chapter two:
Stimulus and Response: Yeats, Soyinka and the Idea of a Theater

1. Brian Farrington. *Malachi-Stilt-Jack: A Study of W.B. Yeats and His Works* (London: Connolly Publications, 1965) p. 5.

2. Biodun Jevifo, "The Artist as an Activist", *Newswatch*, 18 February, 1985, 5.

3. Femi Osofisan, Interview by Olu Obafemi, in "Revolutionary Aesthetics in Recent Nigerian Theater," *African Literature Today*, 12 (1982), p. 119.

4. Cited in Conor Cruise O'Brian, "Passion and Cunning: The Politics of W.B. Yeats," *Literature in Revolution*. eds. George Abbot White and Chris White (New York: Holt, Rhinehart and Winston, 1972.) p. 146.

5. Soyinka, *Myth, Literature and the African World* (London: Cambridge University Press, 1976.) pp. 62–64

6. Soyinka, Preface to *Opera Wonyosi* (Bloomington, Indiana: Indiana University Press, 1981.) p. 147.

7. Conor Cruise O'Brian, "Passion and Cunning," p. 147.

8. Yeats, "The Bounty of Sweden," *Autobiographies* (London: Macmillan, 1955.) p. 559.

9. In the furor surrounding Parnell's affair with Mrs. Kitty O'Shea, this emergent middle class, led by Tim Healy and backed by Murphy's money, emerged as the spearheads of the critical attack against Parnell, the "uncrowned" king of Ireland, thus, subordinating the all-important question of Irish Home rule to Parnell's private morality. The riots which attended the first performances of J.M. Synge's *The Shadow of the Glen* and *The Playboy of the Western World* were engineered by members of the national middle class, who with what Yeats perceived as their hypocritical sense of righteousness, roundly condemned Synge's portrayal of the Irish woman in the figures of Nora Burke and Pegeen Mike and her friends.

10. Conor Cruise O'Brian, p. 166

11. Yeats, "September 1913," *Collected Poems* (London: Macmillan, 1952.) p. 120

12. James Gibbs ed. *Critical Perspectives on Wole Soyinka* (Washington D.C.: Three Continents Press, 1980.) p. 12.

13. Soyinka, *Ake: The Years of Childhood* (London: Rex Collings, 1981.) pp. 180–230.

14. Cited in James Gibbs, "Tear the Painted Masks: Join the Poison

Stains: A Preliminary Study of Wole Soyinka's Writings for the Nigerian Press," *Research in African Literatures,* 14, 1 (1983), p. 5.

15. "Let's Think of the Aftermath of this War," *Daily Sketch,* 4 August, 1967, in Gibbs, "Tear the Painted Masks," p. 7.

16. Soyinka, *The Man Died: Prison Notes of Wole Soyinka* (Middlesex. England: Penguin Books, 1975.)

17. James Booth, *Writers and Politics in Nigeria* (London: Hodder and Stoughton, 1981.) p. 120.

18. Soyinka, *The Man Died,* pp. 179–80.

19. James W Flannery, *W.B. Yeats and the Idea of a Theater* (New Haven: Yale University Press,1976.) p. 73.

20. Flannery, *W.B. Yeats and the Idea of a Theater,* p. 74.

21. Yeats, *The Celtic Twilight* (Dublin: Maunsel and Co., 1905.) p. 138

22. Yeats, *The Celtic Twilight,* p. 31.

23. Yeats, *Uncollected Prose 1* ed. John P Frayne. (New York: Columbia University Press, 1970.) p. 350.

24. Flannery, *W.B. Yeats and the Idea of a Theater,* p. 68.

25. Soyinka, *Ake; The Years of Childhood.* (London: Rex Collings, 1981.) pp. 6–12.

26. Soyinka, *Ake,* p. 16.

27. Soyinka, *Ake,* p. 140.

28. Soyinka, *Ake,* p. 140.

29. Soyinka, *Myth, Literature and the African World,* p. 129.

30. Soyinka, *Myth, Literature and the African World,* pp. 10–26.

31. T.S. Eliot, "Tradition and the Individual Talent," *Twentieth Century Literary Criticism: A Reader.* ed. David Lodge (London: Longman, 1972, pp. 71–72.

32. Yeats, Letter to Katherine Tynan, December 4, 1888; *The Letters of W.B. Yeats,* ed. Allen Wade. (London: Rupert Hart-Davies, 1954.) pp. 75–76.

33. Richard Ellmann, *The Identity of Yeats* (London: Faber and Faber, 1954; 1975 rpt.) pp. 18–19.

34. Soyinka, *Idanre and Other Poems* (London: Methuen, 1967) p. 88.

35. Obi Maduakor, "Cyclic Determinism in Soyinka's "Idanre," *Ufahanu*, 8, 1 (1977), p. 179.

36. Soyinka, *Idanre and Other Poems*, p. 88.

37. Yeats, "The Irish Dramatic Movement," *Plays and Controversies*, New York: Macmillan, 1924.) p. 5.

38. Yeats, "The Irish Dramatic Movement," p. 416.

39. Soyinka, "Penthouse Theater," *In Person: Achebe, Awoonor and Soyinka.* ed. Karen L Morrel (Seattle: Institute of Comparative and Foreign Area Studies, University of Washington, 1975.) p. 105.

40. Yeats, *Autobiographies*, p. 471.

41. Yeats, *Autobiographies*, p. 472.

42. Soyinka, *Myth, Literature and the African World*, p. 43.

43. Soyinka, *Myth, Literature and the African World*, pp. 42–43.

44. George Mills Harper, ed. *Yeats and the Occult. Yeats Studies Series* (London: Macmillan, 1975)

45. Helen B. Blavatsky, *The Secret Doctrine: The Synthesis of Science, Religion and Philosophy*, in Ellmann, *Yeats: The Man and The Masks* (London: Faber and Faber, 1961.) pp. 89–91.

46. Morton Irving Seiden, *William Butler Yeats: The Poet as a Myth Maker.* (Michigan: Michigan State University Press, 1962) pp. 44–45

47. Florence Farr, *A Short Enquiry Concerning the Hermetic Art*, in Ellmann, *Yeats: The Man and the Masks*, pp. 100–101.

48. Flannery, *W.B. Yeats and the Idea of a Theater*, p. 63

49. Ellmann, *Yeats; the Man and the Masks*, pp. 124–25

50. Yeats, *Essays and Introductions.* (London: Macmillan, 1961.) p. 87.

51. Right through the formulation of his plans for the Irish Mystical Order, he was hoping his beloved Maud Gonne would subject herself totally to it. But two factors, her advocating a militant cultural and political nationalism, and as her marriage, in

1903, to Sean MacBride, resulted in a prolonged estrangement between Gonne and Yeats, and put paid to Yeats' plans for the Mystical Order.

52. Yeats, *Essays and Introductions*, p. 518

53. Yeats, *Autobiographies*, p. 191.

54. Yeats, *Explorations*, p. 439.

55. Yeats, *Commentary on The King of the Great Clock Tower* (Dublin: Cuala Press, 1934) pp. 36–38.

56. Yeats, *Essays and Introductions*, pp. 166–167.

57. Cuchulain's significance to the national cause was recognized by the Irish government in its commissioning of a statue of the hero which presently stands inside the General Post Office in Dublin, the scene of fierce fighting during the 1916 Rising.

58. David R. Clark "Yeats, Theater and Nationalism," *Theater and Nationalism in Twentieth Century Ireland.* ed. Robert O'Driscoll. (Toronto: University of Toronto Press, 1971) p. 144.

59. Ellmann, *Yeats: The Man and the Masks,* p. 216.

60. Yeats, "Certain Noble Plays of Japan," *Essays and Introductions* (London: Macmillan, 1961.) p. 113.

61. Richard Taylor, *The Drama of W.B. Yeats: Irish Myth and the Japanese Noh* (New Haven: Yale University Press, 1976.) p. 109.

62. Soyinka, *Myth, Literature and the African World,* p. 2.

63. Soyinka, p. 10.

64. Soyinka, "Drama and the Revolutionary Ideal," *In Person: Achebe, Awoonor and Soyinka,* ed. Karen Morell, pp. 117–118.

65. Soyinka, *Myth, Literature and the African World,* p. 29.

66. Soyinka, p. 26.

67. Soyinka, p. 143.

68. Soyinka, p. 73.

69. Soyinka, p. 33.

70. Soyinka, p. 149.

71. Raymond Williams, *Modern Tragedy* (London: Chatto and Windus, 1966.)

72. Friedrich Nietzsche, "The Birth of Tragedy," *The Basic Writings of Nietzsche*. Trans. and ed. Walter Kaufmann (New York: The Modern Library, 1968.) pp. 56–59.

73. Nietzsche asserts that Attic / Greek tragedy emerged from the fusing of the Dionysian world of intoxication and the Apollonian world of dreams. "The beautiful illusion of the dream worlds", he adds, is the "prerequisite of all plastic art" and ruling over this "beautiful illusion of the inner world of fantasy" is Apollo, the "embodiment of the joyous necessity of the dream experience." The Dionysian, on the other hand, finds expression in 'music', "dancing, intoxication" and "self-forgetfulness." Under the charm of the Dionysian, "not only is the union between man and man reaffirmed, but nature which has become alienated, hostile or subjugated, celebrates – her reconciliation with her lost son, man. ("The Birth of Tragedy," pp. 34–37.)

74. Nietzsche, "The Birth of Tragedy," p. 64.

75. Yeats, *Essays and Introductions,* pp. 502–3.

76. Soyinka, *Myth, Literature and African World,* p. 140.

77. Nietzsche, "The Will to Power," *The Basic Writings of Nietzsche,* p. 539.

78. Nietzsche, p. 539.

79. Yeats, "The Tragic Theater," *Essays and Introductions*, p. 245.

80. Yeats, *Essays and Introductions,* pp. 522–23.

81. Yeats, p. 239.

82. Yeats, p. 287.

83. Yeats, "The King's Threshold," *Collected Plays*, p. 135.

84. Soyinka, *Myth, Literature and the African World,* p. 142.

85. Soyinka, Myth, *Literature and the African World,* p. 29.

86. Soyinka, p. 150.

87. Soyinka, p. 145.

88. Soyinka, p. 148.

89. Soyinka, p. 160.

Chapter three:
The Early Plays: The Quest for a Ritual Format

1. William Butler Yeats', *Essays and Introductions* (London: Macmillan, 1961), p. 516.

2. A. Norman Jeffares and A.S. Knowland, *A Commentary on the Collected Plays of W.B. Yeats* (London: Macmillan, 1975), p. 5.

3. James W. Flannery, *W.B. Yeats and the of a Theater* (New Haven: Yale University Press, 1976), p. 143.

4. All subsequent quotations from Yeats' plays refer to the editions in, *The Collected Plays of W.B. Yeats* (London: Macmillan, 1952). pp. 19–20.

5. *The Countess Cathleen*, p. 4.

6. Ibid., p. 6.

7. Ibid., p. 42.

8. *Cathleen ni Houlihan, The Collected Plays of W.B. Yeats*, p. 81

9. Soyinka, *A Dance of the Forests*, pp. 34–51. All subsequent quotations from Soyinka's plays refer to the editions in *Wole Soyinka: Collected Plays 1* (London: Oxford University Press, 1973).

10. *A Dance of the Forests*, p. 27.

11. Ibid, p. 19.

12. Ibid., p. 51.

13. Ibid.

14. Ibid., p. 56.

15. Ibid, p. 24.

16. Ibid., p. 25.

17. Ibid., p. 55.

18. Ibid., pp. 42–43

19. Ibid., p. 64

20. Ibid., p. 69

21. Yeats, *Letters on Poetry from Yeats to Dorothy Wellesley*, Cited in Flannery, *W.B. Yeats and the Idea of a Theater*, p. 74.

22. Yeats, *Essays and Introductions*, p. 516.

23. *The Countess Cathleen*, pp. 25–26

24. Ibid., p. 26
25. Ibid., p. 27
26. Ibid., p. 33
27. Ibid., p. 43
28. Ibid, p.45
29. *Cathleen ni Houlihan*, p. 83
30. Ibid., p. 88
31. Soyinka, *A Dance of the Forests*, p. 63
32. Ibid., p. 71
33. Ibid., pp 71–72
34. Wole Soyinka, *Myth. Literature and the African World* (London: Cambridge University Press, 1976), p. 413
35. Soyinka, *A Dance of the Forests*, pp. 73–74.

Chapter four:
Cuchulain and Ogun: The Dance of the Mythical Heroes

1. Wole Soyinka, *Myth, Literature and the African World* (Cambridge University Press, 1976), p. 43.
2. Soyinka, *Idanre and Other Poems* (London: Methuen, 1967), p. 11.
3. Cited in James Gibbs, "Tear the Painted Masks, join the Poison Stains: A Preliminary Study of Wole Soyinka's Writings for the Nigerian Press," *Research in African Literatures,* 14, 1 (1983), p. 5.
4. Gibbs, 'Tear the Painted Masks, Join the Poison Stains," p. 5.
5. Cited in Barton R. Friedman, *Adventures in the Deeps of the Mind: The Cuchulain Cycle of W.B. Yeats* (Princeton, New Jersey: Princeton University Press, 1977), pp. 21–22.
6. Soyinka, "Morality and Aesthetics in the ritual Archetype", *Myth, Literature and the African World,* p. 27.
7. Although *On Baile's Strand* was published thirteen years before, for the purposes of this study *At the Hawks Well* will take precedence over *On Baile's Strand*.

8. W.B. Yeats, "Certain Noble Plays of Japan", *Essays and Introductions* (London: Macmillan, 1961), p. 232.

9. Denis Donoghue, "Yeats's Theater," in *William Butler Yeats: Modern Critical Views*, ed. and with an Intro. by Harold Bloom (New York: Chelsea House Publishers, 1986), p. 101.

10. *At the Hawk's Well, The Collected Plays of W.B. Yeats* (London: Macmillan, 1952), p. 208.

11. Reg Skene, "The Sudden Cry of a Hawk", *The Cuchulain Plays of W.B. Yeats*, p. 128.

12. Thomas R. Henn, *The Lonely Tower: Studies in the Poetry of W.B. Yeats* (London: Methuen, 1950), p. 280, cited in Jeffares and Knowland, *A Commentary on the Collected Plays of W.B. Yeats* (London: Macmillan, 1975), p. 89.

13. Peter Ure, *Yeats the Playwright: A Commentary on Character and Design in the Major Plays* (London: Routledge and Kegan Paul, 1963), p. 71.

14 Francis A.C. Wilson, *Yeats's Iconography* (London: Victor Gollancz:, 1960), p.41.

15. Mircea Bliade, *Rites and Symbols of Initiation* (Chicago: University of Chicago Press, 1958), p. x.

16. Leonard E. Nathan, *The Tragic Drama of William Butler Yeats: Figures in a Dance* (New York: Columbia University Press, 1965), p. 183.

17. Yeats, *At the Hawk's Well*, p. 208.

18. Ibid.

19. Yeats, "Among School Children," *Collected Poems* (London: Macmillan, 1952; rpt. 1982), p. 244

20. Nathan, *The Tragic Drama of William Butler Yeats*, p. 189.

21. Yeats, *At the Hawk's Well*, p. 209.

22. Ibid.

23. Ibid., p. 213.

24. Ibid.

25. Ibid.

26. Ibid. p. 214.

27. Yeats, "The Second Coming," *Collected Poems*, p. 210

28. Yeats, *At the Hawk's Well*, pp. 214–215

29. Ibid., p. 215.

30. Ibid., p. 216.

31. Ibid., p. 217.

32. Skene, *The Cuchulain Plays of W.B. Yeats*, p. 142.

33. Yeats, *At the Hawk's Well*, p. 218.

34. Frank Kermode, *Romantic Image* (New York: Macmillan, 1957), pp. 43–44.

35. St. John's Gospel, The Holy Bible – King James Version (London: Catholic Truth Society, 1986), p. 86.

36. Soyinka, *The Road, Collected Plays 1* (London: Oxford University Press, 1973), p. 163.

37. Ibid., p. 164.

38. Ibid., p. 155.

39. Ibid., pp. 205–206

40. Obi Maduakor, "A Reader's Guide to Wole Soyinka's *The Road*," Seminar Paper presented to the Department of English, University of Nigeria, Nsukka, 1983, p. 23.

41. Soyinka, The Road, p. 150.

42. Ben Okri, *The Famished Road* (London: Jonathan Cape, 1991), p. 3.

43. Soyinka, *The Road*, p. 197.

44. Ibid., p. 159.

45. Ibid., p. 157.

46. Ibid., p. 159.

47. Ibid.

48. Ibid., p. 176.

49. Ibid., p. 170.

50. Ibid., p. 182.

51. Ibid., pp. 186–187.

52. Ibid., p. 204.

53. Ibid., pp. 223–224.

54. Ibid., p. 227.

55. Ibid, pp. 228–229.
56. Skene, *The Cuchulain Plays of W.B. Yeats,* p. 168.
57. Yeats, *On Baile's Strand,* pp. 259–260.
58. Ibid., p. 249.
59. Ibid., p. 261.
60. Ibid.
61. Ibid., p. 255.
62. Ibid., pp. 258–259.
63. Ibid., p. 259.
64. Nietzsche, "The Birth of Tragedy," *The Basic Writings of Friedrich Nietzsche,* trans. And ed. By Walter Kaufmann (New York: The Modern Library, 1968), p. 67.
65. Yeats, "Per Amica Silentia Lunae," *Mythologies* (London: Macmillan, 1957), pp. 43–44.
66. In a letter to Frank Fay, Yeats outlines the qualities of the two as follows:
    The touch of something hard, repellent
    yet alluring, self-assertive, yet self
    immolating, is not all but it must be there.
    He is the fool – wandering, passive, houseless
    and almost loveless. Conchubar is reason that is blind
    because it can only reason, because it is
    cold. Are they not the cold moon and
    the hot sun?
    The Letters of W.B. Yeats, ed. Allen Wade. (London: Rupert Hart-Davies, 1954), p. 425.
67. Yeats, *On Baile's Strand,* pp. 260–261
68. Ibid., p. 262.
69. Skene, p. 198.
70. Yeats, *On Baile's Strand,* p. 268.
71. Ibid., pp. 270–271
72. Ibid. p. 276
73. Ibid., pp. 276–277
74. Ibid., pp. 278–279.

75. Soyinka, Author's Note, *Death and the King's Horseman* (London: Methuen, 1975).

76. Mark Ralph-Bowman discusses this idea in his article "Leaders and Left-overs: A Reading of Soyinka's *Death and the King's Horseman*," *Research in African Literatures*, 14, 1 (1983), pp. 81–97.

77. Ibid.

78. Soyinka, *Death and the King's Horseman*, pp. 10–11.

79. Ibid. pp. 13–14.

80. Ibid., p. 14.

81. Ibid., p. 46.

82. Ibid. p. 15.

83. Ibid., p. 23.

84. Ibid., p. 40.

85. Ibid.

86. Ibid., p. 44.

87. D.S. Izevbaye, "Mediation in Soyinka: The Case of the King's Horseman", *Critical Perspectives on Wole Soyinka*, ed. James Gibbs (Washington D.C.: Three Continents Press, 1980), 116.

88. Izevbaye, p. 121.

89. Soyinka, *Death and the King's Horseman*, p. 68.

90. Ibid., p. 69.

91. Ibid., pp. 51–54.

92. Ibid., pp. 60–61.

93. Ibid., p. 75.

94. Ibid.

95. Ibid., p. 76.

Chapter five:
Consciousness of War: Cyclical History and the Apocalyptic Vision

1. Friedrich Nietzscle, 'Thus Spake Zarathustra", *The Basic Writings of Friedrich Nietzsche*, Trans. and ed. by Walter Kaufmann (New York: The Modern Library, 1968), p. 362.

2. Yeats, "Nineteen Hundred and Nineteen", *Collected Poems*, p. 232.

3. Yeats, "Easter 1916", *Collected Poems*. pp.204–205.

4. Yeats, Letter to Olivia Shakespeare, May 1923, *The Letters of W.B. Yeats*, ed. Allen Wade (London: Rupert Hart-Davies, 1964), p. 682.

5. Yeats, "Meditations in Time of Civil War", *Collected Poems*, p. 230.

6. Richard Ellmann, *Yeats: The Man and the Masks* (London: Faber and Faber 1961), and Morton Irving Seiden, *William Butler Yeats: The Poet as a Mythmaker* (Michigan. Michigan State University Press, 1962).

7. By subjectivity, Yeats suggests the ego, the exaltation of individual consciousness and thought that looks inward. Quoting from the Oxford English Dictionary, he defines objectivity as all that is presented to consciousness as opposed to consciousness of self; that is, the object of perception or thought, the non-ego, the treating of outward things rather than inward fact.

8. Ellmann cites Yeats' letter to George Russell, just after the Russian Revolution in which he says, "I consider the Marxian criterion of values as in this age the spearhead of materialism and leading to inevitable murder". (Ellmann, *Yeats: The Man and the Masks*, p. 232).

9. Yeats, "The Second Coming", *Collected Poems*, p. 210.

10. Abiola Irele, 'The Season of a Mind: Wole Soyinka and the Nigerian Crisis", *The African Experience in Literature and Ideology* (London: Heinemann, 1981). p. 200.

11. Tanure Ojaide, *The Poetry of Wole Soyinka* (Lagos: Malthouse Press Limited, 1994), p. 63.

12. Obiajuru Maduakor" "Soyinka as a Literary Critic," *Research in African Literatures*, 17, 1 (1986), p. 9.

13. A.N. Jeffares and A.S. Knowland, *A Commentary on the*

Collected Plays of W.B. Yeats (London: Macmillan, 1975), p. 159.

14. Soyinka, *Madmen and Specialists, Collected Plays II* (London: Oxford University Press, 1974), p. 237.

15. Yeats, "Per Amica Silentia Lunae", *Mythologies* (London: Macmillan, 1959), pp. 354–56.

16. David R. Clark, *Yeats and the Theater of Desolate Reality* (Dublin: Dolmen Press,1965), p. 56.

17. Yeats, *The Dreaming of the Bones*, p. 444.

18. Ibid., p. 436.

19. Ibid., pp. 437–438.

20. Francis A.C. Wilson. *Yeats' Iconography* (London: Victor Gollancz, 1960), pp. 230–31.

21. Ibid., p. 231.

22. Yeats, *The Dreaming of the Bones*, p. 439.

23. Ibid., p. 442.

24. Ibid. p. 443.

25. Soyinka, *Madmen and Specialists*, p. 230.

26. Ibid., p. 233.

27. Ibid., pp 246–247; 255.

28. Ibid, pp. 271–272.

29. Ibid., p. 242.

30. Ibid., p. 241.

31. Oyin Ogunba, *The Movement of Transition* (Ibadan: Ibadan University Press, 1975), pp. 227–228.

32. Soyinka, *Madmen and Specialists*, pp. 225–226.

33. Ibid., p. 259.

34. Ibid., p. 275.

35. Ogunba, p. 228.

36. Soyinka, *Madmen and Specialists*, p. 275.

37. Ibid., p. 276.

Chapter six:
The Dramaturgy of Consciousness

1. W.B. Yeats, "Four Plays for Dances," cited in Russell K. Alspach, ed. *The Variorum Edition of the Plays of W.B. Yeats* (London: Macmillan, 1966), p. 76.

2. For the discussion of the structure in *Death and the King's Horseman*," see Mark Ralph Bowman's article, "Leaders and left-Overs: A Reading of Wole Soyinka's *Death and the King's Horseman*," *Research in African Literatures*, 14, 1 (1983), 81–97.

3. Yeats, *At the Hawk's Well*, p. 20.

4. Yeats, *The Dreaming of the Bones*, pp. 433–34.

5. Soyinka, *A Dance of the Forests*, p. 59.

6. Soyinka, *Madmen and Specialists*, p. 223.

7. Yeats, *The Countess Cathleen*, p. 3.

8. Ibid., p. 49.

9. Yeats, *At the Hawk's Well*, p. 207.

10. Cited in Jeffares and Knowland, *A Commentary on the Collected Plays of W B. Yeats* (London: Macmillan, 1975), pp. 153–155.

11. D.S. Izevbaye, "Mediation in Soyinka: The Case of the King's Horseman", *Critical Perspectives on Wole Soyinka*, ed. James Gibbs (Washington D.C.: Three Continents Press, 1980), p. 119.

12. Yeats, *The Dreaming of the Bones*, p. 443.

13. Ibid., p. 445.

14. Oyin Ogunba, *The Movement of Transition*, p. 119.

15. Yeats, *The Countess Cathleen*, p. 50.

16. Soyinka, *A Dance of the Forests*, p. 31.

17. Ibid., p. 39.

18. Ibid., pp. 35–36.

19. Soyinka, *The Road*, pp. 198–199.

20. Ibid., p. 178.

21. E Bolaji Idowu, *Olodumare; God in Yoruba Belief* (London: Longman, 1962), p. 48.

22. Soyinka, *The Road*, p. 224.

23. Soyinka, *Death and the King's Horseman*, p. 38.
24. Barton Friedman, *Adventures in the Deeps of the Mind: The Cuchulain Plays of W.B. Yeats* (Princeton: Princeton University Press, 1977), p.7.
25. Yeats, *On Baile's Strand*, p. 247.
26. Ibid., p. 248.
27. Ibid., p. 249.
28. Ibid., p. 274.
29. Soyinka, *Madmen ad Specialists*, p. 217.
30. Ibid., pp. 269–270.
31. Yeats, *At the Hawk's Well*, pp. 213–214.
32. Yeats, *The Dreaming of the Bones*, pp. 438–39.
33. Soyinka, *The Road*, p. 220.
34. Soyinka, *A Dance of the Forests*, pp. 59–60.
35. Ibid., p. 63.
36. p. 71.
37. Soyinka, *Myth, Literature and the African World* (Cambridge: Cambridge University Press, 1976), p. 36.
38. Soyinka, *Death and the King's Horseman*, p. 43.
39. Yeats, *The Countess Cathleen*, pp. 47–48.
40. Yeats, *On Baile's Strand*, p. 259.
41. Dan Izevbaye, "Language and Meaning in *The* Road", *Critical Perspectives on Wole Soyinka*, ed. James Gibbs, p. 92
42. Soyinka, *The Road*, p. 220.
43. Izevbaye, p. 92.
44. Soyinka, *The Road*, pp. 201–202.
45. Izevbaye, p. 96.
46. Soyinka, *Death and the King's Horseman*, p. 10.
47. Ibid., pp. 42–43.
48. In the poem "A Coat," Yeats uses this clothing metaphor to describe his poetic theme and style up to a period; his enterprise to walk naked will be his search for a more severe, plain, unadorned style, one reduced to essentials. ["A Coat", *Collected Poems* p. 142].

49. John Millington Synge, Preface, *The Playboy of the Western World, Collected Plays,* ed. Ann Saddlemyer (London: Oxford University Press, 1962).
50. Yeats, *Cathleen ni Houlihan,* p. 79.
51. Emmanuel N. Obiechina, *Culture, Tradition' and Society in the West African Novel]* (Cambridge: Cambridge University Press, 1975), p. 112.
52. Obiechina, p. 189.
53. Soyinka, *The Road,* p. 152.
54. Ibid., pp. 202–203.
55. Yeats, *Cathleen ni Houlihan,* p. 82.

Chapter seven:
Figures in a Dance

1. David R. Clark, "Yeats, Theater and Nationalism," in *Theater and Nationalism in Twentieth Century Ireland.* Ed. Robert O'Driscoll (Toronto: University of Toronto Press, 1971,), pp. 135–136.

References

Primary Sources: Works by Yeats and Soyinka
Soyinka, Wole. *Collected Plays* I. London: Oxford University Press, 1973. [Includes *A Dance of the Forests: The Swamp Dwellers; the Strong Breed; The Road; The Bacchae of Euripides*]

——. *Collected Plays* II. London: Oxford University Press, 1974. [Includes *The Lion and the Jewel; Kongi's Harvest; The Trials of Brother Jero; Jero's Metamorphosis; Madmen and Specialists*]

——. *Camwood on the Leaves*, London: Methuen, 1976.

——. *Opera Wonyosi*, Bloomington, Indian: Indiana University Press, 1981.

——. *A Play of Giants*, London: Methuen, 1985.

——. *Idanre and Other Poems*, London: Methuen, 1967.

——. *The Interpreters*, London: Heinemann, 1970.

——. *Season of Anomy*, London: Rex Collings, 1972.

——. *Aké: The Years of Childhood*. London: Rex Collings, 1981.

——. *The Man Died: Prison Notes of Wole Soyinka*. Middlesex: Penguin, 1975.

———. *Myth, Literature and the African World,* London: Cambridge University Press, 1976.

———. *Isara: A Voyage Around Essay.* Ibadan: Foundation Publications, 1989.

———. *Art, Dialogue and Outrage: Essays on Literature and Culture.* Ibadan: New Horn Press, 1988.

———. *Credo of Being and Nothingness.* Ibadan: Spectrum Books, 1989.

———. *Ibadan: The Penklemess Years: A Memoir, 1946–1965.* Ibadan: Spectrum Books, 1994

———. "And After the Narcissist?" *African Forum*, 1, 4(1966), 53–64.

———. Soyinka, Wole. Declaration of African Writers – January, 1975" *Research in African Literatures,* 6 (1975), 58–59.

———. "Drama and the Revolutionary Ideal." *In Person: Achebe, Awoonor and Soyinka*, ed. Karen L. Morrell. Seattle: Institute of Comparative and Foreign Area Studies, University of Washington, 1975, 61–88.

———. "Television Discussion, Penthouse Theater, Class Discussion" *In Person: Achebe, Awoonor and Soyinka*, Ed. Karen L. Morrell. Seattle: Institute of comparative and Foreign Area Studies, University of / Washington, 1975, 89–130.

———. "Neo-Tarzanism: The Poetics of Pseudo-Tradition" *Transition*, 48(1975), 38–44

Yeats, William Butler, *Collected Plays*, London: Macmillan, 1952; rpt. 1977 [Includes: *The Countess Cathleen, Cathleen ni Houlihan, The Pot of Broth, The Kings's Threshold, Deirdre, At the Hawk's Well, The Green Helmet, On Baile's Strand, The Only Jealousy of Emer, The Unicorn from the Stars, The Player Queen, The Dreaming of The Bones, The Words Upon the Window Pane, The Herne's Egg, Purgatory, The Death of Cuchulain]*

———. *Collected Poems*, London: Macmillan, 1992

———. *The Variorum Edition of the Plays of W.B. Yeats,* Ed. Russell K. Alspach. London: Macmillan, 1966.

————. *Uncollected Prose I*: 1886–1896, Ed. John P. Frayne. New York: Columbia University Press, 1970.

————. *Uncollected Prose II*: 1896–1939, Eds. J.P. Frayne and Coulton Johnson, London: Macmillan, 1975.

————. *The Countess Cathleen and Various Legends and Lyrics*, London: T. Fisher Unwin, 1892

————. *The Celtic Twilight*, Dublin: Maunsel and Company, 1905, New York: Signet Books, 1905, New York: Signet Books, 1965.

————. *Synge and the Ireland of His Time*, Dundrum, Dublin: Cuala Press, 1911.

————. *Plays and Controversies*, London: Macmillan, 1923.

————. *A Vision*, London: Macmillan, 1937.

————. *On the Boiler*, Dublin; Cuala Press, 1939.

————. *Autobiographies*, London: Macmillan, 1955.

————. *Mythologies*, London: Macmillan, 1959.

————. *Essays and Introductions*, London: Macmillan, 1962.

————. *Explorations*: London: Macmillan, 1961.

————. *The Letters of W.B. Yeats*, Ed. Allen Wade. London: Rupert Hart-Davis, 1954.

————. "Nationality and Literature", *W.B. Yeats*, Ed. William H. Pritchard. Middlesex, England, Penguin Books, 1972.

————. "The Symbolism of Poetry", *Twentieth Century Literary Criticism*. Ed. David Lodge. London: Longman, 1972.

Primary Sources II: Works by Contemporary Writers

Aidoo, Ama Ata, *The Dilemma of a Ghost*. London: Longman, 1965.

Al-Hakim, Tewfik, *Fate of a Cockroach*. London: Heinemann, 1973.

Clark, John Pepper, *Three Plays*, Ibadan: Oxford University Press, 1969. [*Song of a Goat; The Masquerade; The Raft*]

————. *Ozidi*, London: Oxford University Press, 1970.

Fugard, Athol, *Three Plays*, London: Oxford University Press, 1962. [*Sizwe Bansi Is Dead; Statements; The Island*].

Gregory, Isabella Augusta, Ed. *Ideals in Ireland: Essays by "A.E." and Others*. London: The Unicorn Press, 1901.

————. *Cuchulain of Muirthemne: The Story of the Men of theRed Branch of Ulster*, London: Murray, 1902.

————. *Gods and Fighting Men: The Story of the Tuatha de Dannaan and the Fianna of Ireland*. London: Murray, 1904.

————. *Visions and Beliefs in the West of Ireland*. London: Pothem, 1920.

————. *Our Irish Theater*. New York: Capricon Books, 1965.

————. *Collected Plays*, Ed. Ann Saddlemyer. Gerard's Cross, Buckinghamshire: Colin Smythe, 1970. [Includes *Twenty-Five, Spreading the News The White Cockade, Dervorgilla*, Vols. I and II

Ibsen, Henrik. *The Oxford Ibsen: Collected Plays*. Trans. and ed. James Walter

MacFarlane, London: Oxford University Press, 1961. [Includes *A Doll's House, Hedda Gabler, The Wild Duck, Ghosts, An Enemy of the People, The Pillars of the Community.*

Ijimere, Obotunde. *The Imprisonment of Obatala and Other Plays*. Trans. Ulli Beier. London: Heinemann, 1966.

Martyn, Edward. *The Heather Field*. London: Duckworth, 1917.

Molloy, Michael J. *Three Plays: The King of Friday's Men; The Paddy, The Wood of the Whispering*. Newark Delaware: Thoe Proscenium Press, 1975.

O'Casey, Sean. *Three Plays: The Shadow of a Gunman, Juno Plough and the Stars*. London: Macmillan, 1975.

————. *Three More Plays: The Silver Tassie, Purple Dust, Red Roses for Me*. London: Macmillan, 1977.

————. *Blasts and Benedictions*. Ed. Ronald Ayling, London: Macmillan, 1967.

Osofian, Femi. *Who's Afraid of Tai Solarin*. Ibadan: Scholar Press, 1978.

————. *Morountodun and Other Plays*, Lagos: Longman, 1982.

————. "Ritual and the Revolutionary Ethos". *Okike*, 22(1982), 72–85.

Robinson, Lennox. *The Big House*. Dublin: Cuala Press, 1928.

————. *Ireland's Abbey Theater: A History, 1899–1951*. London: Sidgwick and Jackson, 1951.

Rotimi, Ola. *The Gods Are Not to Blame*. London: Oxford University Press 1971.

Shaw, George Bernard. *The Quintessence of Ibsenism*, London: Walter Scott, 1913.

————. *How to Settle the Irish Question*. Dublin: Constable, 1932.

————. *Our Theaters in the Nineties*, 3 Vols. London: Constable, 1917.

————. *The Matter with Ireland*. Eds. Dan Lawrence and Dan Lawrence and David Greene. London: Rupert Hart-Davis, 1962.

————. *The Bodley Head Bernard Shaw; Collected Plays with their Prefaces, London: Bodley Head, 1970. [Includes: John Bull's Other Island; Man and Superman; Widowers' Houses; Mrs. Warren' Profession; Pygmalion]* Vols. II, IV, V, & VI.

Sutherland, Efua, *Edufa, London*: Longman, 1967.

————. *The Marriage of Anansewa*. London: Longman, 1975.

Synge, John Millington. *Collected Plays*. 3 Vols. Ed. Ann Saddlemyer. London: Oxford University Press, 1962. [Includes: *Riders to the Sea; The Shadow of the Glen; The Well of the Saints; The Tinker's Wedding; The Playboy of the Western World; Deirdre of the Sorrows*]

————. *An Autobiography of J.M. Synge. Constructed from the Manuscripts by Alan Price.* Dublin: Dolmen Press, 1965

Wa Thiong'o, Ngugi. *This Time Tomorrow*. Nairobi: East Africa Publishing House, 1969.

————. *The Trial of Dedan Kimathi*. London: Heinemann, 1980.

————. *Ngaheeka Ndeenda*. London: Heinemann, 1973.

———. *Homecoming*. London: Heinemann, 1973.

———. *Writers in Politics*. London: Heinemann, 1980.

———. *Barrel of a Pen*. London: Heinemann, 1985.

Secondary Sources – Criticism

Abrahm, M.H. *The Mirror and the Lam: Romantic Theory and the Critical Tradition*. Cambridge, MA: Harvard University Press, 1953.

Achebe, Chinua. *Things Fall Apart*. London: Heinemann, 1958.

———. *Arrow of God*. London: Heinemann, 1960

———. "The Role of the African Writer in a New Nation." *African Writers on African Writing*. Ed. G.D. Killam. London: Heinemann, 1973.

———. *Morning Yet On Creation Day*. London: Heinemann, 1976.

Adams, Henry. "Symbolism and Yeats's *A Vision*." *Journal of Aesthetics and Art Criticism*. 22, 4 (1964), 425–36.

Adedeji, Joel. "Form and Function of Satire in Yoruba Dram." *Odu*, 4, 1 (1967), 61–72.

———. "A Profile of Nigerian Theater, 1960–1970." *Nigeria Magazine*, 107 / 109(1971), 3–14.

———. "Oral Tradition and the Contemporary Theater in Nigeria." *Research in African Literatures*, 2, 2 (1971).

———. "Trends in the Content and Form of the Opening Glee in Yoruba Drama." *Research in African Literatures*, 4, 1 (1973).

———. *Nationalism and the Nigerian National Theater*. *Munger Africana Literary Notes*, No. 54 Pasadena: California Institute of Technology, 1980.

Adelugba, Dapo. *Studies on Synge*. Ibadan: Ibadan University Press, 1975.

Ajayi, J. Francis A. *Christian Missions in Nigeria, 1841–1891*. Cambridge: Cambridge University Press, 1964.

Allt, G.D.P. "Yeats, Religion and History." *Sewanee Review*, 69, 4 (1952), 24–58.

Amankulor. J.N. "Dramatic Technique and Meaning in *The Road*," *Ba' 'Shiru'*, 7, 1 (1976), 53–69.

Anozie, Sunday. "Language and the Modern Experience of Tragedy," *Conch*, 1, 2 (1969), 37–44.

Arnold, Matthew. "On the Study of Celtic Literature." *Lectures and Essays in Criticism*. Ed. R.H. Super. Michigan: Michigan University Press, 1962.

Artaud, Antonin. *The Theater and Its Double*. New York: Grove Press, 1958.

Asanga, Dominic. "Cultural Nationalism and the Dramatic Revival in Ireland and West Africa." Ph.D. Dissertation, University of Ottawa, Canada, 1978.

Auerbach, Erich. *Mimesis: The Representation of Reality in Western Literature*. Trans. Willard R. Trask. Princeton: Princeton University Press, 1953.

Awoonor, Kofi. *The Breast of the Earth: A Survey of the History, Culture and Literature of Africa South of the Sahara*. New York: NOK Publishers International, 1975.

Azikiwe, Nnamdi. *Renascent Africa*, London: Frank Cass, 1968.

Banham, Martin; "Nigerian Dramatists in English and the Traditional Nigerian Theater." *Journal of Commonwealth Literature*, 3 (1967) 97–102.,

———. and Clive Wake, *African Theater Today*, London: Pitman, 1976.

Barthes, Roland. "The Structural Activity." *European Literary Theory and Practice: From Extistential Phenomenology to Structuralism*. Ed. Vernon W. Gras. New York: Delta Books, 1973.

Bates, Walter Jackson. *Criticism: The Major Texts*. New York: Harcourt, Brace, Jovanovich, 1970.

Beier, Ulli. ed. *Introduction to African Literature: An Anthology of Critical Writing from Black Orpheus*. London: Longman, 1967.

Benjamin, Walter. *Understanding Brecht*. Trans. Stanley Mitchell. London: New Left Books, 1977.

Bentley, Eric, ed. *In Search of Theater*. New York; Vintage Books, 1960.

———. *The Playwright as Thinker*. New York: Meridian Books, 1960.

———. *The Theory of the Modern Stage*. Baltimore, Maryland: Penguin Books, 1968.

Bidney, David. "Myth, Symbolism and Truth". *Myth and Literature*. Ed. John B. Vickery. Lincoln Nebraska Press, 1967.

Bishop, Norma. "A Nigerian Version of a Greek Classic: Soyinka's Transformation of *The Bacchae*." *Research in African Literatures*, 14, 1 (1983); 68–80

Bjersley, Bright. *The Interpretation of the Cuchulain Legend in the Works of W.B. Yeats*. Uppsala: Lundegvistika Bokhandan, 1950.

Block, Haskell M. "Yeats's *The King's Threshold*: The Poet and Society." *Philological Quarterly*, 34 (1955), 206–18

Bloom, Harold. *Yeats*. London: Macmillan, 1970.

Booth, James, *Writers* and *Politics in Nigeria*. London: Hodder and Stoughton, 1981.

Brecht, Bertolt. *The Three Penny Opera*. Trans. H. MacDiarmuid. London: Methuen, 1973.

Brooks, Peter. *The Empty Space*. London: MacGibbon and Kee, 1968.

Brown, Malcolm. *The Politics of Irish Literature: From Thomas Davis to W.B. Yeats*. London: Allen and Unwin, 1972.

Brustein, Robert. *The Theater of Revolt*. London, Methuen, 1970.

Bushrui, S.B. "*The King's Threshold*: A Defence of Poetry". *A Review of English Literature*, 4, 3(1963), 81–94.

Cartey, Wilfred. *Whispers from a Continent: The Literature of Contemporary Black Africa*. New York: Random House, 1969.

Carpenter, Andrew Isdell. ed. *Place, Personality and the Irish Writer, Irish Literary Studies I*. New York: Barnes and Noble, 1977.

Cirlot, Joseph E. *A Dictionary of Symbols*. Trans. Jack Sage. London: Routledge and Kegan Paul, 1962

Clark, David R. "W.B. Yeats and the Drama of Vision." *Arizona Quarterly*, 20, 2 (1964), 127–41.

———. "Nishikigi and Yeats's The Dreaming of the Bones." *Modern Drama*, 7, 2 (1964), 111–25.

———. *W.B. Yeats and the Theater of Desolate Reality*. Dublin: Dolmen Press, 1965.

———. "Yeats, Theater and Nationalism." *Theater and Nationalism in Twentieth Century Ireland*. Ed. Robert O'Driscoll. Toronto: University of Toronto Press, 1971.

Clark, Ebun. *Hubert Ogunde: The Making of Nigerian Theater*. London: Oxford University Press, 1979.

Clark, William S. *The Early Irish Stage*. Oxford: Clarendon Press, 1955.

Cook, Mercer and Stephen Henderson. *The Militant Black Writer in Africa and the United States*. Madison: University of Wisconsin Press, 1969.

Corrigan, Robert and James l. Rosenberg. eds. *The Context and Craft of Drama; Critical Essays on the Nature of Drama and the Theater*. San Francisco: Chandler Publishing Co. 1964.

Coxhead, Elizabeth. *Lady Gregory: A Literary Portrait*. Toronto: Macmillan, 1961.

———. *J.M. Synge and Lady Gregory*. London: Longman, Green, 1962.

Cruise O'Brien, Conor. "Passion and Cunning: The Politics of W.B. Yeats." *Literature in Revolution*. Eds. George Abbot White and Charles Newman. New York: Holt, Rhinehart and Winston, 1972.

Curtis L.P. Jr. *Anglo-Saxons and Celts: A Study of Anti-Irish Prejudice in Victorian England*. Bridgeport, Connecticut: University of Connecticut Press, 1968.

d'Azevedo, Warren L. ed. *The Traditional Artist in African Societies*. Bloomington, Indiana; Indiana University Press, 1973.

de Stael, Madame. "De La Litterature" (1800) in Ian Watt, *The Rise of the Novel.* London: Penguin Books, 1963, 66–68.

Dathorne, O.R. *The Black Mind: A History of African Literature.* Minneapolis: University of Minnesota Press, 1974.

Davis, Ann. "Dramatic Theory of Wole Soyinka." *Critical Perspectives on Wole Soyinka.* Ed. James Gibbs. Washington, D.C.: Three Continents Press, 1980.

Donoghue, Denis. *The Third Voice; Modern British and American Verse Drama.* London: Oxford University Press, 1959.

———. , ed. *The Integrity of Yeats,* Dublin: Mercier Press, 1964.

———. *Yeats.* Modern Masters Series. New York: Viking Press, 1971.

Echeruo, Michael J. "The Dramatic Limits of Igbo Ritual." *Drama and Theater in Nigeria: A Critical Source Book.* Ed. Yemi Ogunbiyi. Lagos: Nigeria Magazine Publications, 1981.

———. *Victorian Lagos.* London: Macmillan, 1977.

Ekom, Ernest. "The Development of Theater in Nigeria, 1960–1967." *Journal of the New African Literature and the Arts,* 11 / 12 (1971), 36–49.

Eliade, Mircea. *The Sacred and the Profane.* Trans. Willard R. Trask. New York: Harcourt, Brace, Jovanovich 1967.

Eliot, T.S. "Tradition and the Individual Talent" *20th Century Literary Criticism.* Ed. David Lodge. London: Longman, 1972.

———. "The Function of Criticism". *20th Century Literary Criticism.* Ed. David Lodge. London: Longman, 1972.

Ellis-Fermor, Una. *The Irish Dramatic Movement.* London: Methuen, 1969.

Ellmann, Richard. *The Identity of Yeats*: Oxford University Press, 1959.

———. *James Joyce.* New York: Oxford University Press, 1959.

———. *Yeats: The Man and the Masks.* London: Faber and Faber, 1961.

————. "Yeats Without Analogue." *The Kenyon Review*, 26, 1 (1964), 30–47.

————. and Charles Feidelson, Jr. eds. *The Modern Tradition: Backgrounds of Modern Literature*, New York: Oxford University Press, 1965.

Empson, William. *Seven Types of Ambiguity*. Princeton: Princeton University Press, 1945.

Enekwe, Ossie O. "Myth, Ritual and Drama in Igboland". *Drama and Theater in Nigeria: A Critical Source Book*. Ed. Yemi Ogunbiyi. Lagos: Nigeria Magazine Publications, 1981.

Engelberg, Edward. *The Vast Design: Patterns in W.B. Yeats' Aesthetics*. Toronto: University of Toronto Press, 1964.

English, Horace B. and Ava C. English. *A Comprehensive Dictionary of Psychological and Psychoanalytic Terms: A Guide to Usage:* London: Longman, 1958.

Esslin, Martin. "A Major Poetic Dramatist – Wole Soyinka" *New Theater Magazine*, 12, 2(1972), 9–10.

Fallis, Richard. *The Irish Renaissance*. Syracuse: Syracuse University Press, 1977.

Fanon, Frantz. *The Wretched of the Earth*. London: McGibbon and Kee, 1965.

Farrington, Brian. *Malachi-Stilt-Jack: A Study of W.B. Yeats and His Works*. London: Connolly Publications, 1965.

Fay, Frank. *Towards a National Theater: Dramatic Criticism of Frank Fay*. Ed. Robert Hogan. Dublin: Dolmen Press, 1970.

Feder, Irene. *Ancient Myth in Modern Poetry*. Princeton: Princeton University Press, 1971.

Fergusson, Francis. *The Idea of a Theater*. New York: Doubleday, 1949.

Fergusson, John, ed. *An Illustrated Encyclopaedia of Mysticism and the Mystery Religions*. London: Thames and Hudson, 1976.

Flannery, James. *W.B. Yeats and the Idea of a Theater: The Early Abbey in Theory and Practice*, New Haven: Yale University Press, 1976.

Fletcher, Iain and Frank Kermode, eds. *Poets of the Nineties.* London: John Baker, 1965.

Frazer, James G. Sir. *The Golden Bough: A Study of Magic and Religion.* Abridged Version. New York: Macmillan, 1958.

Freud, Sigmund, *The Standard Edition of the Complete Psychological Works of Sigmund Freud.* Eds. James Strachey and Anna Freud. London. Oxford University Press, 1953-66. [Includes: *The Interpretation of Dreams, Totem and Taboo, New Introductory Lectures*]

Friedman, Barton. *Adventures in the Deeps of the Mind: The Cuchulain Plays of W.B. Yeats.* Princeton: Princeton University Press, 1977.

Frye, Northrop. *Anatomy of Criticism: Four Essays.* Princeton: Princeton University Press, 1957.

———. "The Archetypes of Literature", *Myth and Literature.* Ed. John Vickery. Lincoln: University of Nebraska Press, 1966.

Gassner, John. *Form and Idea in the Modern Theater,* New York: The Dryden Press, 1956.

Gibbs, James. ed. *Critical Perspectives on Wole Soyinka.* Washington, D.C.: Three Continents Press, 1980.

———. "The Origins of *A Dance of the Forests.*" *African Literature Today,* 8 (1976), 66–71.

———. "Tear the Painted Masks, Join the Poison Stains: A Preliminary Study of Wole Soyinka's Writings for the Nigerian Press." *Research in African Literature,* 14, 1 (1983), 3–14.

Graham-White, Anthony. *The Drama of Black Africa.* London: Samuel French, 1968.

Gurr, Andrew. "Third World Drama: Soyinka and Tragedy". *Critical Perspectives on Wole Soyinka.* Ed. James Gibbs. Washington D.C.: Three Continents Press, 1980.

Gurvitch, Georges. "The Sociology of the Theater." *Sociology of Literature and Drama Selected Readings.* Eds. Elizabeth and Tom Burns. Middlesex England: Penguin Books, 1973.

Harper, George Mills. *Yeats' Golden Dawn*. London: Macmillan, 1974.

Henn, T.R. *The Lonely Tower: Studies in the Poetry of W.B. Yeats*. London: Methuen, 1950.

Heywood, Christopher, ed: *Perspectives on African Literature*. London: Heinemann, 1971.

Heywood, Anne-Marie. "The Fox's Dance; The Staging of Soyinka's Plays." *African Literature Today*. 8 (1976), 42–51.

Hogan, Robert. *After the Irish Renaissance: A Critical History of Irish Drama Since The Plough and the Stars*. Minneapolis: University of Minnesota Press, 1967.

———. ed. *A Dictionary of Irish Literature*. Westport, Connecticut: The Greenwood Press, 1979.

Hone, Joseph. *W.B. Yeats, 1865–1939*. London: Macmillan, 1965.

Hyman, Stanley Edgar. *"The Ritual View of Myth and the Mythic."* *Myth and Literature,* Ed. John Vickey. Lincoln University of Nebraska Press, 1966.

Idowu, B.E. Olodumare. *God in Yoruba Belief.* London: Longman, 1962.

Innes, Catherine Lynette. "Through the Looking Glass: Achebe, Synge and Cultural Nationalism." Ph.D. Dissertation. Cornell University, 1973.

———. "Through the Looking Glass: African and Irish Nationalist Writing." *African Literature Today*. 9 (1973), 15–24

Irele, Abiola. "Tradition and the Yoruba Writer: D.O. Fagunwa, Amos Tutuola and Wole Soyinka." *Critical Perspective on Wole Soyinka*. Ed. James Gibbs, Washington, D.C.: Three Continents Press, 1980.

———. *The African Experience in Literature and Ideology.* London: Heinemann, 1981.

Izevbaye, Dan. "Criticism and Literature in Africa." *Perspectives on African Literature*. Ed. Christopher Heywood. London: Heinemann, 1971.

———. "Politics in Nigerian Poetry" *Presence Africaine*, 78 (1971), 143–67

———. "Language and Meaning in *The Road*." *African Literature Today,* 8 (1976), 52–65.

———. "Soyinka's Black Orpheus." *Neo-African Literature and Culture.* Eds. Bernth Lindfors and Ulla Schild. Wiesbaden: B. Heuman, 1976, 147–58.

———. "The African Experience of Comparative Literature." *Comparative Approaches to Modern African Literature.* Ed. Sam O. Asein Ibadan: Ibadan University Press, 1982, 1–8.

———. "Mediation in Soyinka: The Case of the King's Horseman." *Critical Perspectives on Wole Soyinka.* Ed. James Gibbs. Washington D.C.: Three Continents Press, 1980.

Jeffares, A.N. *W.B. Yeats: Man and Poet.* London: Routledge and Kegan Paul, 1962.

———. and G.K. *Cross,* eds. *In Excited Reverie: A Centenary Tribute to William Butler Yeats,* 1865–1939. London: Macmillan, 1965.

———. and A.S. Knowland. *A Commentary on the Collected Plays of W.B. Yeats,* London: Macmillan, 1975.

Jeyifo, Biodun. "The Artist as an Activist", *Newswatch*, 19 February, 1985, 15.

———. *The Truthful Lie: Essays in a Sociology of African Drama.* London: New Beacon Books, 1985

Jones, Eldred Durosimi. "Progress and Civilization in the Work of Wole Soyinka." *Perspectives On African Literature.* Ed. Christopher Heywood. London: Heinemann, 1971.

———. "Wole Soyinka: Critical Approaches." *The Critical Evaluation of African Literature.* Ed. Edgar Wright. London: Heinemann, 1973.

Joyce, James. *A Portrait of the Artist as a Young Man. The Essential James Joyce.* Ed. Harry Levin. Middlesex, England: Penguin Books, 1972.

Jung, Carl. *Psychological Types: Essays on a Science of Mythology.* Trans. R.F.C. Hull. New York: Samuel French, 1953.

Kain, Richard. "Yeats and Irish Nationalism", *W.B. Yeats, 1865–1965: Centenary Essays.* Eds. D.S. Maxwell and S.B. Bushrui. Ibadan: Ibadan University Press, 1965.

————. *Dublin in the Age of W.B. Yeats and James Joyce.* Norman, Oklahoma: University of Oklahoma Press, 1962.

Kant, Immanuel. *Critique of Judgement (1790).* Trans J.H. Bernard. London: Macmillan, 1931.

Kavanagh, Peter. *The Irish Theater: Being a History of the Drama in Ireland from the Earliest Period to the Present Day.* Tralee, Ireland: The Kerryman, 1946.

Kermode, Frank. *Romantic Image.* London: Routledge and Kegan Paul. 1957.

Kesteloot, Lilyan. *The Intellectual Origins of the African Revolution,* Trans. Alex Mboukou. Washington D.C. Black Orpheus Press, 1972.

King, Bruce. *Introduction to Nigerian Literature.* London: Evans, 1971.

Knight, G. Wilson. *The Golden Labyrinth: A Study of British Drama.* London: Phoenix House, 1967.

Ladipo, Duro. *Moremi: Three Nigerian Plays.* Ed. Ulli Beier. London: Longman, 1967.

————. *Oba Ko So / The King Did Not Hang.* Ibadan: Institute of African Studies, 1972.

Laurence, Margaret. *Long Drums and Cannons,* London: Macmillan, 1969.

Laurenson, Diana and Alan Swingewood. *The Sociology of Literature.* London: Paladin, 1971.

Levi-Strauss, Claude. *Structural Anthropology.* Middlesex: Penguin Books, 1972.

Lindfors, Bernth. "The Early Writings of Wole Soyinka." *Journal of African Studies,* 2, (1975), 64–86.

————. "Wole Soyinka Talking Through his Hat." *Commonwealth Literature and the Modern World*. Ed. Hena Maes-Jelinek. Brussels: Didier, 1975.

Loftus, Richard J. *Nationalism in Modern Anglo-Irish Poetry*. Madison: University of Wisconsin Press, 1964.

Lukacs, George. *The Meaning of Contemporary Realism*. London: Merlin Press, 1963.

Lyons, F.S.L. *Ireland Since the Famine*, London: Fontana, 1973.

MacCarthy, J.B. *The Long Road to Garranbraher*, Dublin: Gill, 1928.

MaCanery, Barney C. "Tradition and Satire in Wole Soyinka's *Madmen and Specialists."* *World Literature Written in English*, 14 (1975), 506–13.

Macebuh, Stanley. "Poetics and the Mythic Imagination." *Critical Perspectives on Wole Soyinka*, Ed. James Gibbs. Washington D.C.: Three Continents Press, 1980.

Maduakor, Obiajuru."Cyclic Determinism in Soyinka's *Idanre."* *Ufahammu*, 8, 1 (1977) p.179

————. "Soyinka as a Literary Critic." *Research in African Literature*, 17, 1 (1986), 1–35.

————. *An Introduction to the Works of Wole Soyinka.* New York: Garland Publishing Company, 1986.

Mahood, Molly M. "Drama in New Born States." *Presence Africaine*, 60 (1966), 23–29.

Malone, Andrew E. *Irish Drama*. New York: Benjamin Bloom, 1963.

Marcus, Philip L. *Yeats and the Beginnings of the Irish Renaissance.* Ithaca: Cornell University Press, 1970.

Maxwell, D.E.S. and S.B. Bushrui. Eds. W.B. *Yeats, 1865–1965: Centenary Essays*. Ibadan; Ibadan University Press, 1965.

Mbiti, John S. *African Religions and Philosophy*. New York: Doubleday, 1970.

Moore, Gerald. *The Chosen Tongue*. London. Longman, 1969.

————. *Wole Soyinka*. London: Evans, 1971.

Mootry, Maria K. "Soyinka and Yoruba Mythology". *Ba'Shiru*, 7, 1 (1976), 23–24.

Moyo, Phaniso. "*The Road*: A Slice of the Yoruba Pantheon." *Ba'Shiru*, 2, 1 (1970–71), 89–93.

Mphahlele, Ezekiel: *The African Image*. London: Faber and Faber, 1962.

Murphy, D.J. "Yeats and Lady Gregory; A Unique Dramatic Collaboration." *Modern Drama*, 7, 3 (1964), 322–28

Nathan, Leonard E. *The Tragic Drama of William Butler Yeats: Figures in a Dance*. New York: Columbia University Press, 1965.

Nazareth, Peter. *Literature and Society in Modern Africa*, Nairobi: East African Literature Bureau, 1972.

Nicol, Allardyce. *Late Nineteenth Century Drama*. Cambridge: Cambridge University Press, 1959.

Nietzsche, Friedrich. *The Basic Writings of Nietzsche*. Trans. and Ed. Walter Kaufmann.

New York: Random House, 1968. (Includes, *The Birth of Tragedy, Thus Spake Zarathustra*).

Nkosi, Lewis. *Tasks and Masks*, London: Longman, 1979.

Nwoga, Donatus 1. "Obscurity and Commitment in Modern African Literature." *African Literature Today*, 6(1973), 26–45.

O'Driscoll, Robert ed. *Theater and Nationalism in Twentieth Century Ireland*. Toronto: Toronto University Press, 1971.

O'Farrell, Patrick. *England and Ireland Since 1800*, London: Oxford University Press, 1975.

O'Grady, Standish, *History of Ireland*. Dublin; E. Ponsonby: 1887. 2 Vols.

Obafemi, Olu. "Revolutionary Aesthetics in Recent Nigerian Theater." *African Literature Today* 12(1982), 118–136.

Obiechina, Emmanuel N. "Cultural Nationalism and Modern West African Creative Writing." *African Literature Today*, 1–4 (1970), 24–35.

———. *Onitsha Market Literature*. London: Heinemann, 1972.

———. "Perceptions of Colonialism in West African Literature." *Ufahammu* 5 (1974) 36–53.

———. *Culture, Tradition and Society in the West African Novel.* Cambridge: Cambridge: Cambridge University Press, 1975.

———. "The Writer and His Commitment in Contemporary Nigerian Society." *Association of Nigerian Authors Review,* (1985), 10–11.

———. "Africa in the Soul of Dispersed Children: West African Literature from the Era of the Slave Trade." *Nsukka Studies in African Literature,* 4, 1 (1986), 101–160.

Ogunba, Oyin: "The Traditional Content of the Plays of Wole Soyinka." *African Literature Today.* 4 (1970), 2–18

———. "Language in an Age of Transition: Shakespeare and Soyinka." *Journal of the Nigerian English Studies Association.* 1 (1974), 109–20.

———. *The Movement of Transition: A Study of the Plays of Wole Soyinka.* Ibadan: Ibadan University Press, 1975.

Ogunbiyi, Yemi: "Nigerian Theater and Drama: A Critical Profile." *Drama and Theater in Nigeria: A Critical Source Book.* Lagos: Nigeria Magazine Publications, 1981.

Okpewho, Isidore: "Rethinking Myth." *African Literature Today,* 11 (1980), 5–23.

———. "Myth and Modern Fiction: Armah's *Two Thousand Seasons.*" *African Literature Today,* 13(1983), 1–23.

———. *Myth in Africa.* Cambridge: Cambridge University Press, 1984.

Olafioye, Toye. "Cultural Conventions in Soyinka's Art." *Ba'Shiru,* 7 (1974), 67–70.

Omotosho, Kole: "Wole Soyinka: What Is He to Us?" *Afriscope,* 45 (1974), 58–60.

Osundare, Niyi. "The Artist as an Activist" *Newswatch* 18 February, 1985. 14.

Parkin, Andrew. "Imagination's Abode: The Symbolism of House Settings in Modern Irish Stage Pays." *Myth and Reality in Irish*

Literature. Ed. Joseph Ronsley. Waterloo, Canada: Wilfrid Laurier University Press, 1977.

Peters, Jonathan. *The Dance of the Masks: Senghor, Achebe and Soyinka*. Washington, D.C.: Three Continents Press, 1978.

Plekhanov, George. *Art and Social Life*. London Lawrence and Wishart, 1963.

Povey, John. "West African Drama in English." *Comparative Drama*, 1, 2 (1967), 110.

———. "Wole Soyinka: Two Nigerian Comedies." *Comparative Drama*. 3, 2 (1969), 120–32.

Ralph-Bowman, Mark. "Leaders and Left Overs: A Reading of Soyinka's *Death and the King's Horseman*. "*Research in African Literatures*, 14 1 (1983), 81–97.

Regardie, Israel. *The Golden Dawn: An Account of the Teachings, Rites and Ceremonies of the Order of Golden Dawn*. Chicago: Aries Press, 1937–40. 4 Vols.

Ricard, Alain. *Theater and Nationalism*. Trans. Femi Osofisan. Ife: Obafemi Awolowo University Press, 1983.

Robinson, Lennox: *Ireland's Abbey Theater: A History, 1899–1951*. London: Sidgwick and Jackson, 1951.

Roscoe, Adrain. *Mother is Gold: A Study of West African Literature*. Cambridge: Cambridge University Press, 1971.

Russell, George (A.E.) *Imaginations and Reveries*. Dublin: Maunsel and Co., 1915.

Saddlemyer, Ann "The Cult of the Celt: Pan Celticism in the Nineties". *The World of W.B. Yeats*. Eds. Robin Skelton and An Saddlemyer. Seattle: University of Washington Press, 1965.

———. "J.M. Synge and Modern Comedy: A Lecture Given at the Eighth International Yeats Summer School. Sligo, Ireland, August, 1967." Dublin: Dolmen Press, 1968.

Sartre, Jean Paul. "Orphée Noir" in Anthologie de la nouvelle poesie negre et *Malagache*, Ed. Leopold Sedar Senghor. Paris: P.U.F. 1948.

Schorer, Mark. "Technique as Discovery", *20ᵗʰ Century Literarcy Criticism*, Ed. David Lodge. London: Longman, 1972.

Scott-Kennedy, J. *In Search of African Theater*, New York: Scribner, 1973.

Seiden, Morton Irving. *William Butler Yeats: The Poet as Mythmaker*. East Lansing: Michigan State University, 1962.

Sekoni, 'Ropo. "Metaphor as the Basis of Form in Soyinka's Drama," *Research in African Literatures*, 14, 1 (1983), 45–57.

Skene, Reginald. *The Cuchulain Plays of W.B. Yeats*. London: Macmillan, 1974.

Stock, A.G. *Yeats, His Poetry and Thought*. Cambridge: Cambridge University Press, 1964.

Stock, A.G. Yeats and Achebe. "*Critical Perspectives on Chinua Achebe*, Eds. C.L. Innes and Bernth Lindfors. London: Heinemann, 1978.

Sweeney, Eileen, Sr. "The Irish Literary Revival and the Nigerian Literary Movement in the Sixties," *Comparative Approaches to Modern African Literature*. Ed. Sam O. Asein. Ibadan: Ibadan University Press, 1976.

Taylor, Richard, *The Drama of W.B. Yeats: Irish Myth and the Japanese Noh*. New Haven: Yale University Press 1976.

Traore, Bakary. The Black African Theater and Its Social Functions. Trans. Dapo Adelugba. Ibadan, Ibadan University Press, 1972.

Ure, Peter. *Yeats*. Edinburgh: Oliver and Boyd, 1963.

———. *Yeats the Playwright: A Commentary on Character and Design in the Major Plays*. London: Routledge and Kegan Paul, 1963.

———. *Yeats and Anglo-Irish Literature*. New York: Harper and Row, 1974.

Vendler, Helen. *Yeats's Vision and the Later Plays*. Cambridge, Mass: Harvard University Press, 1963.

Vico, Giambattista. *The New Science*; (1744) Trans. T.G. Bergin and M.H. Fisch. New York: Cornell University Press, 1948.

References

Vincent Theo. "The Modern Inheritance: Studies in J.F. Clark's *The Raft* and Wole Soyinka's *The Road*," Oduma, 2, 1 (1974), 38–49.

Wauthier, Claude. *The Literature and Thought of Modern Africa.* London: Heinemann, 1978.

Welleck Rene and Austin Warren. *Theory of Literature.* Middlesex, England: Penguin Books; 1963.

Wilkinson, Nick. "Demoke's Choice in *A Dance of the Forests.*" *Journal of Commonwealth Literature.* 10 3 (1976), 22–27.

Williams, Raymond: *Drama From Ibsen to Brecht*, London: Oxford University Press, 1968.

————. *Marxism and Literature.* London: Oxford University Press, 1977.

————. *Modern Tragedy.* London: Version Editions, 1979.

Wilson, F.A.C., *W.B. Yeats and Tradition*, London: Victor Gollancz, 1958.

————. *Yeats Iconography.* London: Victor Gollancz, 1960.

Wimsatt, William and Cleanth Brooks, *Literary Criticism: A Short History.* Chicago: University of Chicago Press, 1975, Vols. I and II.

Zell, Hans and Helene Silver: Eds. *A Reader's Guide to African Literature.* London: Heinemann, 1972.

Zwerdling, Alec. *Yeats and the Heroic Ideal.* New York: New York University Press, 1965.

Index